Balcony
Over
Jerusalem

Balcony Over Jerusalem

JOHN LYONS

with Sylvie Le Clezio

HarperCollins*Publishers*

HarperCollins*Publishers*

First published in Australia in 2017
by HarperCollins*Publishers* Australia Pty Limited
ABN 36 009 913 517
harpercollins.com.au

HarperCollins*Publishers*
Level 13, 201 Elizabeth Street, Sydney NSW 2000, Australia
Unit D1, 63 Apollo Drive, Rosedale, Auckland 0632, New Zealand
A 53, Sector 57, Noida, UP, India
1 London Bridge Street, London, SE1 9GF, United Kingdom
2 Bloor Street East, 20th floor, Toronto, Ontario M4W 1A8, Canada
195 Broadway, New York, NY 10007, USA

National Library of Australia Cataloguing-in-Publication entry:

Creator: Lyons, John, 1961- author.
Title: Balcony over Jerusalem : a memoir of the Middle East /
John Lyons with Sylvie Le Clezio.
ISBN: 978 1 4607 5256 2 (paperback)
ISBN: 978 1 4607 0742 5 (ebook)
Subjects: Lyons, John, 1961-
Journalists – Israel – Biography.
Jerusalem – Biography – Anecdotes.
Middle East – Biography – Anecdotes.
Israel – Social life and customs.
Other Creators/Contributors:
Le Clézio, Sylvie, author.

Cover design by Darren Holt, HarperCollins Design Studio
Front cover image by DEA / W. BUSS/De Agostini/Getty Images
Back cover image by Sylvie Le Clezio
Internal images, courtesy Sylvie Le Clezio and John Lyons
Typeset in Baskerville MT by Kirby Jones
Printed and bound in Australia by McPhersons Printing Group
The papers used by HarperCollins in the manufacture of this book are natural,
recyclable products made from wood grown in sustainable plantation forests.
The fibre source and manufacturing processes meet recognised international
environmental standards, and carry certification.

To Sylvie, my great love, and Jack, our wonderful son,
who shared this extraordinary adventure.

CONTENTS

Prologue   The Handshake   1

Chapter 1   A Balcony Over Jerusalem   5

Chapter 2   My Long Journey to Jerusalem   13

Chapter 3   Arriving to a War   28

Chapter 4   A Shadow across the Balcony   42

Chapter 5   Welcome to the Islamic Republic of Iran   58

Chapter 6   The French School of Jerusalem   74

Chapter 7   Dirty Tricks   91

Chapter 8   The Arab Spring   104

Chapter 9   'I Think Egypt is Going to Blow'   119

Chapter 10   Colonel Gaddafi's Gangster Regime   137

Chapter 11   Frankenstein's Monster   145

Chapter 12   Coffee with the Israeli Army   184

Chapter 13   Walking into Syria   217

Chapter 14   The American Factor   229

Chapter 15   The Lobby   250

Chapter 16   Eight Dead Omars   289

Chapter 17   Sunset in Gaza   293

Chapter 18   Returning to Iran   300

Chapter 19   The View from Palestine   310

Chapter 20   Netanyahu's Israel   326

Epilogue   Farewell, Jerusalem   353

Endnotes   369

The Handshake

13 September 1993

My fascination with the Middle East began with a handshake. Standing in front of me were Bill Clinton, Yasser Arafat and Yitzhak Rabin. It was one of those moments that makes being a journalist worthwhile. I was the Washington correspondent of *The Australian* newspaper, and on this crisp autumn morning I found myself standing on the South Lawn of the White House, 30 metres from history.

These three men had a chance to resolve one of the most damaging conflicts in the Middle East, one which has impacts through the region. There had been doubts about whether Arafat, the leader of the Palestinian Liberation Organization, and Rabin, the Prime Minister of Israel, would shake hands. At a private meeting inside the White House before the ceremony, the Israeli and Palestinian delegations had refused to do so. As the *New York Times* reported:

They both walked to the Blue Room, where several people were already drinking coffee and orange juice ... The Israelis clustered at the southern end of the oval room, with Mr Arafat and Mr Abbas [later Arafat's successor] gravitating to the west end, about 15 feet away. After all the other dignitaries filed out of the Blue Room to be introduced, Mr Clinton, Mr Arafat and Mr Rabin were left alone together for a minute in the diplomatic entrance and it was then that the two old antagonists exchanged their first words.

'You know, we have a lot of work to do,' Mr Rabin said sombrely, according to a Clinton aide.

'I know, and I am prepared to do my part,' Mr Arafat answered.[1]

Outside, hundreds of us waited. I sat next to Michael Stutchbury, Washington correspondent for the *Australian Financial Review*. For me, at age 31, this was more than I could ever have hoped for as a boy from Christian Brothers' College St Kilda, in Melbourne, whose father had left school at 14 and worked as a printer's assistant at Fairfax in Sydney. When I got a cadetship at the *Herald* in Melbourne as an 18-year-old, Dad told me how proud he was. He said that when he worked at Fairfax it was a big thing if, during the evening meal break, the journalists would speak to him – because the journalists were considered at the top of the pile and the printers at the bottom.

Now, I was one of those guys, not just at the top of the pile, but sitting at the White House watching history being made.

At 11.43am, Arafat and Rabin stepped forward to sign what would become known as the Oslo I Accord. Both men had enemies on their own sides who were prepared to kill them for what they were about to do.

What President Clinton had done that day was extraordinary: he'd brought two bitter enemies together. He'd come closer than almost any other president to bringing peace to the Middle East. For both sides he had that most valuable asset: credibility.

Then came the moment of truth. They'd signed the deal, but now Clinton was determined that they shake hands. As a president he wanted a peace agreement, but as a politician he wanted a photograph.

Arafat extended his hand. Rabin stared at Arafat. For a second that seemed an eternity, Arafat stood with his hand poised in the air. This could have been one of the most famous snubs in history. Then Rabin raised his hand. The men shook. The crowd erupted.

As a journalist, it's the most powerful moment I've ever experienced. The world was on the brink of resolving one of the most relentless conflicts in history.

As I stood there in Washington, I knew that I wanted to be part of the momentous events in the Middle East – somehow. When I finally arrived on 2 January 2009, as *The Australian*'s Middle East correspondent based in Jerusalem, I landed with great expectations.

Over the next six years, through experiencing life in the suburbs of Jerusalem to spending time with senior political and military officials in Israel and beyond, I would come to understand how Israel works. I would also come to realise the belief that peace was possible had gone. The notion that Israelis and Palestinians could co-exist had gone. The ultra-Orthodox had gained greater power. And the settler movement – represented by the 'national religious group' – had become the dominant power.

I would get to know the Middle East. I would cover the collapse of corrupt regimes during the Arab Spring. I would speak to jihadists in Lebanon who had just fought in Syria. I would interview families in Turkey who had just fled from Islamic State.

This is the personal journey of a foreign correspondent – my Middle East memoir.

CHAPTER 1

A Balcony Over Jerusalem

January 2009 to January 2015

WE HAD THE BEST BALCONY IN JERUSALEM. FROM IT, WE could see the best and the worst of this ancient city – the extraordinary past and the beguiling present. The good and the bad, the hope and the despair. And it was from this balcony that I would go forth around the Middle East, flying to wherever yet another dictator was slaughtering his people.

It was from this balcony that I would travel to a meat refrigerator in Libya where Colonel Gaddafi's body had been taken. Muammar Gaddafi lived in obscene wealth. Yet for all the family's trappings, his end was appalling.

It was from this balcony that I'd travel to Egypt to cover the fall of Hosni Mubarak, and his security forces would blindfold me and tie my hands with electrical cord. Soon after doing so, they used the butts of their guns to bash the Egyptian man sitting in front of me.

From this balcony I'd travel to Iraq. 'We think Islamic State might be close to taking Baghdad,' one of my editors said to me. 'Can you get there as soon as possible?' That's the sort of phone call you get in journalism: while everybody else is scrambling to get out of a place, you're trying to get in. Islamic State – the most savage terrorist group of our age – was within 50 kilometres of Baghdad and it was thought they might take the capital. As the plane came in to land at Baghdad International Airport, I wondered what I'd do if Islamic State *did* make those last 50 kilometres. But I'd been in journalism long enough to know that I could worry about that later.

And it was from this balcony that my paper sent me to South Africa to cover the funeral of Nelson Mandela, the man who slayed apartheid. In Pretoria, I joined the long queue and filed past his body. I then drove 16 hours to the Eastern Cape for the funeral in Qunu and walked with locals along a dirt road as the coffin of 'Madiba' was pulled on a carriage to the family cemetery. Overhead, helicopters from the South African Army flew in formation – the same army which once would have targeted Mandela because of the colour of his skin.

On that trip, I teamed up with Or Heller, the military correspondent for Israel's Channel 10. We rented a car and drove to various memorial events. At one point, Heller, whose grandmother survived Auschwitz and then Bergen-Belsen, turned to me and said: 'You know, Nelson Mandela was on the right side of history. In Israel we're on the wrong side of history. South Africa used to be an apartheid state and Mandela changed that but I fear that for us apartheid may be ahead of us, not behind us.'

For me, my wife Sylvie and our son Jack – eight when we first arrived – so much of family life during our six-year adventure in the Middle East happened on this balcony. The balcony became not just our base, but also our favourite place. On warm evenings, we'd have dinners with friends out here as we looked over the Dead Sea to Jordan. We could see below to the place where, according to Jewish history, Abraham stood 4000 years ago on the site of what would one day be Jerusalem. He then had his famous meeting with King Melchizedek, a man whose name resonates to this day for both Jews and Christians.

From our balcony, we looked across an extraordinary landscape: rows of gnarled olive trees; the Old City of Jerusalem with its golden Dome of the Rock, sombre-looking al-Aqsa Mosque and Western Wall; the grandeur of Mount Zion; historic Mount Moriah; the Mount of Olives; and the Judean desert. If we looked to the left we could see the Garden of Gethsemane, where Judas Iscariot betrayed Jesus Christ with a kiss to the cheek, condemning him to a death that would echo for the next 2000 years.

And while we could see the Old City, we also had a view of modern Jerusalem, with all its high-tech entrepreneurs, who have made Israel the largest foreign contributor after China to New York's Nasdaq stock exchange.

From our balcony, we could see the old government house, now the United Nations' Middle East headquarters. I always found it incongruous that the blue UN flag flew so triumphantly, given the powerlessness of the UN in this part of the world.

In front of our apartment, as well as the Western Wall, we could see the other famous 'wall' – the concrete snake that separates Israel from the occupied West Bank. As with everything there, people can't even agree on its name: the Israelis call it a 'security fence', the Palestinians an 'apartheid wall'. Israel's supporters in Australia prefer not to call it a wall but a fence.

Every day we would see Israeli Army Jeeps driving along the 'wall', checking on a new Israeli settlement that was being built on the outskirts of a Palestinian village.

Our balcony became our private time machine. We could fast-forward from the biblical past to the troubled present. We would see tear gas being fired at Palestinians and rocks being thrown at Israeli soldiers.

On Fridays – the Muslim holy day and start of the Jewish Shabbat – I developed a routine. As soon as I woke I'd go onto the balcony, where I could see this conflict in the Middle East taking place right in front of me. If there were merely police helicopters circling the hotspots, I knew it was a run-of-the-mill confrontation. When Israeli police prevented access by males aged five to 55 to the al-Aqsa Mosque on the Temple Mount, I knew the violence would be much worse. If things were really bad, an army blimp would fly above. On those days, Sylvie and I would jump into our car and head towards the trouble spot. Sylvie would take photographs and videos for *The Australian*, as well as for other media outlets.

These Friday clashes were mainly unremarkable. Locals dismissed them as 'a bit of Tom and Jerry'. Usually at about two o'clock the Israeli soldiers and the Palestinians would go back to their lives until the following week. We were watching the world's slowest war.

In front of our balcony was the 'peace park'. Not once did we see an Israeli talking to a Palestinian. This was part of the unwritten code of Jerusalem: Israelis would place their picnic baskets on the higher parts and the Palestinians on the lower parts.

On Friday evenings, when a siren announced the weekly Shabbat, Israelis would walk to their Shabbat dinners. This was the cue for Palestinians to appear, carrying plates of kebabs and tabouli. For 24 hours, the Palestinians would move to the higher parts. You could set your clock by this changing of the guard. Jack and I would hear everyone in the park speaking Hebrew at five o'clock and everyone speaking Arabic at six o'clock. In one extraordinary hour, one religion, language and culture would be replaced by another. Then on Saturday evening, as Israelis returned to the park, Hebrew again became the language of the higher parts, and the Palestinians moved back down the hill. Every weekend I wondered: how was it, amid all the wreckage of the Middle East, that these rituals endured?

So much of this conflict happened quietly.

From our balcony, if we looked really carefully at the rolling hills between us and Jordan, we could see a tiny Palestinian house 300 metres in front of us, in East Jerusalem. It had a single light, and two or three goats in the yard. From a distance, we got to know this family – its habits, its movements, its celebrations. We'd see the children head off to school each morning. During the day their father herded goats on the hill.

The oldest child was doing his final year at school, and there's a Palestinian tradition that if a student graduates the family lets off fireworks. It's a way of letting the neighbourhood know the news. We knew what day the results of the final exams were due so we watched to see whether fireworks were let off that night. We saw several other homes in the valley celebrating – then came fireworks from the little house. The boy had passed.

Then one morning the little house was gone. The Israeli Army had come while we were asleep and bulldozed it, claiming it was an illegal structure. The little house had been a part of our lives. Sylvie, Jack and I decided to walk down the valley to speak to the family. The army had demolished everything except the stairway. When we arrived we found the owner sweeping it.

It was one of the saddest things I've ever seen. A broken man sweeping his stairway to nowhere.

*

Yet it was also from our balcony that I saw one of the only rays of hope in six years. As the Middle East deteriorates – the situation has dramatically worsened with the emergence of ISIS – I often think back on this moment. I believed then – and still do – that if the right people built on such goodwill then perhaps peace would come.

It was 27 September 2009, our first Yom Kippur in Jerusalem. Yom Kippur is the Day of Atonement, one of the holiest days of the Jewish calendar. For one day of the year, this stressed-out city, trying to function on 17th-century donkey tracks, stops.

In the hours leading up to Yom Kippur, police close roads. As the sun sets, traffic lights begin flashing. Cars disappear, as if we have rewound to a time before they existed. If you drive a car during Yom Kippur you may be stoned by religious Jews.

People dress in white clothing to symbolise the purity of angels. Thousands of families walk together to their synagogues.

Although a solemn holiday, there was one wonderful feature of Yom Kippur: with the roads free of cars, children would take bikes and roller skates and become the masters of the streets. Jack invited his friend Mark over and they revelled in the freedom. For one day, Jerusalem – one of the most remarkable cities in the world – was ours.

Our apartment was technically in 'no-man's-land': in front of us was East Jerusalem, and the Palestinian village of Jabal al Mukaber, but from a smaller balcony off our bedroom at the back we could see West Jerusalem, which was mainly Jewish. On the 'Jewish side' there were some 20 synagogues within 2 square kilometres.

When we finally arrived home at the end of that first Yom Kippur, Sylvie and I took a bottle of red wine to the main balcony. Below us was dead silence. Normally, a Sunday night in East Jerusalem would be full of life. We knew that West Jerusalem would be quiet, but we were looking across the Palestinian suburbs of East Jerusalem. We sat there as the moon rose over Jordan. Every village below us was silent. We found out later that out of respect for Yom Kippur, the Palestinians remained quiet for 24 hours.

'We don't drive our cars on Yom Kippur out of respect for the Jewish holiday,' one Palestinian told me. 'Palestinians and Jews have coexisted peacefully here for hundreds of years. Our argument is not with Jews, it's with the policies of the Israeli Government, such as the occupation.'

Over our six years in Jerusalem, we experienced the same thing each Yom Kippur: a serenity that proved to be a rare glimmer of hope.

Our balcony was an important part of our life, but nothing was more important than the fact that from up here, each Yom Kippur, we heard what peace sounded like. Never had silence sounded so good.

*

This book covers much of the Middle East and North Africa (particularly Egypt and Libya), which was also part of my brief.

But, because we lived in Israel and observed daily life in that country in intimate detail, much in the following pages focuses on Israel and its major political problem – the occupation of the territory of 2.9 million Palestinians in the West Bank. That occupation turned 50 in 2017, making it one of the longest occupations in modern history. I came to realise that it was an extraordinary case of social engineering.

Whether one is passionately pro-Israel, anti-Israel or neutral depends largely on the information one consumes. My view is that, ultimately, the Israelis and Palestinians have to sort out their own problems. Both sides detest each other, both sides have done bad things to each other. This is a physically, emotionally and psychologically abusive marriage, yet they share the same house. The answer, I have come to believe, is in divorce – but who would broker this divorce and on what terms?

Among other things, this book examines how the media report on Israel. It is the result of interviews with the leading foreign correspondents in Jerusalem – including journalists from the *New York Times, Die Welt, The Guardian*, Reuters, Agence France Presse and *The Economist*.

As for my own perspective, I approach reporting of Israel from a 'pro-journalist' stance. I'm neither 'pro-Palestinian' nor 'pro-Israel'. My home is in Australia, on the other side of the world. To use an old Australian saying, I don't have a dog in this fight.

CHAPTER 2

My Long Journey
to Jerusalem

1961 to 2009

That moment on the White House lawn in September 1993, watching two men who had long despised each other shaking hands under the encouragement of Bill Clinton, had become seared into my memory. Reporting on such a momentous international event confirmed my decision to become a journalist.

At high school in Melbourne, I had my heart set on becoming a barrister. As a 16-year-old during school holidays, I'd take a tram into the city to the County Court. I took delight in opening any random door of the court complex and then sitting in the public gallery. I loved the intellectual challenge: what was the case about? How strong was the prosecution? Was the accused's lawyer doing a good job? Was the judge being fair? Which way was the jury leaning? Sometimes I'd get hooked on a particular trial and return to it day after day after day.

When I achieved 100 per cent in my Higher School Certificate for what was called Commercial and Legal Studies it validated my career choice. I succeeded in getting into Law and Commerce degrees at Melbourne University.

But it was literally on my last day at school that one of the teachers put the idea of journalism into my head. Pat Brown, a gentle man who all the boys felt they could trust, shook my hand as I was about to leave the school for the last time. For a reason I've never understood, he said to me: 'I know you want to be a lawyer, but why don't you think about journalism? It's about observing the world around you then translating that into words.'

His question echoed with me for days. I had also wanted to travel, and the idea that as a journalist I could live almost anywhere in the world was what, in the end, won me over. I wrote to the papers.

After several interviews with the Melbourne *Herald*, I was one of the five chosen out of a field of 400 and I deferred my Law degree. After completing my cadetship with the *Herald*, *The Australian* offered me a job in Melbourne in 1984. I was then posted to their bureau in the press gallery in Canberra and from there I moved to Sydney to be the National Chief of Staff – a tough job for a 24-year-old. In that role I met David Leser, one of the reporters on the paper. So began not just a lifetime friendship but what amounted to a 30-year discussion (which continues until today) about the Middle East. David's passion for all things Middle Eastern and his belief that one day there could be an end to the Israeli–Palestinian conflict fired my interest in the region.

Then in 1989 John Alexander, the Editor-in-Chief of the *Sydney Morning Herald* offered me a job as a senior writer, with the strong possibility that I could become a foreign correspondent. I took the job and three years later would be posted to New York, then later re-hired back to *The Australian* by Paul Kelly to be Washington correspondent. It had been a whirlwind first 15 years in journalism.

In 1994, a year after the signing ceremony at the White House, my phone in Washington rang. It was my former Editor John Alexander, who'd been brought back to run the *Sydney Morning Herald* and try to stem a serious fall in circulation. The paper had gone down-market chasing a broader audience but instead had shed a large number of readers.

Alexander wanted me to be one of his deputies, with the strong prospect of becoming the Editor. The chance to be the Editor of the *Sydney Morning Herald* at 33 was too good to pass over. So I accepted and returned from Washington to Sydney.

*

It was around this time that I met Sylvie Le Clezio, a Mauritian-born film director and producer and still photographer. She'd produced many films, particularly documentaries.

I met Sylvie in Sydney through a mutual friend in 1994. She was then directing a documentary about a young Catholic nun who worked on the Sydney waterfront. When I met Sylvie I thought it would be good to work on a project with her.

Growing up in Elwood and going to school in St Kilda, I'd been in the heart of a very Jewish part of Melbourne. I played a lot with Jewish kids and became a very close friend of Moishe Gordon, a Chabad Orthodox Jew. We decided that a documentary on Jewish identity would be interesting. We began looking at whether Judaism was a religion, an ethnicity or a nationality – or all three. We would examine the culture, the challenges it faces, the humour and the future.

We worked on the Jewish-identity project in our spare time, filming about 64 interviews, including with luminaries such as Lord Jonathan Sacks and Rabbi Adin Steinsaltz, a scholar who translated the Talmud into modern Hebrew. We interviewed Rabbi Steinsaltz on a visit to Israel in 1998.

Sylvie and I married in 2000. Later that year our son Jack was born. Jack is the third of Sylvie's children – he has an elder brother, Nicolas, 30, an engineer, and a sister, Isabelle, 27, a social worker assisting with refugees.

*

As SMH Deputy Editor, I found my phone began ringing with requests for meetings with leaders of the Jewish community. I only learnt later that once you have 'deputy' in your title or are perceived as being on the rise within your media organisation you become a target for cultivation by the fiercely efficient pro-Israel lobby.

Usually the caller was Robert Klarnet, the public affairs director of the New South Wales Jewish Board of Deputies. The board would later coordinate tours in partnership with the Melbourne-based Australia/Israel and Jewish Affairs Council (AIJAC). It has become almost a rite of passage for deputy editors of any major Australian news outlet to be offered a 'study trip' to Israel. Colin Rubenstein, the head of AIJAC, told me that AIJAC has sent at least 600 Australian politicians, journalists, political advisers, senior public servants and student leaders on these trips over the last 15 years. It is my assessment that by 'educating' rising media executives, the Israeli lobby has in place editors who 'understand' the Israeli-Palestinian conflict. Today, I barely know an Australian newspaper executive who has not been on one of these trips.

Klarnet was good company, but invariably at the end of each meeting came; 'We'd like to invite you on a trip to Israel.' After a year or so of phone calls and meetings, I accepted his offer. And so it was that two years after 'the handshake' – in 1996 – I made my first trip to Israel, courtesy of the NSW Jewish Board of Deputies.

My group included Bruce Guthrie, Editor-in-Chief of *The Age*, and Tony Parkinson from the Melbourne *Herald Sun*. We flew through Athens to Tel Aviv for our five days of wining, dining and briefings (including a stay in a kibbutz).

Once in Israel, though, I quickly realised how narrow a range of opinions we were receiving. The organisers set us up for an hour or so with some Palestinians to hear the point of view of the Palestinian Authority, but apart from that we were getting only one side of the story – and a hardline side at that. It became clear to me that the whole point of the trip was to defend Israel's settlements in the Palestinian territories.

To give myself a broader perspective, I asked to go to Hebron, in the occupied West Bank. I'd read enough to know that in Hebron you can see the raw conflict. Hebron is instructive because it's the only Palestinian city where there is an Israeli settlement in the middle of the Palestinian population; normally, the settlements are separated. In Hebron several hundred settlers live in the middle of 200,000 Palestinians. It's therefore easier for visitors to see the reality of life for the Palestinians. In Hebron the same Israeli Army that occupies the West Bank operates; in Hebron the same rules of engagement for the army apply.

I told my hosts that I wanted to go, and set out with my paper's correspondent Ross Dunn. Guthrie and Parkinson also took a trip to Hebron, after telling the Israeli hosts that they wanted to hear more of the Palestinians' side.

The cruelty of Hebron is there for all to see. I saw how the conflict between the settlers and Palestinians played out at the most basic level. In Hebron, the streets are empty; Palestinians are not able to drive on some roads or walk on others. As my own editor Paul Whittaker would remark when I took him there years later, 'It's like Dresden after the bombing.'

Whittaker had broken away from the group he was with – as his correspondent, I had picked him up after the day's meetings and driven him to Hebron. We arrived late at night. The heavy Israeli Army presence, the lights and the empty streets gave the city a certain eeriness. Whittaker was confronted by what he saw. He asked one soldier at the closed checkpoint into the Old City: 'Where are the Palestinians?'

The soldier smiled and replied: 'They're all tucked up in bed!'

On this first trip I believed the claims that Hebron is an exception – but I would come to realise it's only different because you can see everything.

In Hebron, Palestinians have put wire over their market stalls to stop them being hit when Jewish settlers living above them throw bricks, chairs, dirty nappies and rotting chickens onto them. Israeli soldiers will sometimes decide, without notice, to lock the Palestinians into the old part of the city at night, behind big security gates that look like cages.

I thought to myself that *this* was where the real story was, not in all the fine restaurants paid for by the organisers of our trip. I also took Paul Whittaker to Bethlehem, where we stood under the 'fence'. He looked up at the structure, more than twice the size of the Berlin Wall.

'Is this a wall or a fence?' I asked.

'A wall,' he said.

'So can you remember this next time you get a letter complaining that I refer to it as a wall?'

What I had not realised when I first arrived in Israel was that wave after wave of journalists, editors, academics, student leaders and trade union officials were taken to hear the same spin from the same small group of people used to defend Israel's policies in the West Bank – that is, the occupation through settlements.

*

I came back from that trip and said to Sylvie, 'We really must push ahead with our Jewish project.'

Meanwhile, in 1998, John Alexander appointed me the Editor of the *Sydney Morning Herald*. I'd been determined to get back to Israel with Sylvie, and during our holidays that year we finally managed it.

We interviewed Shimon Peres, former Israeli Prime Minister and future president, a man who was older than the State of Israel itself. Peres's staff had agreed to a 15-minute interview. Peres walked into the room. He'd done thousands of interviews, and the prospect of yet another one no doubt loomed heavily. At first his answers were dour. But one question changed everything.

'Mr Peres, when was the first time that you felt Jewish?'

Time became irrelevant: Peres talked for the next 90 minutes. He described what it was like to be a boy in Poland in 1931. Anti-

Semitism had been on the rise and he recalled walking down the street with his grandfather, the famous Torah scholar Rabbi Tzvi Hirsh Meltzer. When people shouted anti-Semitic abuse, Peres had been frightened. 'My grandfather reached down and took my hand,' Peres told me. 'At that moment, through my grandfather's hand, I felt for the first time a connection to my Jewish ancestry.'

Two days after that interview, Sylvie and I were in a different world. We wanted to understand the mindset of Israel's enemies, so we drove south and walked into Gaza. Thanks to a Palestinian journalist contact, we were able to meet with all three major Palestinian factions: Fatah (Yasser Arafat's party), Hamas and Palestinian Islamic Jihad (PIJ).

The PIJ was founded in 1981 by disillusioned members of the Egyptian-based Muslim Brotherhood. According to the US's Council on Foreign Relations, the PIJ violently opposes the existence of Israel. Hamas was founded in 1987 and also emerged from Egypt's Muslim Brotherhood. In 2006 Hamas defeated Fatah in an election in Gaza, and has ruled since then. Hamas opposed Fatah's engagement in the Oslo peace process.[1]

Sylvie and I visited the home of Ismail Abu Shanab, the number two Hamas official in Gaza, second only to founder Sheikh Ahmed Yassin. Shanab met us at his front door. He was not a typical Hamas leader: the 43-year-old with 11 children had a Masters degree from Colorado State University. His children played in the backyard as we sat talking. We were there as part of our research into the Jewish identity – I wanted to try to understand how a group such as Hamas viewed the Jewish people in general, rather than the State of Israel.

Shanab was at first surprised when I asked him about Abraham. But then he drew on the Old Testament to support his view that Israel was in this part of the world illegitimately. 'You should take note,' he said, 'that in the Old Testament Abraham has to buy the burial site in Hebron to bury his wife Sarah. If the Jews owned the land he would not have had to buy it.'

Shanab quickly changed the conversation. He talked about how Israeli bulldozers were demolishing houses, how Israeli settlers were killing Palestinian farmers and the Israeli Army was killing Palestinian children. This, he said, was terrorism. 'We do not justify violence, we defend ourselves from very heavy attacks from the Israelis – the settlers, the government, soldiers, tanks – and the stealing of our land.' Then he added: 'We can make the strongest military in the Middle East cower. There is no atomic bomb and no weapon against the human being bomb. We have a million of them. There are children here in this refugee camp that have nothing to live for. They have no hope. They have no future. We tell them to go into Israel to do this and they will go into Israel and do this. So who's got the power here? You know?'

When you grow up in a country like Australia, you think there is always a chance for negotiation and peace. I said to him, 'Surely this is not the way. This is not the future.'

He replied, 'It's easy for you to say this from Australia but we are under occupation. This is a war. The Israelis are bombing us and we respond. It's a war. This is not coexistence. For Hamas there is no grey, just black and white, it's just, "Forget about negotiation. One day Israel will accept the fact that they can't be the occupier and until that day we are at war with them."'

Next our journalist contact took us around and around the back blocks so that we would not be able to remember where we had driven, and finally to a tall building where we went up to the 10th floor and then down to the ninth floor and met a senior member of Islamic Jihad. Then word came through to us that if we came to 'Chairman Arafat's' compound we might meet the PLO leader himself. That evening, with a breeze blowing from the Mediterranean, we walked through the compound. As we looked up we could see security guards on the rooftops watching us. Given the number of assassination attempts on Arafat – both from Israel and from Palestinian militant groups – this was no surprise. In the end Arafat did not appear.

The Peres and Shanab interviews in particular had challenged us. So complicated were the politics of the Middle East that the public positions of these two men apparently differed from their private positions. Internationally, Peres is hailed as a peace-maker – he won a Nobel Peace Prize for his role in the Oslo Accords – but within Israel he was known as one of the strongest supporters of settlements and the Hilltop Youth, a hardline group of national religious settlers who would take hilltop after hilltop and turn them into outposts which were illegal even under Israeli law.

And while Ismail Abu Shanab talked about 'human-being bombs', within Hamas he was known to argue against the use of bombs, and to have advocated a long-term political solution with Israel. He once told the Israeli media: 'Let's be frank, we cannot destroy Israel. The practical solution is for us to have a State alongside Israel. When we build a Palestinian State, we will not need these militias. All the needs for attack will stop. Everything will change into a civil life.' In 2003, Shanab would be assassinated by an Israeli helicopter as he drove his car through Gaza City, leading Hamas to declare an end to a truce with Israel. Two months before his assassination, Shanab told American television journalist Ted Koppel that Palestinians were willing to renounce violence and accept Israel's existence in return for Israel withdrawing from the West Bank.[2]

The Peres and Shanab interviews had shown Sylvie and me that in the Middle East what people say is not necessarily what they believe. We were determined that we would come back.

*

So how would we get back to the Middle East? For the next 10 years this was an issue ticking away in the back of my mind. After editing the *Sydney Morning Herald* for another three years, I moved to *The Bulletin* then joined the Nine Network's investigative program *Sunday* for seven years. By this point I was quite keen to get back into newspapers, and it felt like the right time to start thinking seriously about the Middle East. Sylvie and I wanted to go to Israel to finish our Jewish-identity series; you can't understand modern Judaism without understanding Israel.

One day I ran into Paul Whittaker of *The Australian,* who suggested I have lunch with him and his boss, Editor-in-Chief Chris Mitchell. They offered me a position on the paper. My one request was to be the paper's next Middle East correspondent, based in Jerusalem. They agreed.

I worked at *The Australian* for just over a year, then the Middle East position came up when the current correspondent, Martin Chulov, went to *The Guardian.*

Despite the dangers of living in such a politically volatile region, Sylvie was just as keen as I was to move there. But we would be taking an eight-year-old child with us. So we looked into the security situation. We ascertained that there was an official French Government school similar to the one Jack had been attending in Sydney, the International French School in Maroubra. Jack was not so keen to leave his friends but took it in his stride.

One thing that weighed on my mind was that Jack might absorb the idea that the world is full of hate and conflict. So we resolved to shield him as much as possible. We decided that when I returned from a work trip I wouldn't tell Jack about the things I'd seen in places like Iran, Egypt, Libya and Gaza.

Still in Sydney, Sylvie and I began Arabic classes and I decided that I would learn Hebrew in Jerusalem. Then, in October 2008 – two months before I flew out – *The Australian* put me into 'hostile environment safety training'. For this I travelled south of Sydney to bushland with Michael Sainsbury, a colleague from *The Australian* who was being posted to Beijing. We were coached in navigation, the use of cover, satellite communications, evacuation and how to react when under attack in a vehicle.

*

I would soon learn that, as far as the Israeli lobby groups are concerned, there are two phases for Israeli correspondents: before a correspondent arrives in Israel and once they are there. My experience is that once a correspondent is announced by a news organisation, the lobby makes a decision: whether to charm or to attack.

I was charmed. At a personal level, and as Editor of the *Sydney Morning Herald*, I'd always had good relations with leaders of the Australian Jewish community. But I'd never received as many invitations to lunches or dinners as when I was announced as *The Australian*'s new Jerusalem-based correspondent.

One of the officers from the Israeli Embassy in Canberra wanted to meet me for coffee. We met at the Hilton Hotel in Sydney. Then, a few days later, he wanted to meet again at another hotel. It sounded urgent. I arrived, and this time he had reserved the business lounge in the hotel and had an extensive spread of food and drinks for me. The two of us sat in this palatial environment with little to say beyond what we'd said a few days earlier. But this would be a short honeymoon: it would end as soon as I began doing my job.

In my final weeks in Australia, I contacted various ambassadors. The Iranian Ambassador was very tentative at first, finally agreeing to meet at the Hilton Hotel in Sydney. He was keen to tell me that Iran – despite being an Islamic republic run by clerics – is wonderful for women, and urged me to do stories on higher education in there.

I met the Lebanese Ambassador in Canberra and he told me that Lebanon would be 'the last country on earth' to recognise Israel. The two countries had been bitter enemies ever since Lebanon began harbouring the PLO in the 1970s, leading to the 1982 Lebanon War and an 18-year Israeli occupation of South Lebanon; more recently, powerful Lebanese militant group Hezbollah had declared war against Israel, resulting in the 2006 Lebanon War.

I had an amusing exchange with the Syrian Embassy. In 2009 Syria was relatively peaceful and I wanted to be able to take Sylvie and Jack on a trip there, so had applied for visas for all three of us. A few weeks later, the Syrian Embassy called me. 'Mr Lyons,' said the officer on the other end of the line. 'We're honoured that you want to come to our country. We're going to give you multiple-entry six-month visas,'

I was thrilled. But then he told me: 'The ambassador thinks you're the best equestrian writer in the world.'

Equestrian writer? We were so close to having excellent visas, but on the basis that the Syrians thought I was the world's leading horse writer?

'Thank you, but I don't write about horses,' I said.

'Aren't you the famous John Lyons?' he asked. 'We in the Arab world love our horses. They're so important to us.'

'Unfortunately,' I replied, 'I'm not the famous one.'

There was an awkward moment before he said: 'Because you have been honest, we will give you the visas anyway.'

As for the Israelis, once the word went out that I was to be the Middle East correspondent of *The Australian*, based in Jerusalem, the charm offensive went into overdrive. I had one memorable lunch in Canberra with Israel's Ambassador, Yuval Rotem. As I walked towards the restaurant I noticed security men along the street, and at the front and back of the restaurant. The wine flowed freely; Rotem enjoyed the good life. A few weeks later, he wanted to see me again before I left. He suggested we meet at *The Australian*'s headquarters in Surry Hills in Sydney. His security detail was a combination of his own staff and Australian Federal Police. As they took up their positions around News Limited, Rotem joked about how he'd recently climbed Uluru and his security detail had insisted on going with him. He laughed at the memory of struggling to get to the top followed by a bunch of security men.

Seated in the News cafeteria, Rotem turned on the charm. 'I enjoyed your stories on Captain Chaos!' he said in reference to a series I'd just written detailing the dysfunction inside the office of Prime Minister Kevin Rudd. 'I read them on the plane and couldn't stop laughing. You know, the Israeli media is one of the toughest in the world – they're always running those sorts of articles about their leaders.' Rotem, as it turned out, would not be as enthusiastic when I was equally tough on Israel.

But it was his next comment that resonated. 'The settlers are nutters,' he told me, referring to Israeli citizens who move to live in the occupied West Bank. It was a fascinating comment from a high-ranking Israeli official. Was he was one of the 20 per cent of Israelis who opposed the settlements?

As I would soon discover, he had touched on the single most important issue preventing a resolution of the Israeli–Palestinian conflict.

CHAPTER 3

Arriving to a War

January 2009

ON THE NIGHT OF FRIDAY, 2 JANUARY 2009, SYLVIE, JACK and I stepped off the plane at Tel Aviv's Ben-Gurion Airport. We landed at the same time as a planeload of Russians, many of whom had come to do Aliyah – the Hebrew word for 'Ascent', or Jewish immigration to Israel. The Russians have given a huge boost to Israel's scientific and military capability. But, as Bill Clinton once observed, they have also dramatically changed the country.

The 'Russian factor' is a highly sensitive issue in Israel. But Bill Clinton clearly felt it was one he could discuss after his presidency. Clinton placed the blame for the failure to achieve a Palestinian State firmly at the feet of the new Russian immigrants. 'An increasing number of the young in the IDF [Israel Defence Forces] are the children of Russians and settlers, the hardest-core people against a division of the land,' he told a discussion group in New York. 'This presents a staggering problem. It's a different Israel, 16 per cent of Israelis speak Russian.'[1]

Under Israeli law, any person anywhere in the world deemed to be Jewish by a rabbi is entitled to take up Israeli citizenship. Part of Aliya involves the government assisting people with bank accounts, housing and employment. Israelis hope that this will guarantee a true 'Jewish Homeland' and defuse what they refer to as the 'demographic time bomb' of a growing Palestinian population in Israel and the West Bank. For Israel it is becoming increasingly difficult to attract Jewish migrants: the waves who migrated there in the 1980s and 1990s, particularly from the former Soviet Union, have dried up and most of the 7.8 million Jews who live outside Israel appear to have no urgent desire to move there.

As I walked through Ben-Gurion Airport that afternoon, I reflected on my own preconceptions about Israel: a military and economic powerhouse in a volatile neighbourhood. Just a week earlier, a six-month truce with Hamas had ended, and, since 27 December, rockets and air strikes had been occurring in Gaza and Israel. The original trigger had been the capture by Hamas of Israeli soldier Gilad Shalit in June 2006, and more recently there had been an escalation in rockets coming from Gaza in response to a long-running Israeli blockade. Speculation had been building that Israel might launch a ground attack. (We would see this pattern every two or so years on average over the period we were there.)

As Editor of the *Sydney Morning Herald*, I'd had long conversations with Jewish leaders who'd argued strongly that Israel was a victim of unfair media reporting. I'd always found it strange that a country exercising military authority over 2.9 million Palestinians in occupied territory could be a victim. This would make Israel simultaneously an occupier and a victim.

Nonetheless, Israel's lobby groups had convinced the majority of the media to present that perspective, at least in the US and Australia.

*

We woke on our first morning in Jerusalem – the Jewish Shabbat – and went to look at Jack's new school, the French School of Jerusalem. We walked from the Old City through the neighbourhoods of ultra-Orthodox Jews, or Haredim. We walked along HaNevi'im – the Street of the Prophets. A strong, chill wind was blowing. Coming towards us was a Haredi with a long beard. The wind made it part down the middle, like the Red Sea before Moses. 'Did you see that man?' Jack asked. 'He had two beards!'

We found the school, in the centre of Jerusalem, next to the ultra-Orthodox neighbourhood of Mea Shearim. I didn't tell Jack that seven years earlier the head of a Palestinian suicide bomber had been blown over the school wall. The Palestinian had dressed as a Haredi Jew, but there had been frequent bomb explosions and everyone was on alert – even the Haredim, who tend to live in their own world. Two real Haredim had noticed the man – an Israeli and a Palestinian can spot each other a mile off – and alerted police.

The terrorist, wearing a vest packed with explosives, had been heading into crowded Jaffa Street to cause maximum casualties, but when confronted by police had detonated himself, and his head had flown over the school wall. This had all happened at eight o'clock in the morning. An adult in the schoolyard had thrown a jacket over the head so children wouldn't see it. Many already had.

As I lifted Jack onto my shoulders to look into his new school, I thought of this incident but decided not to tell him about it. He soon found out anyway; such stories are spoken about openly in Jerusalem.

We went home after our day of exploring to our short-term rental accommodation in Yemin Moshe, a picturesque old suburb with a windmill, just outside the walls of the Old City. I told Sylvie I was going to make sure we had everything organised before I began writing stories. Because I'd already been a foreign correspondent, I knew the importance of organising yourself. I told Sylvie that I'd spend the first few days trying to obtain a rental car, apartment, mobile phone and internet before I began filing stories.

My plans quickly collapsed. That night, I turned on CNN to discover that Israel had launched a ground invasion of Gaza. A period of heightened violence had just turned into a full-blown conflict, which would become known as Operation Cast Lead.

Suddenly I had a war to cover.

*

How do you cover a war? Firstly, you need to work out how to get as close to the front line as possible. Israeli journalists are never allowed into Gaza, but most of the time foreign journalists are. However, during Operation Cast Lead the Israeli Army decided *not* to allow foreign journalists to cross from Israel into Gaza. Israel would later regret the decision, as it meant the foreign media were largely reliant on journalists in Gaza – most of whom were Palestinian.

The war continued for another two weeks, most of which time I spent on the border between Israel and Gaza – on the

Israeli side. I travelled to Bethlehem in the West Bank, where the information from Gaza was filtering through via videos and online means. Huge banners showing pictures of dead children had been hung in the public square. Most Israelis and Palestinians only see one perspective, but by travelling along the border I started to understand how the two sides' reactions to the war are so different.

Three of the main spokespeople for the Israeli side were Australian: Mark Regev, chief spokesman for the Prime Minister, and Benji Rutland and Guy Spigelman, spokesmen for the army. Regev was from Melbourne like me, and we got on very well. He, Rutland and Spigelman were always accessible, and Regev and Rutland gave me daily updates.

The Palestinian side was harder to get; I didn't have a fixer in Gaza yet, having only just arrived. But I was able to get information about deaths and injuries from Palestinian spokesmen in the West Bank and aid organisations or the UN in Gaza. I also monitored the Palestinian media, such as Maan News Agency, which carried regular updates from the Red Crescent ambulance service. Sometimes I looked at Jordanian newspapers or other Arab-language newspapers from other places. Agencies like Reuters and Agence France Press tended to be much more down the middle than the Israeli or Palestinian media.

But not being in Gaza, I wasn't able to confirm information I was being given. My solution was to report as 'the Israelis claimed' and 'the Palestinians claimed'. The he-said-she-said form of journalism is not ideal but preferable to stating facts you can't verify.

In Israel, I could feel the mood change on both sides. Parents at Jack's school started to get nervous. In shopping centres people would stand around television screens watching the war. We'd be in a sports store trying to find some shoes for Jack, or buying meat at the butcher's, and people around us would be saying, 'The Israelis are doing well. Let's get in there and clean out Hamas.' And, 'Our boys are doing what they need to do.'

As a foreign journalist, you learn very quickly not to take sides. I'd often be asked: 'What do you think of the situation in Gaza?' And I always used to give the same answer, whether it was a Palestinian or an Israeli asking the question: 'Look, I'm not there. I can't tell.'

As frustrating as it was to cover a war from the outside, it gave me insight into the 'bubble' many Israelis lived in. At the Malha Mall in Jerusalem, I walked into a newsagency. Media from France, Britain and Germany carried photographs from Gaza: pictures of dead babies, deformed children and bodies half buried in rubble after Israeli air strikes. The material had come from Palestinian photographers and journalists in Gaza. The Israeli newspapers next to them showed pictures of Israeli soldiers fighting their enemies.

The contrast could not have been stronger. One newsagency, two different wars.

The war the Israeli public saw was one in which it was defending itself against its aggressive neighbours. The one the international community saw involved enormous civilian casualties in Gaza. It helped me understand the genuine perplexity Israelis feel when others gather in the streets of London or Sydney and protest against the Israeli Government's actions. Israelis, not having seen any of the images that have fired these protests, dismiss them as anti-Semitic. As Aluf Benn, Editor of Israeli newspaper *Haaretz*, has written: 'Israel's image problem abroad is down to one issue:

the stark and growing difference between how Israelis view their country and how it is seen from outside. This explains the anger and insult that Israelis feel when they watch themselves on the BBC or CNN. It can't possibly be us, they protest, the networks must be biased and pro-Arab.'[2]

In times of war most of the Israeli media adopt a clear policy: any criticism of Israel is held off until the war is over, and instead the media swing behind the Israel Defence Forces (IDF). The Palestinian media do the same: they only highlight their own victims. In wartime, both sides seem to have an inability to see the other one as human.

There is also a strong commercial imperative determining what material is shown: in general, Israelis do not want material critical of their army, given that it is a conscript army and most of their children at some point are part of it.

According to Arad Nir, Foreign News Editor of Israel's Channel 2:

> The Israeli media allows itself to be controlled by its
> consumers. In Protective Edge [the 2014 Gaza War],
> out of the 15 hours of straight news coverage per day
> showing what happened in this war, there were only
> 10 or 15 minutes dedicated to what happened on the
> other side ...
>
> I have some news for you. Even the decision-makers in
> Israel ... wanted us to show what was happening on the
> other side – they were under the impression that the public
> doesn't understand how much they were doing or how hard
> they were hitting the other side. So they complained to us.
> It's not that we are serving the regime, the government –

we are serving the consumerist regime, and those are not necessarily the same interests.

But sometimes Israelis do become angry about their media. 'During all the wars we covered on Channel 2 News, during our post-mortem meetings there were many times that we made a mea culpa and admitted that perhaps the public's feelings of bitterness in the wake of the war were because we did not show what was happening on the other side. That is, we didn't show the public the blood spilled in its name on the other side.'[3]

Significant stories by the Israeli media about the IDF must be cleared by the military censor, which can ban publication. According to the Montreal-based Centre for Research on Globalisation, from 2011 to 2016, between 13,000 and 14,000 items were submitted each year to the IDF censor for review before publication. The centre found that from 2011 to 2013 between 20 and 22 per cent of items submitted were redacted either in part or in full.

*

Over three weeks, two different wars had occurred: one that Israelis watched and one that the rest of the world watched. As soon as the war was over, I wanted to get into Gaza to work out which war actually happened.

Despite being one of the world's best locations, right on the Mediterranean, Gaza is one of the world's most tragic places. Gaza has been bombed so many times that when you are there it sometimes appears to be one large rubble pile with a few buildings in between. Electricity often doesn't work for days on end, water doesn't run. There's a huge refugee population and hardly any economic activity relating to the outside world. The biggest industry by far is United Nations welfare; 60 per cent of the population is on the UN payroll.

Former British Prime Minister David Cameron called Gaza 'an open-air prison'. About 1.8 million Palestinians are squeezed into a sliver of land that's 40 kilometres long and, at some points, just six kilometres wide.

From Israel, the only way for journalists to enter Gaza is through Erez Crossing, a 90-minute taxi ride south from Jerusalem. It's a facility the size of an airport terminal, with state-of-the-art security, including cameras filming your every move. As you walk through the first section, a voice gives instructions: 'Turn left', 'Go straight', 'Hold your arms in the air', 'Open your bag'. The person voicing instructions guesses what language you will understand from what you look like on the wall of monitors in the control room. The instructions are usually in English or Arabic. If you don't understand, the voice speaks louder. It's like having a cameo role in a bad science-fiction movie.

At the end of this first section, a massive concrete door opens, and you begin a long and eerie walk along a caged metal corridor. I never got used to it. Here you are, walking between Israel, one of the wealthiest nations in the Middle East, and Gaza, one of the most bombed places on earth, and you barely see a single human.

The one-kilometre-long cage traverses a no-man's-land that is technically Gaza, but no Gazans are game to come into it. Occasionally, quite a distance away outside the cage, you'll see Palestinian children with buckets clambering over the rubble of destroyed buildings, collecting concrete to be recycled. But some children have been shot by Israeli soldiers, so few risk coming here. This is a walk that journalists and aid workers mostly make alone.

By now, through other correspondents, I'd found a reliable fixer. He was waiting for me at the end of the cage. He drove me a further kilometre to a Hamas checkpoint. The Hamas officials always search your bags. It took me a couple of visits to realise what they were really looking for. A sign in their office says: 'Do not bring alcohol into Gaza.' And then, as if they know how to punish journalists, they add: 'If you try, we will pour it out in front of you.'

My fixer and I decided to drive along the border. This was where the Israeli tanks had come and where most of the fighting had taken place. We visited house after house. I could see the Israeli border, its concrete wall with army checkpoints snaking its way to the Mediterranean. All there was between us and Israel were magnificent strawberry fields and rubble. The Palestinians grow remarkable strawberries that often the Israelis don't let them export.

As the day wore on I learnt more about the reality of the Gaza War. I interviewed three farmers in a strawberry field, standing near tyre marks made by the tanks, about what they saw when the Israeli soldiers came in. I was eating some of the strawberries, which the farmers had insisted I try.

Suddenly, the three started running. 'Drone!' one of them shouted. 'Run!' I followed them.

They told me afterwards that they heard a drone get louder, and often a loud drone would be followed by a missile, particularly if the Israelis saw three or four men standing together in a field. The claim was that the men could be Hamas fighters preparing to fire a rocket into Israel.

Over the course of a day I heard many times about an incident on 4 January. I met three Palestinians who said that at about 4pm they were on a crowded tractor in the village of Beit Lahiya. Two of them were on a trailer being pulled by the tractor and one was sitting on the tractor's wheel covering. Israeli soldiers, who had taken over a house along the street, shouted at them all to stop the tractor and get off.

Two men on the tractor got off with their hands in the air. People I spoke to said the two men were shot several times; one died instantly, the other shortly after. A few minutes later, two others who had been on the tractor–trailer, Nabeela Abu Halima and Omar Abu Halima, were also shot, but survived; I interviewed them both. Nabeela said she was shot in the arm because she refused to leave the scene, wanting to help the injured, while Omar said he was shot through the arm because he refused to strip. This was interesting; it contradicted what the Israeli lobby had been telling me about the conduct of the IDF: that it was 'the most moral army in the world'.[4]

I wanted to double-check the story, so I went back the next day and tracked down the three witnesses at different locations so I could speak to them separately. I took each of them back to the location and asked them to walk me through what happened. They showed me the building the Israeli Army took over; they said an Israeli tank later crushed the tractor. I visited the garage where the remains of the tractor were taken. I cross-checked with human rights workers, who independently verified the incident.

I then contacted the Israeli Army, putting to them the entire incident – the time, the location, the names of those killed. They replied with the following statement: 'In this incident, two armed militants were spotted riding a tractor along with an infant's body.

The militants opened fire on IDF troops, and both the terrorists were killed in the following exchange of fire.'

The story was published on the front page of the *Weekend Australian* on 31 January 2009, with the IDF response included prominently. The IDF had no problem with it. In fact, they said that they appreciated the fact I gave them enough time – 48 hours – to provide a statement. But the AIJAC lobby group in Melbourne opened fire.

Under the headline 'Atrocity or atrocious reporting?' AIJAC and the *Australian Jewish News* based an entire attack on an anonymous blogger who was 'left asking many questions'. The blogger queried whether one man I mentioned had actually been shot in the arm and run away, because the Israeli human rights group B'Tselem had not mentioned him. It didn't matter that we ran a photograph of the injured man in the paper. Because B'Tselem had not mentioned this man then it might well have been 'atrocious reporting'.[5]

For me this raised a question that I would ask about many other stories over the next six years: how would a lobby group in Melbourne know that something in Gaza had not happened while I had gone to the spot and investigated it? I would come to realise a favourite tactic of AIJAC: they cherry-picked the articles they liked and talked up the journalist responsible, but personally attacked journalists who wrote stories they didn't agree with. When I covered human rights abuses in Iran or Lebanon or Syria, I was a leading Australian journalist; when I reported what I had seen done by the Israeli Army, I was an unreliable reporter.

The first AIJAC attack on me would be followed by years of abuse by sections of the Jewish community. A frequent abuser from the Melbourne community dubbed me 'Ayatollah Lyons'. In another email, he referred to me as 'naturally Hamas smelly used tampon John Lyons'. In case I hadn't got the message, he added: 'Fuck yourself John.' Another email from the same person said: 'Can't single Jews out forever Lyons as world history has shown that Jews and Israel have outlived their enemies like the scum that you are.'

After receiving this sort of abuse, I asked some of the other foreign correspondents in Jerusalem about their experience. The bureau chief of Reuters newsagency, Crispian Balmer, told me this story. 'One time I got something absolutely foul from somebody on Facebook who wrote to my own personal Facebook address. There she was in her picture sitting down with her baby in her arms and she was basically saying, "I hope the next time a bomb goes off in Jerusalem that you and your family are sitting on it."' When Balmer asked her what gave her the right to be so abusive to someone she had never met, she replied: 'Because you are journalist scum.'

I was coming to realise that when you write about Israel you are open to a level of abuse I had never seen before. As a journalist, you quickly learnt that you could have a very pleasant life if you wrote what Israel wanted you to. In contrast, if you wrote what you saw in front of you – such as the massive growth in Israeli settlements in the West Bank – your editors would be hit with complaints and your professionalism would be impugned.

As the Editor of the *Sydney Morning Herald*, I'd dealt with our network of correspondents, who were often travelling to dangerous places. I'd worked as a foreign correspondent myself. I regarded myself as experienced and pretty tough.

But the pressures of being a foreign correspondent are particularly acute when you're covering a sensitive part of the world and are coming under attack. And the problem for me with the attacks that AIJAC and other groups made was that they would slowly chip away at my credibility, often without my even knowing. Sometimes I only found out about them much later.

CHAPTER 4

A Shadow across
the Balcony

February 2009

JERUSALEM: A BEGUILING CITY, WITH ITS OWN HIDDEN rhythms. One moment normal, the next frenzied; one moment enchanting, the next a battleground. Things are rarely what they seem.

After a month in our temporary accommodation, we'd found an apartment at the end of the Haas promenade in what was 'no-man's-land' – in front of our balcony was Palestinian East Jerusalem and behind us was Jewish West Jerusalem. We'd been in contact from Sydney with a wonderful agent called Eva Aviad. She dealt with most of the foreign media and started referring possible options to us.

One day, she showed us an apartment. We loved it. It was a warm family home, but what charmed us was the stunning balcony with panoramic views over Jerusalem and Jordan. It was huge and beyond our budget, but the owner and Eva had a solution – we could take half of the apartment on our budget.

We met the owner, Avi Murdoch, who told us that even though this was his dream home he'd decided to move his family to the beaches near Tel Aviv. 'It's time for me to show my children a normal childhood,' he said. A secular Jew, he disliked the growing influence of ultra-Orthodox Jews and what he believed was the growing number of Palestinians. (Avi reflected the view of many Israelis that the number of Palestinians in Jerusalem was increasing, when in fact it was falling.)

Our view was so spectacular that Avi had once invited Ehud Olmert, then Mayor of Jerusalem and later Prime Minister, to bring a foreign delegation here. 'You are now on the roof of the world!' Olmert told them.

We would move into another place during our last year in Jerusalem, but for the next five years Avi's dream apartment, with its amazing views, would be our home.

*

In our first months in Jerusalem everything seemed exotic. As the sun set over the Old City we'd enjoy a religious symphony from our balcony. First came the Muslim call to prayer from the mosques below. '*Allah hu Akbar*!' – 'God is Great!' – echoed across the valley. The green lights of the mosques would glow as the sky faded. From each mosque a muezzin would chant through a microphone.

Then at sunset on Fridays the 'Shabbat siren' would sound, ushering in 24 hours of prayer and family time for Jews. I loved the way the different sounds blended into one; they'd hit the hills of Jordan then bounce back.

Our Jewish neighbours would recite Shabbat prayers. In the apartments around us we could see them light candles and sway back and forth as they prayed towards the Western Wall, the holiest place for Jews. We could see the Western Wall from our balcony. On Friday nights the beautiful, ancient stones would be illuminated to create a wall of light. Some worshippers would place their hands against these stones, reciting prayers that were thousands of years old. Others pushed pieces of paper with handwritten prayers between the cracks.

Amid the Friday night Hebrew songs and Muslim calls to prayer, my own tribe – the Christians – doggedly refused to concede defeat. Although Christians are now very few in the Holy Land, the bells of the Catholic and Armenian churches would ring out across the Old City. From our balcony, we'd have to listen carefully to hear them; in this battle of the airwaves between the three monotheistic religions, the Christians came in a distant third. But every so often – between the 'Allah hu Akbar's and the Hebrew psalms – you could hear them. It might have been due to my days at Christian Brothers' College, or perhaps because I've always supported the underdog, but those Christian bells always gave me a lift. Two thousand years – and still hanging in there. Just.

I would realise how much Christianity in Israel was struggling, though, when I visited holy sites such as the place near Nazareth where Mary, mother of Christ, was born. There was not even a plaque. On the spot where Jesus is believed to have delivered his famous Sermon on the Mount, there was not a single reference to him. Bethlehem, his birthplace, was now a town virtually crippled by Israel's occupation.

Life for Christians is not easy in the Holy Land – it can be quite hostile. We spoke to priests who told us they do not walk in the Old City in their cassocks, as this makes them a target. One afternoon Sylvie saw an ultra-Orthodox man spitting at an elderly nun walking near Jaffa Gate, in front of Israeli Border Police; they did not react. A few weeks beforehand, a member of the Knesset, Michael Ben-Ari, tore up a copy of the Christian Bible and threw it into a bin in front of a television camera crew. The Bible, he said, was an 'abominable' book.

*

As a family, we embraced local life with gusto. We enrolled Jack in an Israeli judo school and summer camp, and he made friends with some Palestinian students at the French school, while I began to study Hebrew and learnt to read and write it to a basic level. The street signs in Jerusalem were in Hebrew, English and Arabic, and traffic was appalling, so I used the time to teach myself the Hebrew alphabet. I would later take formal lessons at an *ulpan*, or language school.

There are almost 800 foreign journalists registered to work in Israel, second only to Washington DC. I found it useful comparing stories – what we had seen or done, where we had been, and our attitudes to the situation in Israel. We soon got to know a large number of journalists and diplomats – but many of them would only stay two or three years, which made it difficult in terms of friendships, especially for Jack. On the other hand, locals knew that we would be going home at some stage too. But gradually we did make friends, mainly through Jack's school, and in our building and our neighbourhood. An Israeli couple on the floor below, Ilan, a historian, and Stephanie, a museum curator, became very good friends; we regularly had dinner in each other's apartments, and they arranged lunches for us to meet their Israeli friends.

We lived near the wonderful Jerusalem Cinematheque and the German Colony neighbourhood, a famous inner-city area. It also had a local swimming pool, so sometimes on Fridays, after I'd filed for the weekend paper, I'd go there with Jack. In West Jerusalem, most things close on Friday nights for Shabbat, so if we wanted to go out we'd head to the Arab section in East Jerusalem.

Everything around us was new – and much of it unexpected.

There was a ritual at our swimming pool in the German Colony that I watched with fascination. The ultra-Orthodox Jewish men refused to swim with women, so the management insisted that once a week – Thursday nights – all the women leave. I'd be in the changing room as scores of ultra-Orthodox men came in to take off their religious garb. It felt like a scene from Isaac Bashevis Singer's novel *The Slave*, set in 17th-century Poland. The women from 21st-century Israel filed out of the gates so the men from the 17th century could swim for a couple of hours, freshening themselves up for the next day's Shabbat. From women to men, from one century to another. All happening at our local swimming pool.

On the buses in ultra-Orthodox areas, men sit at the front and women at the back. Sometimes the men insist on this outside their neighbourhoods. Once, an ultra-Orthodox man told two women on a bus in central Jerusalem to move to the back. The women ignored him. He kept insisting. Finally, one of the women, who had just returned from overseas, said to her friend: 'I thought I'd landed in Israel but there must have been a mistake – I've arrived in Iran!' The man angrily moved to another seat.

Many secular Israelis told us they wanted to live in a 'normal country'. But the ultra-Orthodox want Israel to be religious, and their numbers are growing. Their attitudes alienate many secular Israelis, like our landlord Avi. At a lunch with our neighbours, a British-born Israeli likened the ultra-Orthodox to the clerics of Iran. '*Our* men in black coats and beards are just as bad as *their* men in black coats and beards!'

This was one of the changes that had taken place since Sylvie and I had last been here a decade earlier. But the biggest difference was that there was no significant contact any more between Israelis and Palestinians. On our previous visit, Sylvie and I had gone to a place called Neve Shalom – New Peace – where Jews and Palestinians would live together and make a point of discussing peace and other issues. In those days, there were student-exchange programs to foster mutual understanding between Palestinian families in Ramallah and Jewish families in Tel Aviv. I realised almost all of that had stopped.

Civilians walking around Jerusalem with guns was another big surprise. We were having lunch in a sushi restaurant three months after our arrival when we noticed a man wearing a Glock handgun. He told us he was from New York and had moved to a settlement in the West Bank. 'I love it here!' he said. 'We have a lot of guns in the US but I can't walk around New York with one of these!' We would be surprised going to a supermarket or café and having to be searched and go through a metal detector while heavily armed Israeli youths passed through without being checked.

Many people in their 20s had come from overseas – including Australia – to join the 'messianic mission' to build up the settlements in 'Greater Israel', or the biblical land of Israel.

They talked of 'reclaiming Judea and Samaria' (i.e. the West Bank) from the Palestinians who, in their view, were wrongly given it by the United Nations in 1947, even though Israel agreed to that deal.

Another thing that surprised us was how small this part of the world is. When we travelled to the Golan Heights we could look into Israel, Lebanon, Syria and Jordan. In southern Israel, we could swim in the Red Sea and look into Egypt and Saudi Arabia.

In the Middle East you see wars close up. Locals told us how, during the Gulf War in 1990 to 1991, scud missiles ordered by Saddam Hussein in Baghdad could be seen flying past Jerusalem on their way to Tel Aviv. Television crews set up on rooftops to film them. Once, a siren warned of an incoming scud; it led to a famous photograph of patrons at the Jerusalem Theatre wearing gas masks and listening to Isaac Stern playing with the Israel Philharmonic Orchestra. Saddam Hussein could not stop the Sarabande from Bach's D Minor Partita for solo violin.

War had become part of daily life. In Israel we discovered the 'Code Red' app, which alerts people to where rockets from Gaza are falling. People sit in cafés in Israel and look at their phones for Code Red alerts – 'A rocket towards Ashkelon', 'A missile fired towards Efrat'.

We heard that Israelis were taking folding chairs and binoculars to a hill in Israel looking into Gaza and would cheer when missiles exploded there. Sylvie and I went to see if it was true. It was quite obscene – it was like an outdoor café, with an old sofa, lots of chairs and someone had even set up a barbecue. People cheered and took selfies with bombs exploding as a backdrop.

Even around Jerusalem, we watched wars in the skies. One night Sylvie, Jack and I went for dinner at the Hosh Jasmin Restaurant near Bethlehem in the West Bank, only 15 minutes from our apartment. It was a beautiful evening and we were eating outside. A siren began and we saw a missile shooting across the sky. Then a second missile appeared, pursuing the first. The first was a Hamas rocket from Gaza and the second a rocket fired by Israel's 'Iron Dome', designed to destroy the first.

The Iron Dome is a brilliant device: a computer system that can tell within seconds the trajectory of a missile and whether it is heading for a populated area. If so, it will fire a missile to hit the incoming missile. If the incoming missile is heading into the sea, or the desert, the Israelis will save the US$90,000 that each missile costs.

On this night in Bethlehem, we watched one rocket chase the other. Finally the Israeli rocket caught up with the Hamas rocket and we heard a massive clash of metal. Seconds later we heard a thud as all this metal crashed to earth. We looked at each other, realising what an extraordinary new life we had.

*

It's no surprise that people who have lived in this atmosphere for 50 years have been affected by it. Israelis are some of the most stressed people in the world. Israelis near the Gaza border have lived for years with Code Red sirens, bomb shelters and psychological trauma. I interviewed a psychologist in Sderot whose entire practice was dealing with traumatised Israeli children.

The conflict is not the only cause of stress – there are also financial pressures. Israel has a high cost of living due to the lack of competition among retailers, and wages are low. This pressure creates a culture of distrust.

So notorious are many tradespeople at over-charging that Israel's Channel 2 runs a show called 'Yatzata Tzadik' – 'You Emerged as Honourable'. Filmed by hidden cameras, tradesmen, dentists and other professionals are asked to give quotes. The dishonest are humiliated on national TV; the 'honourable' are given a medal.

Daily life is frantic and pressured. In West Jerusalem, which is predominantly Israeli, arguments and tension are commonplace, whether you are in a bank or a post office. And when you go into the Old City or East Jerusalem, with a high Muslim population, you can get caught up in the Israeli–Palestinian tensions.

The pressure-cooker atmosphere extends to the roads. There are constant traffic jams, noise and stress as people travel around in the heat. In car parks, when two cars are trying to push ahead of each other, the battle becomes which driver will lose their nerve first. I told a shopkeeper that I'd never experienced anything like driving in Jerusalem. 'People here aren't very nice sometimes,' he said. 'They won't back down.'

One of our neighbours – a diplomat from the European Union – argued at a traffic light with another driver. He gave her 'the finger'. She reached into her glove box and pulled out a gun. He panicked and took off. 'I'm always giving people the finger in Brussels,' he told me later, 'and no one gets upset.'

In the space of four months, we had two car accidents. First a bus filled with settlers travelling to Hebron ripped off the front of our car, knocking our bumper bar 15 metres up the road. The next accident happened when we stopped for pedestrians at a zebra crossing: a taxi smashed into the back of us. The driver told us he was distressed and needed to collect his thoughts, then sped off the minute our backs were turned. When we told an Israeli friend about the accident, she said: 'In Israel you need to make it clear to pedestrians that you're not going to stop and then they won't cross.'

Many months and $2400 in repairs later, we were told that if we wanted to get any of that money back we'd have to take the driver to court. But there are so many car crashes in Israel that chasing him down was the last thing the police wanted to do. The Hyundai Getz we'd bought, a former Avis rental car, was getting newer all the time: it now had a new front and back.

*

The apparent threat of missile attacks seemed to justify the heavy Israeli security presence we noticed everywhere we went. That was how we felt at first, but as time went on we were no longer so sure. As the months went by, a shadow began to creep across our balcony, as we began to realise the situation in Israel was not all it seemed.

Many insights came from passing through Israeli checkpoints.

We would sometimes go to Bethlehem to do our shopping. One day I arrived at the checkpoint between Jerusalem and Bethlehem to find the gates shut.

'What's the problem?' I asked.

'Security,' the soldier said.

'Has there been an incident?' I asked.

'Security,' he repeated.

What I discovered was that the gates had been closed for nine days for the Jewish holiday of Sukkot (the Feast of the Tabernacles). I had not realised that for each Jewish holiday, Israel sealed off the West Bank, with only Israeli West Bank settlers allowed to travel into Israel or Palestinians with special permits.

I gradually learnt these border rules can change according to the soldier of the day. On one occasion, an Israeli border policeman in East Jerusalem would not let me speak to a group of Palestinians who were being intimidated by young Israelis during a rally. As a journalist you receive a media card that's meant to give you access to all public areas. I showed the policeman my card, explaining that it was an official accreditation from the Israeli Prime Minister's office.

'Then telephone the Prime Minister,' he said.

When I responded that that was unfair, he challenged me to a physical fight. 'Push me!' he said. 'Push me here!' he repeated, pointing to his chest.

I told him I didn't want to fight and left, finding a side street which allowed me to interview the Palestinians.

To travel by land from Israel to Jordan, you need to cross the Allenby Bridge. Because Israel has no diplomatic relations with most of the Arab world – Egypt and Jordan being the main exceptions – to fly to countries such as Lebanon, Iran or Libya I first had to travel to Amman in Jordan. Foreigners such as me have the option to fly from Tel Aviv to Amman, but this is not an option for Palestinians – they are not allowed to use Tel Aviv airport.

Allenby is the only land crossing that Palestinians are allowed to use. It's therefore a place where foreigners can observe the interaction between Israeli authorities and Palestinians. You need to get a bus across the no-man's-land border into Jordan. One time in 2009 I got onto a waiting bus, assuming it was for all passengers.

'Only Palestinians!' an Israeli guard insisted.

'Why?' I asked.

'Palestinians here, foreigners there,' he replied, pointing at another bus.

When I asked again, he said: 'That's the way it is.'

One of the most unpleasant things I saw at Allenby was when Sylvie, Jack and I were returning to Israel after a holiday in early 2010, and waiting, among hundreds of Palestinians, to go through security. Next to us was an elderly Palestinian woman whose trolley was overloaded – blankets, bags, water. It looked as if it was about to topple over. Then an Israeli security guard walked by. Seeing the woman's trolley, he kicked it, causing much of the contents to fall off.

Jack helped the woman load it all back on. The guard returned and kicked it off again. 'Why did he do that?' Jack asked. All I could say was 'I don't know.'

On my next visit to Allenby, with Sylvie in mid-2010, Israeli security wanted to examine my bag, so I was taken to a private room. There was a large metal table in the middle of the terminal for Palestinians only. Later we saw an Israeli security officer holding up the clothes of a Palestinian man's wife. The officer ran his hand along the woman's underwear. He then held up the woman's bra. The man stared across the table at the officer while his wife sat nearby with her head in her hands.

To Sylvie and me, the way the security officer was running his hand along the underwear was offensive. This seemed to be about humiliation, not security.

On another occasion at Allenby, Sylvie, Jack and I were waiting alongside an elderly Palestinian man in a wheelchair and his nephew. The man had just been in a car crash; his nephew told us it was a hit-and-run. His leg was bleeding, the blood dripping into a plastic container. He had passed through the security check, openly bleeding, but no official was helping.

His nephew tried to gain the attention of the official behind the counter. She ignored him. The nephew then asked if I, as a foreigner, could help, so I approached two other officials. They pointed me back to the woman in the booth.

I went back and told her that the man needed help. She waved me off, telling me she would attend to him when she'd finished dealing with the line of people at her window. I asked the people in the line whether they would let the injured man go ahead of them, and they agreed. I raised my voice, telling her this was unacceptable.

The woman then turned to the official who had entered the booth next to hers and, indicating me, said I should be 'punished'. When our turn came, the second official took our passports. She handed back Sylvie's and Jack's passports, but not mine. Instead, she gave it to an official from the Interior Ministry, who took it away.

After 20 minutes I sought out Baruch, the manager of the centre, who I knew. I told him that a clearly injured elderly man had been made to wait and that my passport had been taken without reason.

I was then called into an office inside the terminal for a meeting with Interior Ministry officials. When I walked in, the first woman who had refused to help was present. She threatened to cancel my press accreditation. I told her it was a Government

Press Office (GPO) card, which she could not cancel. The woman said she wasn't threatening me, but handed me a new visa – no longer my B1 journalist's visa but a B2 'Not Permitted to Work' visa.

Instantly my work status had been downgraded. From then on, each time I entered Israel my passport was stamped 'Not Permitted to Work'. The GPO, however, told me that I could continue to work.

*

The shadow even invaded our balcony when Sylvie and I entertained our friends. We quickly learnt to keep two different beers in our fridge: Goldstar for Israelis and Taybeh for Palestinians. We would sometimes put on a kosher dinner for our Israeli friends and the following night a dinner for our Palestinian friends. Often the conflict became the main topic of conversation. Many Israelis are automatically hostile towards foreign journalists – but even at social functions, I soon realised that I shouldn't offer an opinion on the conflict to anyone, no matter what it might be.

On one occasion we were invited to one of our neighbours' apartments for a Saturday lunch and the conversation turned to the Palestinians and the Israelis. I said something about how I thought the situation with the Palestinians needed to be resolved, and a woman at the lunch turned to me and said, 'Well, *you* can't talk. Look how you've treated the Aboriginals. It's a disgrace what you've done to the Aboriginals.'

I said, 'I agree with you.'

'What do you mean?' she responded.

I told her that I agreed that the way we'd treated our Indigenous population was appalling.

She said, 'But you're an Australian.'

I replied, 'Well, yes, and I think it's wrong, and we're trying to rectify it. But why should that stop me from having an opinion on the Palestinians?'

It taught me how sensitive Israelis are to criticism from foreigners. After that I became careful never to reveal my personal views.

On another occasion, some Australian friends invited us to their house to watch a rugby game between Australia and South Africa. They also invited some South Africans.

It was a thoroughly enjoyable event: Australia won 21–6. Afterwards, the conversation turned to politics. They said they had been surprised to discover that there were 'dozens' of different permits which covered Palestinians – indeed, what I did not know then until I began researching it was that there were 101 different permits which Israel had devised to apply to Palestinians. I asked the three South Africans how they saw the situation between Israelis and Palestinians. The South Africans were from three different backgrounds: a white English South African, a white Afrikaner South African and a black South African. Each of them said that the permit system which Israel used in the West Bank was worse than the notorious 'pass system' used during apartheid. Their verdict was that in terms of movement, Israel's permit system made daily life more unpredictable than the pass system in South Africa.

Their reasoning came as a complete surprise to me. They said apartheid was designed to be an ongoing economic system based on race. White South Africans relied on workers from the townships to perform the blue-collar work. It was about segregation, not expulsion, because if the blacks had left, the economy would have collapsed. But to them, it appeared that the Israelis wanted to make the lives of Palestinians so difficult they would eventually leave.

I'd just watched a great Wallabies win, but as Sylvie and I drove home I wasn't thinking about the rugby – but about how three South Africans from different backgrounds believed that Israel's occupation was worse than apartheid.

CHAPTER 5

Welcome to the Islamic Republic of Iran

June 2009

WITHIN A MONTH OF MY ARRIVAL IN ISRAEL, IN FEBRUARY 2009, I went from covering a war to covering an election: a battle between the far-right Benjamin Netanyahu, who led the Likud Party, and the centre-right Tzipi Livni, who led Kadima. Livni won more votes, but was unable to form a coalition, so Netanyahu – who had already served as prime minister between 1996 and 1999 – was declared the leader.

Many commentators made clear their view: that Israel had re-elected a man who did not want peace with the Palestinians. Gradually, too, I would become convinced that Israel's two-State solution died the night Netanyahu was reinstated as prime minister.

Meanwhile, Lebanon and Iran both decided to try to convince the world that they were vibrant democracies.

In the lead-up to the Lebanese national election on 7 June, neither major candidate appeared in public for fear of assassination. Sheikh Hassan Nasrallah, who led the 8 March Coalition – which is dominated by Hezbollah – addressed his supporters by video from bunkers. Saad Hariri, who led the 14 March Coalition, campaigned from Saudi Arabia. Hariri was worried (justifiably) that Hezbollah would try to assassinate him, while Nasrallah was worried (justifiably) that Israel would try to assassinate him.

Saad Hariri's own father Rafik, a former Prime Minister, had been killed years earlier by a massive bomb. Both 8 and 14 March were the dates of major demonstrations in the aftermath of that assassination.

*

Just days later I was in Iran, covering yet another national election. For a country that normally restricts foreign journalists, suddenly Iran had put out the welcome mat.

Every four years Iran elects a president. These events are always choreographed – the ruling Ayatollahs choose four acceptable candidates – so they rarely mean real change. But in 2009, one of the four candidates, Mir Hossein Mousavi, went rogue. Either he fooled the Ayatollahs during the vetting process, or he decided afterwards to seize the day. The election became real.

On the flight from Amman to Tehran, I met an English woman who spoke fluent Farsi, or Persian. She regularly visited Iran for business. To protect her identity, I'll call her Susan. She introduced me to many Iranians during what would be a turbulent time.

We landed at Imam Khomeini International Airport two nights before the election. My taxi could barely move as thousands of Mousavi supporters filled the streets. They were keen to replace Mahmoud Ahmadinejad – the hardline Holocaust-denying President.

A record number of foreign journalists arrived, and we were all required to stay at the Laleh Hotel, where government officials could keep an eye on us. As I walked into the 1970s-style reception area I noticed several intimidating-looking men sitting around the foyer watching everyone.

The hotel said I must hand over my passport and contact the 'Ministry of Islamic Guidance', which would assign me a fixer at US$150 a day. I put this off – the idea of being accompanied everywhere by a government spy had no attraction. I calculated that there were so many journalists that by the time the ministry discovered I hadn't contacted them I would have bought a few days of freedom, and hopefully found some real stories.

I met with Susan, who knew Tehran well. The buses in Iran have a pole across the middle; men are required to stay in the front half and women in the back. Just like the ultra-Orthodox neighbourhoods of Jerusalem.

Susan and I were talking across the pole when a woman demanded of her in Farsi: 'Are you married?' Under Iran's version of sharia law, men and women are only allowed to talk in public if they are related.

'Yes,' said Susan, wanting to avoid a confrontation. She told me later that the 'Islamic police' had sometimes walked up to her and said that her scarf did not hide her hair. Once, two policewomen told her to wipe lipstick off her face and she pretended she could not speak Farsi and kept walking. Back in

Australia, before I'd begun my posting, Iran's Ambassador had told me how good life was for women in Iran – now I was getting the chance to see for myself just how much equality women really enjoyed.

*

Friday, 12 June 2009: election day. In the capital there seemed to be strong support for Mousavi. But Tehran was a stronghold for reformists, whereas Ahmadinejad was popular in rural areas.

At polling booths I did my own poll – most Iranians speak some level of English. Every person I spoke to who used the internet said they would vote for Mousavi, while those who had never touched a computer – particularly the elderly and the poor – supported Ahmadinejad.

On Friday night, only three hours after the polls had closed, Ahmadinejad went on television to claim victory – overwhelmingly. People were stunned.

It was inconceivable that all the votes could have been counted within three hours, particularly given it was done by hand, and the results were too neat. In region after region, the result was 63 per cent for Ahmadinejad and 34 per cent for Mousavi. Ahmadinejad had received about 10 million more votes than expected. He'd even beaten the other candidates in their home towns by two to one.

One candidate, Mehdi Karroubi, received only 300,000 votes. With a campaign team of 400,000, an outraged Karroubi asked: 'Did 100,000 of my campaign workers sleep in?'

Next morning, I was at an intersection in Tehran where hundreds of young people gathered. They seemed angry. Police began trying to break them up. Some resisted, and the police attacked with batons. The mood turned nasty.

American journalist Joe Klein reported that a number of journalists were coming back to the Laleh Hotel badly beaten. Australia's Ambassador to Iran, Marc Innes-Brown, went for a walk, and as he passed the Interior Ministry a plain-clothes official pushed his finger into the ambassador's chest, telling him to leave.

Around Tehran, I watched a regime prepare for war against its own people. Riot police stood on every corner. Snipers took up positions on rooftops. And the most feared unit of all, the paramilitary Basij militia, roamed with batons, knives and truncheons.

*

Not having a government minder meant I could break away. Not only was I freer but so were the people I was able to speak to.

One of the things I investigated was an alleged massacre at Tehran University, whose students were driving many of the protests. There were suggestions that the Basij had attacked students in a dormitory, an allegation I wanted to check.

At the university, several students agreed to talk about the killings. I found out that five students had been killed. It appeared that *basijis* had stormed a dormitory and begun a killing spree. The students told me they'd placed the names of the five on noticeboards but the police had taken the list down.

Back at the Laleh Hotel I discovered media teams preparing to depart. Officials had been going from room to room demanding that journalists leave the hotel. Embarrassed by huge protests, the regime wanted foreign reporters gone from the country. 'We're out of here,' one television journalist said to me. 'Every time we pull out our camera someone tries to stop us.'

But for me this was a rare opportunity: I had a 15-day visa, I hadn't registered with the Ministry of Islamic Guidance, and this was a big story. If I could get my passport back from the front desk, the authorities would have no idea where I'd gone.

*

Tehran was erupting. Even the executive editor of the *New York Times*, Bill Keller, was unable to get his visa extended. 'Visa extensions have been denied across the board', he wrote.

I emailed Sylvie in Jerusalem to ask her to help me find another hotel. Through the *Lonely Planet Guide – IRAN*, she found a backpackers' hotel, the Firouzeh. The *Lonely Planet* summary read: 'If ever there was a hotel whose atmosphere revolved around one man, this is it. Mr Mousavi is the personification of Persian hospitality and his enthusiasm, useful information and help with bookings make an otherwise unremarkable little hotel in an unlovely part of town into the city's backpacker centre. Toilets are shared.'

But I needed to get back my passport from the Laleh Hotel without any suggestion that I was remaining in Iran. After checking out, I declined the hotel's offer to organise a taxi for me because I didn't want them knowing that I was going to another hotel. I walked outside and took a random taxi instead.

I arrived at the Firouzeh Hotel. It was so small you could barely see it.

A man at the front desk smiled.

'Mr Mousavi?' I asked. He nodded. 'I've been reading about you in the *Lonely Planet* guide!'

He greeted me like a long-lost friend. He gave me a room at US$10 a day – then informed me that for an extra dollar I could also get the internet. I decided to 'lash out' and go for the US$11 package.

I slipped into backpacker mode, having breakfast with a Swedish man who was on a motorbike trip 'across the world' and a New Zealander who was riding his pushbike across Iran and complained that the roads were terrible. 'I've gone through 10 tyres,' he said. This was not a good time to be a foreign journalist in Tehran, so I didn't reveal my occupation.

Near the hotel I could hear tear gas and bullets being fired, so I went to have a look. For the first time, I heard a sound I would soon come to dread: the sound of metal shutters being pulled down. Often it means the end of the working day, but in this climate it meant something very different: fear.

On my first day at the Firouzeh, the shutters were being pulled down in nearby Amir Kabir Street. Supporters of Mousavi were clashing with police. The Basij arrived on motorbikes. 'Go!' one shopkeeper shouted at me. 'Basij!'

*

The next morning I noticed a man at breakfast typing furiously on a laptop. When you're a journalist on the road you learn to spot other reporters; it's almost a sixth sense. He was from Mexico.

A day later I spotted a woman who also had the look of someone on a deadline; she was a British journalist. The three of us had all fled the official hotel and we began to travel around

Tehran together. Being a team gave us some protection. At one protest, police grabbed the Mexican and were about to put him into a car when I appeared from down the road; this confused them and they let him go. Two days later, the three of us became concerned to hear that officials had rung the hotel to ask if there were any journalists staying there. We needed to move out of the Firouzeh. The visas of the other two were about to expire, so they decided to leave. One of the Iranians I'd met through Susan had an apartment down a back lane where I could come and go without being noticed. This became my home. I slept on the floor, and each day I took a bus into central Tehran to cover the protests.

I frequently dropped into internet cafés. Social media was driving this uprising. This was confounding the regime, which struggled to manage the new communication form. For me, these internet cafés became a valuable way of finding out the sort of material being circulated, and of talking to protesters. The clientele tended to be young and examining videos – often gruesome – from the protests. The common message from these people – who supported what came to be known as the 'Green Revolution' – was that they wanted choice over their government.

*

Sunday, 20 June. I walked into a café to see several young people around a computer. A man called me over and played a video of a young woman lying on the ground, looking traumatised. Then I saw a trickle of blood from her mouth. Then from her nose. Her eyes widened and took on a haunted look. The people showing the video looked up at me. 'Her name is Neda,' one said.

Neda Agha Soltan, 26, was a student who had been at a protest when a sniper shot into the crowd. Within 24 hours, this woman would become the face of the brutality of the regime.

Another man in the café showed me a picture of a friend killed the day before. A woman showed me a picture of a young man lying on a slab with white patches over his eyes. She also showed me a picture of militiamen wielding knives at protests; this was proof, she said, that it was the Basij who were using weapons on protesters.

By posting this material, these young people were shaping international opinion. Internet cafés had become the command-and-control centres of the opposition movement. In the Middle East, social media was changing the power balance. This would be confirmed just a few months later when the Arab Spring erupted.

Not all the cafés were so friendly, though. I was on a deadline to file a story – it was 7pm Sydney time – and I needed the internet. The café I entered did not have an air of youthful enthusiasm. I sat at a booth as far away from others as possible and began writing a story about the massacre at Tehran University. A man came and sat in the next booth. It was a fixed computer, not a laptop, so I couldn't angle it for privacy. I kept writing, but I noticed he was trying to read it. It might have been simple curiosity, or he might have been a government official. I quickly logged off and left.

The message that I wasn't welcomed by some was made clear as I walked with protesters towards Azadi Square in the centre of the city. Two men on a motorbike came up behind me and pushed the motorbike into my heels. They did it again, and again, and stared at me. I climbed over a fence on the side of the road, which meant they could no longer follow me.

Conversely, many Iranians showed great concern. As violence broke out in Engelab Square, another Tehran focal point, two young men beckoned me into their mobile phone shop 'You should not be out there,' one said. From the shop door I was still able to see everything going on in the square.

But a day later, I found myself between the riot police on one side of an intersection and protesters on the other. Behind the lines of riot police were hundreds of police on motorbikes. It was clear the riot police were not just going to stand there; the regime was determined to crush the uprising.

The scene was chaotic: in the midday sun, car sirens were sounding and people were shouting. A man had run up some stairs, but had been caught and was being clubbed by police.

Police on motorbikes were coming down the street, brandishing wooden truncheons. I saw a woman standing by the side of the road. As the police rode past, one of them bashed the woman with his truncheon. The sound of the wood hitting her head was awful. The woman fell backwards and because she was next to a deep drain there was nothing to break her fall. The sight of that woman falling back into the drain imprinted itself on my visual memory.

All this brutality brought people together: the woman who had been hit was not religious, judging by her dress, but several women in black hijabs climbed into the drain to help her. One of the women charged up to a police commander and put a finger close to his face, then pointed to the woman lying unconscious.

At the next Friday prayers, Ayatollah Khamenei warned that organisers would be responsible for the consequences of any future protests. While in the first few days people were bringing children, everyone realised that if you turned up to a rally now you risked being killed.

At one protest, three days after the election, panic set in, and people were running to get into buses headed towards Azadi Square, one of the most violent battlegrounds. Four o'clock came and the battle began. The regime was becoming more strategic: the police sealed off streets, quarantining the protesters into small zones. This prevented the trapped protesters from bringing in reinforcements and meant the regime could dramatically outnumber them.

It felt like a scene from Dante's *Inferno*. There were fires everywhere, and the smell of burning tyres. People were running in all directions and there was a constant high-pitched sound of sirens and shouting. Police began running into Azadi Square from a side street.

I was witnessing a grim daily ritual. Thousands of people came to demonstrate against their government, which was telling them it was prepared to kill them. In this gladiatorial contest, the police and militia gathered to meet them. It was now a civil war in which only one side had weapons.

'We have the numbers, they have the weapons,' one protester said. But the opposition had added another 'weapon' to their armoury: each night at 9pm, opposition sympathisers had started turning on all their electrical appliances. This would make the grid crash, plunging the city into darkness.

*

It was clear that the Basij militia were critical. I asked a few of the protest leaders to guide me towards anyone who had ever been in the Basij or a related part of the Iranian military.

After a couple of days I was given the name of a man who'd held a senior position in the Revolutionary Guards but become appalled by their methods and left. He was prepared to explain the Basij's role. The reason, he explained, why the regime was able to turn fear on and off was because of a force it had been building methodically (since the toppling of the Shah in 1979): the Army of the Guardians of the Islamic Revolution.

The most feared weapon of the army is the Basij, Iran's secret police. The full name is Sazeman-e Basij-e Mostazafan, or the Organisation for the Mobilisation of the Oppressed. While the name suggests defenders of the weak, in fact the Basij are the enforcers for the Ayatollahs. Whoever controls the Revolutionary Guards and the Basij controls Iran.

There are about 2 million members of the Revolutionary Guards, which includes about 100,000 *basiji*. The Basij can afford to have such large numbers because it is a volunteer organisation. Its members receive rewards rather than money. The biggest reward is tertiary education: university places in Iran are scarce. To enter university you must sit an examination called the Konkoor (from the French *concours*). The regime gives exemptions only for those who have shown exceptional loyalty. First among these are young people who have signed up to the Basij. The Konkoor works on a points system; although those who enlist with the Basij need to sit the exam, their membership gives them bonus points.

Joining the Basij also takes a year off the compulsory military service Iranian men must do when they turn 18. This means *basijis* can do other jobs and earn more than they would as a soldier. They also receive immunity from prosecution. In return for these 'privileges', Basij members must 'protect the revolution' in whatever way required. When civil unrest breaks out they must be prepared to turn on their own people.

Around Tehran at this time, the Basij seemed to be everywhere. Chains and batons in hand, *basijis* turned up wherever crowds were gathering and attempted to break them up. Part of their power was that they were virtually impossible to identify. Some wore balaclavas.

*

Mahmoud Ahmadinejad had amassed great power due to his patronage of the Basij. While the Supreme Leader, Ayatollah Khamenei, appointed the head of the Revolutionary Guard – which gave him unprecedented power – Ahmadinejad had shrewdly cultivated his own people in the Guards and the Basij. He had purged the public service of many mandarins and replaced them with Guards.

The former Revolutionary Guard I interviewed said his ex-colleagues had a power additional to violence. 'They have the ability to destroy reputations,' he said, citing the case of a radio broadcaster who the regime thought was becoming too powerful. The broadcaster had come up with an idea to challenge the government: each Friday, after his show, he would set off from the radio station for a walk with listeners. The regime felt threatened, and soon afterwards the broadcaster was photographed at a party dancing with two women who were not wearing scarfs: a breach of Iran's religious laws. He was also holding a drink that the regime said was wine. The photographs were given to a newspaper and the journalist lost his job.

'It's called wringing,' the former Guard told me. 'Anybody who has something to say and is listened to by the people is dangerous and should be "wrung" of it. They take away your name, your friends. When you wring [clothing], what happens? It stretches, loses water, becomes fluffy, there is nothing left of it and it should be left on the rope to dry.'

He told me about another public figure the regime thought was 'too big for his boots', against whom corruption charges were fabricated. At his trial, the man testified that the Revolutionary Guard had said to him: 'We will break you.' The man was found guilty and became unemployable.

Even as a foreigner, I felt a sense of menace about the Basij – Iran has set up an extraordinary machine, oiled by the dark art of fear creation.

The Iranian regime had won – in the short term at least. They'd used such violence that few people would now come onto the streets.

*

I woke up on the 15th day of my visa. I had until 5pm to get to the airport.

I was warned by an Australian diplomat that the authorities at the airport were taking journalists away for questioning. I asked the diplomat what I should do if that happened to me. 'Fucked if I know!' he said. That didn't reassure me.

An American journalist trying to leave had been taken away by Revolutionary Guard. Fearing that he would be uncontactable, he shouted his name and media organisation in the hope that others in the queue, when they reached their destinations, would telephone his editors. Someone did, so his organisation knew he'd be detained.

One of the trickiest things about being based in Israel was that I needed two passports to travel in the Middle East: one with my Israeli work visa and one with no Israeli stamps – a so-called 'clean' passport. Australia's Department of Foreign Affairs and Trade will give a person a second passport if you travel frequently in the Middle East, because some countries, such as Iran and Lebanon, will not allow you to enter if you have an Israeli stamp.

And so, with my 'clean' passport in my top pocket and my Israeli-stamped passport hidden in the lining of my computer bag, I headed to Tehran Airport.

The hardest part of having two passports is remembering the travels in each one. It's a bit like long division. On one passport you've been to Ankara, Malta and Cyprus. On the other to Beirut, Amman, Dubai. In the taxi ride I tried to memorise my travels in the passport I was about to use to leave Iran.

Passport checks at the airport were being done by officers from the Revolutionary Guards. They were interested in trying to find inconsistencies in people's stories. Due to their fear that Israel would try to sabotage their nuclear program, the number one target Iranian officials look for is agents from Mossad, Israel's intelligence service, posing as journalists or businesspeople. And it's known in the Middle East that for Mossad an Australian passport is gold.

I handed my passport to the Guard, and he and a woman went through it.

'What is your destination?' the man asked.

'My eventual destination is Australia,' I said. Which, technically, was true.

'Where do you go from here?' he asked.

'I go to Kuwait, then Jordan,' I said.

'Do you travel to Jordan a lot?' he asked.

This was the long-division moment: the real answer was that I travelled to Amman on almost every trip out of Israel. I knew that in the passport I was hiding from him there were many Amman stamps, but I was trying to remember if there were many Amman stamps in the one he was looking at.

'Not much,' I guessed.

He flicked through the passport and looked back at me. 'You say you do not travel much to Jordan but there are four stamps here.'

'That was in transit,' I said. I tried not to show it but I was nervous. This was not a good time to be taken away for questioning by Iranian authorities.

'Why would any country put in a stamp for a transit stop?' he asked: a reasonable question.

'I really don't know,' I said, hoping it was enough.

He and the woman had another discussion. Then he said: 'The Arabs do all sorts of things that cannot be explained.' They laughed furiously. The age-old Persian rivalry with the Arabs had kicked in.

He handed back my passport. 'Thank you,' he said. 'I hope you enjoyed the Islamic Republic of Iran.'

I went through, sat down and had a coffee. I felt a huge sense of relief – it could have ended badly. Once the plane took off, I watched a remarkable scene: several women around me dressed in burkas or niqabs took off their robes. Underneath, many wore designer clothes. Some took high-heeled shoes and lipstick from their hand luggage. From Basij to Prada – before the dinner was served.

But beyond my relief at leaving Iran I also felt anger. Those of us on the plane were leaving behind millions of trapped people.

CHAPTER 6

The French School of Jerusalem

July 2009

WE'D NOW BEEN IN JERUSALEM FOR SIX MONTHS AND THE attitude we'd arrived with was beginning to be challenged. We were seeing things that we'd not read about in our preparations to come here. We needed to look no further than Jack's school, which proved to be a mine of stories, a perfect microcosm of life in a conflict zone.

Six years of hearing real-life stories through the French School of Jerusalem would allow me to give the conflict a human dimension. I'd be able to gain a knowledge of how the system worked from direct experience.

Run by the French Government, the Lycée Français de Jérusalem was housed in a magnificent old stone convent rented from the St Joseph's nuns. It had a French director and mainly Jewish Israeli teachers. Some of the parents were diplomats, aid workers and journalists. The school held fundraising lunches on Fridays that proved interesting; I would find myself having a beer with a diplomat who'd just spent a week in Gaza or Syria.

A lot of the students lived in the West Bank. Students were mainly Palestinian, with some French and other internationals. During the Second Intifada (second Palestinian uprising) between 2000 and 2005 – in which 3057 Palestinians and 918 Israelis were killed – many foreigners fled Jerusalem, leaving vacancies at the school. France offered them to Palestinian children.

I've always savoured the challenge of trying to decode scenes and conversations. Often in Israel you come across what Israelis call *balagan* – a Hebrew word meaning 'chaos'. Our initial parent– teacher meeting, halfway through our first year in Jerusalem, turned into serious *balagan*.

I was approaching the event with great enthusiasm. At Jack's school in Sydney, these meetings had been a good way to make friends. Before the meeting at the new school in Jerusalem, I even bought a barbecue for our balcony so we could entertain the friends we'd hopefully meet.

The day came. Parents began to arrive – and hostilities quickly emerged. A French parent accused the Palestinian parents of holding a secret advance meeting to plan their strategy for today's meeting. The French parents wanted to increase the fees so the school could provide better facilities, while the Palestinians said the French Government should pay more.

When a French parent said there should have been no preliminary meeting, a Palestinian shouted: 'Why is it always the fault of the Palestinians?'

A Palestinian woman began speaking in Arabic.

'Speak French, this is a French school!' a French mother yelled.

The Palestinian woman glared at her: 'I will speak my language when I am in Palestine!'

'This is not Palestine!' the French woman responded. 'This is Israel!'

The room erupted. A French diplomat involved with the school called for calm. A Palestinian father replied: 'Under what authority are you standing there?'

The Palestinian had wounded French pride. 'With the full authority of the French Government, which pays for this school!' he replied.

The meeting went downhill from there. No barbecue tonight, I thought. As we left, a French woman, making a point, put a finger on the shoulder of a Palestinian woman.

'Don't touch me with your condescending French finger!' the Palestinian snapped.

At another meeting, in mid-2010, Palestinian parents turned on each other. One group said the school should register as an Israeli school to receive tax concessions, while others objected.

'I will not take one shekel from the occupying power!' one man shouted.

I was sitting next to a UN official – a parent – who said: 'Here we go – Fatah versus Hamas!'

In Jerusalem, you could never escape the conflict.

Later we saw how it had taken hold even at a suburban level, when we were invited to the 13th birthday of a friend of Jack's from school. His house was just near the German Colony, a mainly Jewish area of West Jerusalem.

The boy's father, a New Zealander, and his mother, a Palestinian, were getting the backyard ready. His Palestinian uncle lit the barbecue, which gave off some smoke – nothing dramatic – but it unleashed a loud verbal attack from a neighbour. The boy's family had been living in the house since 1968, coexisting peacefully with their Jewish neighbours. But a Jewish family from Morocco had recently moved next door.

'Why are you living here?' the Moroccan neighbour shouted in English. 'You should go and live in one of the Arab neighbourhoods!'

The following argument ensued.

The uncle: 'Our family has been living here since 1968!'

The neighbour: 'Yes, that's enough – you've been here too long!'

The uncle: 'But you've only been here from Morocco for a year!'

The neighbour then switched to Hebrew. He shouted: '*Anachnu mishtaltim alechem*' – 'We are taking control over you.'

The uncle: 'If you think you have control over me let's meet in a stairwell and see who controls who.'

The boy's family called the police, fearful that if they didn't then the neighbour would. In the battle between Palestinians and Israelis, there's always a first-mover advantage. The family then filmed the backyard to prove it was a birthday party. I sat there thinking how horrible it was to live like this.

The Israeli police turned up and began interrogating the family, even though they'd done nothing wrong. When the police discovered that foreigners were present – us   they became conciliatory.

We discovered that much of the hatred towards Palestinians came from more recent immigrants. And older Israelis often had a more benign attitude than their children. They had had regular contact with Palestinians for decades, and many acknowledged that 700,000 Palestinians were exiled or fled when the State of Israel was established in 1948.

Batsheva, who lived in the apartment below us, was in her 60s and a fifth-generation Israeli. Her gardener was an elderly Palestinian who had worked for her for 10 years. 'But my children want me to sack him,' she told us. 'They say one day he'll slit my throat.' Her view was that the occupation guaranteed endless conflict; her children's view was that God had given the Jewish people 'Judea and Samaria', the Palestinian Territories.

One day around this time, while dropping Jack at school, a parent told us that gas masks were being handed out at the Talpiot Mall. Crowds had gathered in the mall and were pushing towards boxes of the masks. Officials shouted for them to calm down.

'What's happening?' I asked one man.

'We're preparing for war,' he replied.

'Who against?' I asked

'Maybe Iran, maybe Hezbollah, maybe Hamas – but somebody is going to attack.'

Israel is that sort of place. People either talk about the war just passed or the war about to begin. Enemies are over the horizon – it's just not certain who. I got into the queue to get masks for Sylvie, Jack and me, but was told the masks were only for Israelis.

That night Jack, then 11, wrote in his diary: 'There is one thing that everybody is preparing for – war. Iran was saying they have a nuclear bomb. In the malls people were giving out gas masks for free and the Prime Minister [Benjamin Netanyahu] was thinking about attacking first. I knew that they [Iran] would not aim at Jerusalem, since a lot of Palestinians live there and there is the

Dome of the Rock mosque. Things in Syria are getting out of control. That's all. Apart from that, everything is peaceful.'

*

We wanted Jack to experience both Israeli and Palestinian cultures, so in our first summer in Jerusalem – June 2009 – we enrolled him in our neighbourhood Hebrew-language judo and gym clubs and the Palestinian soccer club and summer camp.

The Hand in Hand summer camp was one of the few in Jerusalem that accepted both Jewish and Palestinian students. At the end of the first day I asked the director, an Israeli, how Jack had been.

'No complaints, but I can tell you he's unlikely to be worse than the Israeli kids,' she said. 'A lot of Israeli children are on Ritalin and their parents think it's good to give them a break over the holidays. So the kids come off Ritalin and become my problem.' She told me Israeli kids often became aggressive towards their teachers, so Ritalin was used 'like a blanket thrown over the children'. Local media reported a lot of violence in Israeli schools.

Through Jack's school I discovered that some Palestinian children also had behavioural problems. It seemed the conflict fed on itself in terms of violence.

We saw first-hand how Palestinians in Israel lived in fear. One of the Palestinian boys in Jack's class was playing with friends in Bethlehem when Israeli soldiers arrived. Jack's friend escaped but others did not: they returned to school days later with cuts and bruises.

One day in 2010 a car driving past Jack's school lost control. Because there were no railings, the car careered onto a footpath, killing a student, six-year-old Farid Abu Katish. Jerusalem's streets are narrow; it's a 17th-century city with 21st-century demands. In an effort to get railings and speed humps installed, the parents – including Sylvie and me – held a protest outside the school, complete with banners in Hebrew. We walked to the office of the Mayor, Nir Barkat. One of the parents, Nicolas Pelham, the correspondent for *The Economist*, led the way. We wanted to give Barkat a petition. Looking up at Barkat's office, Pelham chanted through a megaphone: 'Barkat! Barkat! Come down now!'

Finally, Pelham needed a rest. He turned to some Palestinian parents and tried to hand them the megaphone. They backed away. Even though we'd obtained a permit for the demonstration, the Palestinians were too fearful to take a prominent role. And although the protest was legal, Israeli police told us to close it down. 'You have a permit for the demonstration but not for the megaphone,' one said. In the end, the municipality agreed to put up a barrier outside the gate and paint a crossing.

Palestinian parents later told me that one of the reasons for their fear was Israel's right to revoke work permits or residency for 'Jerusalemites' – Palestinians living in Jerusalem. These Palestinians don't have the same rights as Israelis – for example, they are not allowed to vote in Israel's national elections. For those parents living in the West Bank the permit situation made them even more vulnerable. In the West Bank, the Israeli Army will not allow Palestinians to gather for a protest in a group of more than 10.[1] Permits are rarely granted, meaning demonstrations are effectively prohibited. The maximum sentence for protesting is 10 years – which means the army can go into a crowd of 10 or more Palestinians that they claim is a demonstration and send someone to prison for 10 years. The only evidence they need to show for a conviction is a photograph of what appears to be a protest.

This was just one of many kinds of discrimination we noticed. One day, not long after we arrived in Jerusalem, Sylvie was picking up Jack from school and mentioned to the Palestinian woman in charge of the playground that she looked good. 'I washed my hair!' she replied. She explained that in her West Bank village of Taybeh they got water on Saturdays, and the moment they heard water hit their tanks they began washing their houses, their clothes, their children and their hair and then filling up bottles. For many, Saturday was their only day off work.

From this moment, we started to inquire about the water situation in every Palestinian village we visited. We learnt that an Israeli uses between 240 and 300 litres per day, compared with the Palestinian average of 73 litres. Many Palestinian families spend up to 40 per cent of their salary on water, according to *Haaretz* newspaper. In Area C of the West Bank – which is under total Israeli control – average water consumption for Palestinians is 20 litres per person each day.[2] This compares with an average of 270 litres per person each day for neighbouring Israeli settlers.

Many Palestinian parents at the school were also not allowed to live in Jerusalem. Israel does not allow the immigration of Palestinians from the West Bank to Israel, which would change the demographic balance. In 2003, Israel passed a law[3] that prevents Palestinians from the West Bank who marry Palestinians who are Israeli citizens from living in Israel. One Palestinian man that we knew – an Israeli citizen – was married to a Palestinian from the West Bank. His wife was not legally allowed to work or drive in Israel, so she held a job in secret and lived in fear of having the smallest car accident that would bring her to the attention of Israeli police.

One woman we knew needed a visa for a work trip to the US. As a Palestinian, she was not allowed to travel to Jerusalem without a permit. Because the US Consulate is in Jerusalem, the only way she could get a visa was to illegally visit the city. At checkpoints into Jerusalem, Israeli soldiers stop anyone who looks Palestinian, so to get through, the woman took off her scarf, let her hair down, put on lipstick and wore sunglasses. The soldiers, presumably thinking she was either a foreigner or a settler, waved her and her female friend through. The women called it their 'Thelma and Louise moment'.

Each morning the school provided a bus for students – both French and Palestinian – who needed to travel from Bethlehem, in the West Bank, to Jerusalem. They needed to cross an Israeli Army checkpoint. Most soldiers waved the bus through. But we were told that once in 2008 a soldier had decided to make all the children get off. It had been a hot day, and about 15 children, some as young as four, had been forced to stand for hours in the sun. Many had cried and several had wet themselves. French diplomats had been outraged.

To make sure it did not happen again, each day a French diplomat in Jerusalem would rise at 6am and drive to Bethlehem to accompany the bus into Jerusalem. If a soldier tried to board the bus, the diplomat would hold up his or her credentials and tell the soldier the bus was French territory and could not be entered.

Most days this worked, but one day a soldier decided that while the French official had diplomatic protection, the driver did not; the soldier insisted that he could board the bus. A stand-off went on for hours until Israeli and French officials worked out a solution.

Many of the parents in the West Bank were not able to attend school concerts. Many never met their children's teachers, as they could not travel to Jerusalem.

One Palestinian boy was preparing for his final exams, the Baccalauréat. Because he had turned 18, he needed an 'adult permit' to travel from his home in Bethlehem to the school in Jerusalem. The Israelis would not give him one. This meant he could not sit the exams in Jerusalem even though he'd been preparing for six years.

A French mother, angry about this, smuggled the boy in her car to a hotel in East Jerusalem. The boy was terrified there would be a knock at the door and it would be Shin Bet (the Israel Security Agency). There was no knock, and he passed with distinction.

In 2016, after our return to Australia, a new hotel would open opposite the school. A group of fathers who had dropped off their children tried to order coffees. 'We don't serve Arabs here,' they were told. Such discrimination, in my view, creates a long-term disaster: these men are moderate, well-educated professional Palestinians who should be bridges to a peaceful future. Instead, they felt humiliated, and it reinforced to them that such discrimination goes on openly, and unpunished, every day.

*

About six o'clock one morning, the mother of one of the Palestinian boys from Jack's school phoned. 'We need your help,' she told me. 'As a foreigner you will have more influence than us.'

She said the police had come to their house in Jerusalem and taken away their 16-year-old son. He was now being interrogated, without a parent or lawyer, by Shin Bet.

Someone had gone into the family's garden and cut down their olive trees, and written 'Price Tag' in Hebrew. 'Price Tag' was a policy of violence used by some Israeli settlers in the West Bank to protest against government decisions they didn't like. They would write these words after they burnt down mosques or cut down olive groves.

Sometimes Jewish extremists in Israel vandalised Christian churches and spray-painted graffiti such as 'Price Tag' or 'Mary Was a Whore'. But while Christians were sometimes targeted in Jerusalem, if Palestinians were now facing 'Price Tag' inside Israel it was a big story. The French media in particular were interested.

'They say my son cut down the trees,' the mother told me. To me this was completely implausible – the notion that he would cut down his own family's olive trees then write 'Price Tag'. But that was what Shin Bet was arguing.

This fitted with a pattern I had started to see of how Israel muddied the waters. It was much harder for the media to report that 'Price Tag' was spreading among Israeli extremists when a Palestinian youth was being interrogated for the crime.

The boy was an Israeli citizen and had a working knowledge of Hebrew. His parents had decided he would need it if they were to remain in Israel. During the interrogation, Shin Bet officers handed him a piece of paper and asked him to write 'price' and 'tag' in Hebrew. He knew 'price', but not 'tag'.

For 16 hours, different interrogators tried different approaches – sometimes threats, sometimes sympathy – to get him to confess. But he simply did not know the Hebrew word for 'tag'. They let him go, but Shin Bet had made it difficult for journalists to write that 'Price Tag' had come to Jerusalem and, secondly, should they have any concern about this youth in future they could argue that he was a risk, as they had previously had to interview him.

*

Such interrogations of children occur every day in the West Bank.

In 2012, a British delegation of lawyers and judges, including former British Attorney General Baroness Patricia Scotland, called for Israel to video-tape interrogations to reduce the chances of assault. As a result, Israel introduced audio-visual recording in 'non-security' cases – but it soon emerged that they were using a system of double interviews.

It became clear that in some cases the first interview was the 'real' interview, in which the child continued to be threatened or tortured until agreeing to confess. Some children told human rights lawyers they were tortured with hand-held electrical devices, or threatened with rape, until they either confessed or provided information about others, and were asked to become regular informants. Children reported that they were then brought back for a second interview, which was conducted lawfully and video-taped: the child was read his rights before, usually, confessing.[4] A UNICEF report stated: 'In the majority of cases, the principal evidence against the child is the child's own confession ... although many children reported providing confessions as a result of ill-treatment, few raise this matter before the court for fear that their complaints would lead to harsher sentences, even though international law prohibits the use of evidence obtained under duress by a court'.[5]

When it came to detaining Palestinian children for questioning, in most cases soldiers would force their way into a house at two or three in the morning. Children as young as 12 were routinely taken by soldiers from their beds to unknown locations, denied access to a parent or lawyer and sometimes kept in solitary confinement.

Enough Palestinian children have talked about the notorious Cell 36 in Al Jalame children's prison in the north of Israel for lawyers to have built up a picture. Harriet Sherwood of the UK's *Guardian* newspaper carried out an investigation into the cell. She reported: 'The room is barely wider than the thin, dirty mattress that covers the floor. It is one of a handful of cells where Palestinian children are locked in solitary confinement for days or even weeks. One 16-year-old claimed that he had been kept in Cell 36 for 65 days.'[6]

The Guardian's investigation was based on affidavits by minors to Defence of Children International. Most of the children were accused of throwing stones and most maintained their innocence, even though they signed confessions. Australian lawyer Gerard Horton, who through his group Military Court Watch monitors this situation, said the quickest way to get out of the system is to plead guilty. He said: 'The system, particularly the solitary confinement, breaks the spirit of the child and what we find is that the children often say that after a week of this treatment they confess simply to get out of the cell.'[7]

Again, under international pressure, Israel agreed to a trial whereby a summons would be issued in lieu of night arrests – as occurred with Jewish children in neighbouring settlements. But after media attention had died away, Israel stopped the pilot program altogether. The army claimed that no statistics were kept during the program to enable assessment.[8]

*

I saw the boy from Jack's school shortly after his 'Price Tag' interrogation; he seemed traumatised. For Israel, that was one more way in which their policy worked – in the short term, at least. After such experiences, youths tend to retreat into themselves. But there was another possibility. One day they could snap.

The ultimate authority over the 2.9 million Palestinians in the West Bank is the Israeli Army. For the 600,000 Israeli settlers it is the Israeli civil courts. Since 1967, at least 770,000 Palestinians – including children – have been detained, and many of them prosecuted in the military court, whose judges are soldiers.

I was interested in how a country could operate two different legal systems in the same area: a civilian law for Israelis and a military law for Palestinians. I would research the operation of the West Bank military court for more than a year, and finally the IDF would give Sylvie and me rare access. They would at last accept my argument: if you're proud of your system, why not let us visit?

November 22, 2010. A brilliant sunny morning when we picked up Captain Arye Shalicar and made the 25-minute drive to the military court at Ofer, in the West Bank. (Following that visit, Sylvie and I conducted a year of research into the military court system, before returning for a second visit to check our information with the Israeli Army prosecutors.) It was a grim place, with an entrance of barbed wire. Twice a week they had 'children's days', when children as young as 12 faced army judges.

As we waited to go in, Captain Shalicar said he thought foreign journalists needed to do more positive stories about Israel – such as features on its booming wine and hi-tech industries. Just at that moment we heard the clink of metal. Through a gate came a Palestinian man, shackled and handcuffed.

We entered the courtroom. The guards were clearly trying to keep the doors shut until the last moment, but one opened them too early and I caught a glimpse of what Israel's long-term grip on the West Bank looked like.

Four young boys, in small brown prison overalls, shuffled across the courtyard. They were handcuffed and shackled at the feet. At that moment I thought: If the most powerful army in the Middle East thinks it's acceptable to treat children like this, then something has gone badly wrong.

That was not to say, of course, that some of these children should not be seriously dealt with. I had gone to hospital to visit a three-year-old Israeli girl, Adele Biton, who had suffered brain damage from rocks thrown by Palestinian youths as her family drove to their West Bank settlement. She later died.

But it could not be denied that these Palestinian children were not being given the same justice before the law as would be guaranteed to a Jewish child who lived in a settlement next door.

The most stunning aspect of the military court was its conveyor-belt nature. So quick were the appearances that sometimes the judge did not even look at the children. Some of the cases I witnessed lasted less than 60 seconds – just long enough for the child to plead guilty and to hear their sentence. A lawyer told me how even though one boy banged his head repeatedly against the metal rail, the judge did not look at him.

Sometimes the children didn't even have a chance to talk to their lawyer. Those who did were usually advised to plead guilty: in 99 per cent of cases – the IDF's statistic – there was a conviction. These must be the most guilty children in the world.

If police or soldiers in Australia took Aboriginal children from their beds at three in the morning and did what Israel does there would be an uproar. So why did those who financially support this army have no problem with it? Even Israel's Foreign Ministry spokesman Yigal Palmor told me that the military court system was a 'wart'. He quipped: 'Let's face it – military courts are to justice what military bands are to music.'

As we finally left the military court, Captain Shalicar remarked: 'It's not a very nice place, is it?'

More than two years after Sylvie and I began researching this story, and after two visits to the military court, I sat down and wrote the following words:

> You hear them before you see them. The first clue that a
> new group of children is approaching is a shuffle of shoes
> and a clinking of handcuffs and shackles. The door to the
> courtroom bursts open – four boys, all shackled, stare into
> the room. Four boys looking bewildered. They wear brown
> prison overalls and they trail into the room where their fate
> is to be decided by a female Israeli Army officer-judge, who
> is sitting at the bench, waiting. The look on the face of one
> of the boys changes to elation when he sees his mother at the
> back of the court. He blows her a kiss. But his mother begins
> crying and this upsets the boy. He begins crying too ...
>
> This courtroom has become a front line of one of the
> oldest conflicts in the world, the Israeli–Palestinian conflict.

It is Israel's conveyor belt of justice, but it is a world away from Israel: in Israel a child cannot be sent to prison until 14; in Israel there are laws against a child being taken away at night; and in Israel a child cannot be interrogated without a parent.

The Israeli Defence Forces, concerned at the growing debate about Israel's treatment of children, has given *The Weekend Australian Magazine* rare access to the court. They say too many journalists write about it without visiting it. They are keen for me to spend time with the army prosecutor in charge of the cases who will be my guide during three visits to the court. I have a briefing with him before the trials begin. The main point he wants to emphasise is that, two years ago, the army set up this military juvenile court to take note of children's needs. If a child needs a welfare officer or a psychologist, they are available.

Inside the courtroom, the army's public relations unit wants the IDF guide to sit next to me to explain each case. I'm told I can quote him as 'my guide' but not name him and we are allowed to photograph some of the older children but not the younger ones. Nor will they allow us to photograph children handcuffed and shackled trying to walk – 'absolutely not', my guide says. The army obviously realises that such a photo would be enormously damaging. After September 11 I'd seen images of alleged terrorists walking like this but I'd never seen children treated this way. It's not surprising that Israel doesn't want this image out there – it would look uncomfortably like a Guantanamo Bay for kids.[9]

CHAPTER 7

Dirty Tricks

August 2009

IT WAS ONE OF THE MOST EXTRAORDINARY 'DIRTY TRICKS' operations I've ever witnessed. Over 35 years in journalism, I've reported on a few, as they tend to make intriguing stories. But there was something very different about this one: the target was me.

The saga began with a story I'd written for the *Weekend Australian Magazine*, published on 22 August 2009. It was about a man called Nasser Jaber, a Palestinian travel agent whose family had lived in the Old City of Jerusalem for generations. In 2009, he moved out of his house so it could be renovated. A group of seven armed Jewish settlers living nearby saw that he had moved out, and, at 2.30 in the morning, broke in and changed the locks. They refused to leave. A few days later they put Jaber's furniture onto the street, and to this day he has not been able to return to his house.

What appealed to me about doing this story for an Australian audience was that it helped explain the daily battle in the Old City of Jerusalem. The aim of some Israeli hardliners is to 'Judaise' the

Palestinian parts of the Old City – to get as many Jewish families as possible into houses currently occupied by Palestinians. By doing this, they can improve the 'demographic balance' of the Old City. There are powerful groups behind this Judaisation, such as Ateret Cohanim, whose funding comes from Jewish groups in countries such as Australia and the US. Ataret Cohanim operates in the shadows – run by an Australian, Daniel Luria. It works to create a Jewish majority in the Old City as well as in East Jerusalem.

My interest in the general issue of evictions had been increased by the eviction a couple of weeks earlier of several Palestinian families from their homes in East Jerusalem to make way for Jewish families. The families had lived in their homes for generations and the evictions meant 19 children were left homeless. Both British and US officials had issued statements of concern. The British Consulate in Jerusalem said: 'We are appalled by the evictions in East Jerusalem. Israel's claim that the imposition of extremist Jewish settlers into this ancient Arab neighbourhood is a matter for the court or the municipality is unacceptable. Their actions are incompatible with Israel's professed desire for peace. We urge Israel not to allow extremists to set the agenda.'

The US State Department said: 'We urge that the government of Israel and municipal officials refrain from provocative actions in East Jerusalem, including home demolitions and evictions.'

I started following the story of Nasser Jaber 12 hours after his home was invaded by armed settlers and spent four months researching the story, which included going to all the court hearings. I interviewed Jaber, and approached the lawyer representing the settlers at the court hearings. His clients did not want to comment. But I viewed the documents he produced for the court, as well as Jaber's title deed for the house. The settlers were claiming they had bought the house, but where was their record of purchase? Did they trust this Palestinian man so much that they had paid him a large sum of money but had not asked him for a receipt?

I discovered that the ownership of the house had been challenged in court by Israeli settlers nine years earlier. In that dispute the judge had ruled that under Israeli law the property belonged to Jaber. I interviewed people who lived in the same part of the Old City who confirmed that Jaber's family had lived there for decades.

The court process seemed to be going Jaber's way. The judge told the settlers she had two questions for them: what time did they enter the house, and how? Jaber told me after that hearing, 'When we heard those questions we thought everything would be OK. Obviously if you have good documents you can enter in the light of day.'

But Jaber's faith in the Israeli legal process was soon eroded. In subsequent hearings, those two questions were never asked again, and at the end of each hearing the judge ordered that the status quo be maintained. This meant the settlers would be able to remain in the house until the case was heard in full. But in Jerusalem these cases often go on for years, so Jaber was locked out of his home indefinitely. 'If I was Jewish and seven armed Palestinians had broken into my house, the case would have been dealt with within the hour,' said Jaber.

Jaber's lawyer argued that in the lead-up to the break-in the Israelis had offered to buy the house. During one court hearing, Jaber's lawyer asked the settlers: 'If you say you own the property why are you still making offers to buy it?' The settlers did not respond.

Three lawyers from the UK were monitoring the case, and one of them remarked to me that given the settlers had entered the property at 2.30am and could not produce any evidence that they had bought the property, the case would be thrown out in almost every jurisdiction in the world. At the very least, he argued, the presumption of ownership would have been given to the man who had lived in the house for 38 years and had produced titles to the property for an Israeli court nine years earlier. On that occasion the judge ruled that the documents the settlers were presenting were fakes and they were ordered to leave immediately. Jaber produced the deeds again in this case.

*

I realised that the Israeli lobby in Australia was not going to like this story. But early in my posting, when those first attacks had started arriving, I'd decided that if I were going to pull my punches for fear of the inevitable attacks by AIJAC and other groups then I would be acting as a diplomat rather than a journalist and would be short-changing the readers of *The Australian*.

I'd written the story and it was going through the production process for the *Weekend Australian Magazine*. The Editor of the *Weekend Australian*, Nick Cater, dropped by the office of Steve Waterson, the Editor of the magazine. Waterson told me later that Cater warned him about the possible reaction of Colin Rubenstein, the head of AIJAC: 'If there's one mistake in this article Colin will come down on us like a ton of bricks.'

Waterson resented the warning, and said he responded: 'I was Editor of Time Australia for more than ten years. I check everything. We're aware of how sensitive this subject is, and we've been through the story very carefully. John is a hugely experienced editor and correspondent, and I have no doubt his piece is accurate in every respect. Besides, I don't report to Colin, I report to Chris [Mitchell].'

As expected, AIJAC was not happy with the story. It unleashed an attack against me, declaring on its website that a key fact in the story – that Israeli police had provided food to the settlers who had moved into the house – was wrong. I began receiving emails from members of the Australian Jewish community who questioned whether Jaber even existed – despite the fact that his photo appeared alongside my article. One emailer told me he believed Jaber was a fake because he'd checked on the internet and could find no reference to his travel agency, and 'obviously a travel agency would have a social media presence'.

The Israeli Embassy in Canberra joined the attack. Hearing that SBS's *Dateline* was soon to run a story by Sophie McNeill on the same issue, Dor Shapira, the embassy's Political Officer, phoned the Executive Producer of *Dateline*, Peter Charley. Shapira asked Charley whether he was proceeding with McNeill's story on Nasser Jaber. Charley was somewhat taken aback but insisted that he was. Shapira told Charley that my story in the *Weekend Australian Magazine* was 'inaccurate' and that he wanted to provide McNeill with contacts in Jerusalem to give the *Dateline* story 'balance'. Charley asked McNeill to communicate with Shapira to get these contacts but stressed that she should report the story exactly as she saw it.

Fresh from ringing SBS, Shapira went to Nick Cater and asked that *The Australian* publish a letter stating that the story contained factual errors. When I heard through a colleague on the paper that Cater was planning to publish it, I contacted Chris Mitchell.

I explained that the letter – which was meant to detail the errors I had made – was itself full of errors. I talked Mitchell through them. Shapira had even got Nasser Jaber's name wrong, calling him 'Naber Jasser'. Shapira repeated the criticism made against me by AIJAC: 'The police never cooperated with the Jewish residents and never supplied them with food.' I explained to Mitchell that what Shapira didn't know was that Sophie McNeill had spent several days in the Old City filming the police as they helped the Israelis move goods into the house and took them food. I'd gone through the footage frame by frame. SBS was about to broadcast the vision. The story, 'Hot Property', aired on *Dateline* on 1 November.

Chris Mitchell decided not to run the letter in the paper. That's the sort of backing that is invaluable for a correspondent. If a story contains errors then the media outlet should correct it quickly, but if the story is correct and the letter is wrong that is, in my view, a different matter.

There was one bizarre aspect of Shapira's letter: he claimed that my article had harmed the peace process. 'In publishing this story, the *Weekend Australian* damages the ability of parties to the peace process to negotiate with trust and credibility.' In response to Dor Shapira, Steve Waterson wrote: 'If you really believe that we are the obstacle to the peace process, I fear your priorities are sadly misplaced.'

*

I'd headed off the attacks from the Israeli Embassy and AIJAC, but now an entirely new assault began – the Dirty Tricks campaign. This new campaign would be led by a mystery Israeli journalist.

The first hint I had of it was when I rang Nasser Jaber in September, a month after my article was published, to check if there were any developments in his case. He told me, 'I've had a call from a woman who says she's an Australian journalist based in Jerusalem and she wants to do a story on me.' This intrigued me: there were only three Australian journalists based in Israel, and I knew them all. Jaber continued, 'She wanted me to say that you misquoted me, and I said you had not.' Jaber told her that if she wanted to interview him she would need to do it in person. She left her name – Noga – but would not leave her telephone number. Jaber found this odd; why would a journalist not leave a telephone number? She said she'd ring back. When she did call back, she insisted – for a second time – that he had been misquoted in the story. Jaber insisted – for a second time – that he had not been misquoted. This time she left her phone number, which would prove her one mistake when it came to me discovering her identity.

I checked through the list of journalists in Israel. The only Noga was Noga Tarnopolsky. It would not be her – we'd spent our second Friday night in Jerusalem having Shabbat dinner at her place with a mutual friend, and Noga had been to our house for lunch.

I would subsequently uncover the movements of this 'Noga' in the weeks after my article was published. She was aware that there was a television program on the ABC in Australia called *Media Watch*, dedicated to keeping journalists accountable. But how would she get material to them without revealing her identity? She knew a journalist at the *Sydney Morning Herald*, Asher Moses, so she decided to use him as a middle man. She told him that she thought my story had been made up. Moses would later tell me that Noga had told him that for many Palestinians, the fabrication of facts was considered normal. It was clear she believed that Nasser Jaber was one of these Palestinians. Moses told me that Noga said: 'It's a world view in which "facts" do not exist independently, but as objects one can manipulate to one's benefit, thus racking up points in a long-term struggle.' In contrast, Israel had an admirable approach to correcting anything that it said that was wrong. She sent Moses material to pass on to *Media Watch*, but told him that to protect her identity she would use the name of a friend, Lydia Rener, a bag designer. Noga, who was apparently part of the foreign journalists' community, didn't want her fingerprints anywhere near what she was about to do.

Moses then got in touch with Mark Franklin, a producer at *Media Watch*, to tell him that he would soon be contacted by someone with strong credentials – a leading journalist who had written for the *Jerusalem Post* and the *New York Times*, among other publications. But the need for secrecy was paramount. Moses wrote, 'I won't tell anyone else about it before you broadcast.'

Noga then sent Moses material that she hoped would discredit both me and Jaber, exposing me as the typical biased foreign journalist and Jaber as the typical Palestinian with a flexible view of the truth. She explained that Micky Rosenfeld, the official spokesman for the Israeli Police, knew nothing about the Jaber case. Noga didn't realise that the police who attended Nasser Jaber's house were the Border Police – who come under the army, not the police.

She had also contacted Israeli human rights group Ir Amim. 'Very significantly, Ir Amim has no record of this case at all,' she wrote to Asher Moses. Ir Amim, however, had never had anything to do with the case. Peace Now was the human rights group that had been attending the court hearings. Had she rung them her entire attack would have collapsed.

But Noga was convinced that the whole story was a fabrication. She wrote to Asher Moses: 'It really appears that *The Weekend Australian* simply got the story wrong – the heart of the story, not just tangential details. In other words, it's not the story of the midnight highway robbery of a house, it's the complicated story of one member of an Arab family screwing another member, and a Jewish non-profit organisation taking advantage of that situation. Life in the Middle East (and especially in the Old City of Jerusalem) is filled with complexities, and superficial or not properly researched stories just muck things up.'

Moses passed the information on to *Media Watch* in Sydney. He pointed out to me later, 'My only involvement was forwarding an email.' One day in early September, Noga took a bus from Jerusalem to Lydia Rener's house in Tel Aviv. Using Lydia's email address, she wrote to Mark Franklin at *Media Watch*: 'I am glad that Asher [Moses] forwarded you all the phone numbers and info I had sent him. Great news.' Noga wanted her material on me to be seen not just as an isolated story but as an illustration of how the foreign media in general cover Israel. 'The contacts that I sent along will be useful for you and grant legitimacy to any other incident that might arise from Israeli news coverage', she told Franklin. She talked about 'the general failures in Israel coverage'.

Noga also told Franklin, 'I am personally friendly with Foreign Ministry personnel who were involved with drafting the Israeli response [to my article].' I'd heard separately from a contact inside the Israeli Foreign Ministry that its legal team had indeed been told to attempt to find faults in the story.

On 22 September, Noga made another bus trip from Jerusalem to Lydia Rener in Tel Aviv. She wanted to give Franklin a push-along. Her email read: 'Hi Mark, Shana Tova [Happy Jewish New Year]! Any progress? Any interest? All best, Lydia.'

Franklin was nervous about having *Media Watch* base an attack on someone not prepared to use their real name. He was worried that because 'Lydia' had concealed her identity she might not be accountable for the information she provided. Franklin told 'Lydia': 'I have to say … it troubles me that you are using a false name. I have to be suspicious of sources who ask for anonymity and I can see no good reason why you won't even tell me your name. How do I know that you're a journalist who has been published in the J-Post and NYT? Really, I'm only pursuing this story on the strength of your credentials, and I can't even verify those.'

'Lydia' replied: 'I understand the suspicions you feel. For many reasons, both personal and professional, it is inappropriate for me to be involved in this story. I know both the journalist involved and his competitors … also, I know the Australian media world is a firey and divey thing.'

She continued: 'I feel very awkward, of course, because I *have* published in the NYT and other fab places! But truly, this has nothing to do with my ego or my credentials, or, you know, anything other than your own professional judgment about whether this story is worth pursuing for your very excellent program. If so, let me know, I'll be happy to help, and I trust we'll find a way around my temporary anonymity. Incidentally, I am a real *Media Watch* admirer, and under my own name will be happy to assist you with other stuff should you ever require some local footwork.'

'Lydia Rener' added a note of intrigue. She told Franklin: 'Just to let you know, the AJN have contacted me and have a researcher working on this case.' How would the *Australian Jewish News* know to contact someone who was hiding her identity about a story with which she had no association?

About the same time, I got a call from Bob Magid, the owner of the *Australian Jewish News*. I didn't know him but he was in Jerusalem for Shimon Peres's presidential conference and wanted to meet. When we met at the conference, he told me that he'd engaged Haviv Rettig-Gur, a journalist with the *Jerusalem Post*, to check the veracity of my story about Nasser Jaber. Rettig-Gur was attending the conference, so I suggested that the three of us get together so I could answer any questions they had.

The three of us sat down together. The next 20 minutes were truly odd. To find out what research Rettig-Gur had done, I asked him whether he'd checked the court records, including the statement of claim of both sides. He said no. I asked whether he had spoken to Nasser Jaber. He said no. (I gave him Jaber's phone number.) I asked whether he had been to look at the house in the Old City. He said no. The expression on Magid's face when Rettig-Gur kept saying no to all my questions was one of 'Then what am I paying you for?' Rettig-Gur said that if I could help him prove that the story was true then 'perhaps the *Jerusalem Post* can campaign on behalf of Nasser Jaber'. I told him I did four months' research into the story and we proved it was true; that was why we published it. I also found his comment about the *Jerusalem Post* campaigning on behalf of a dispossessed Palestinian ludicrous. I never heard from Rettig-Gur again.

For weeks I'd refused to believe that the 'Noga' running the campaign could be Noga Tarnopolsky. It was inconceivable that someone who knew Sylvie and me would engage in such a cloak-and-dagger operation. But a nagging doubt grew in my mind.

I telephoned Nasser Jaber and asked if he still had the telephone number that Noga, the 'Australian journalist', had given. He looked around for the piece of paper then rang me back.

It was Noga Tarnopolsky's telephone number. The whole campaign had been run by Noga – our friend.

I decided that she and I should meet and discuss what it was that she was upset about. We sat down in a café in the German Colony and I told her I knew all about her operation.

She looked stunned.

'Why did you do it? I asked.

'I think the foreign media cover Israel unfairly and I thought you were doing the same thing,' she said.

Over the next hour, she explained the whole operation. She said that when Micky Rosenfeld knew nothing about the Israelis who had moved into Jaber's home she became suspicious that it had never happened. When she called Ir Amin and they, too, knew nothing about it, it seemed to confirm to her that the whole thing had been made up. She said if she'd known it was the Border Police, rather than the regular police, and that it was Peace Now, rather than Ir Amim, she would never have pursued the operation to feed material to *Media Watch*.

'But couldn't you have rung me and asked me?' I said.

'Yes,' she said, clearly embarrassed.

The whole saga confirmed something about Israel that I had begun to understand. If a foreign correspondent writes about 'Palestinians' as a generic group there is no problem. But if a journalist gives a Palestinian a name as I did – an identity, an ambition, a profession, a life – it can bring down the wrath of Israel's supporters, even acquaintances such as Noga Tarnopolsky.

A few months later, a leader of the Melbourne Jewish community visited Israel. Over lunch, I asked him why he thought the Nasser Jaber story had caused such a fuss.

'You portrayed him as a professional, middle-class Palestinian,' he told me.

'But he *is* a professional, middle-class Palestinian,' I replied. 'It's just that now he's a professional, middle-class Palestinian who can't live in his own home.'

CHAPTER 8

The Arab Spring

December 2010

FEW DEATHS IN MODERN TIMES HAVE HAD SUCH AN IMPACT.
In life, Mohamed Bouazizi was an unremarkable character – a
26-year-old fruit seller with a modest stand in the small village
of Sidi Bouzid in central Tunisia. Bouazizi's life had been
tough. He'd left school early to provide for his widowed mother,
Manoubia. He'd set up his fruit stall and diligently attended each
day. But on 17 December 2010, a council worker made the fateful
decision to tell Bouazizi that he was not allowed to operate at that
spot, and confiscated his cart. Bouazizi snapped. What he did
next would engulf the Arab world in what became known as the
'Arab Spring'.

Bouazizi set himself alight. His suicide unleashed the anger
of Tunisians against the dictatorship of Zine El Abidine Ben
Ali. After they took to the streets the regime cracked down with
brutality. For two weeks Tunisia was crippled, until El Abidine
Ben Ali fled to Saudi Arabia.

Manoubia Bouazizi later said the municipality had long made trouble for her son, often taking away his weighing scales. She could never have imagined his act would lead to the ousting of the president. 'I thank God we were sent this caring boy who opened the gates for all the people of Tunisia – and for all the Arab world,' she said.[1]

There have always been pressure points in the Middle East, but what happened in Tunisia was something that the Arab world rarely sees: big crowds in the streets demonstrating against their leader. For decades, many Arab nations had been ruled by nepotistic, hardline regimes. It was the same formula almost everywhere: dictators who abused their power and abused human rights. Those regimes were all based on fear. Often people did not know whether their neighbour was going to inform on them.

The situation in these countries deteriorated because the cronies of the dictators were awarded key parts of the economy, and it became corrupted. These regimes might have survived, but oppression and no jobs were a lethal combination.

Inspired by Tunisians, a powerful mood of optimism soon developed: people in Egypt, Jordan, Syria, Yemen, Saudi Arabia and Bahrain believed that they, too, might be able to dislodge their dictators.

The 'Arab Spring' – a misnomer if ever there was one – meant that I needed to fly from one uprising to the next in the Middle East and North Africa. As it turned out, the West's belief that Arab nations could go from dictatorship to democracy overnight was hopelessly naïve.

*

Our first trip to Syria as a family had been in August 2010. It was seven months before Syria descended into civil war. When Sylvie, Jack and I arrived in Damascus, the city had been booming: luxury hotels had been fully booked and the Al-Hamidiyah Souq (market) had been bustling with ice-cream shops, clothing boutiques and antiques stores. The *New York Times* had even listed Syria as one of the world's hottest travel destinations. Young entrepreneurs had renovated old mansions into magnificent hotels, charging US$400 a night per room.

From Jerusalem we'd taken the 35-minute drive to Allenby, the land crossing into Jordan. Another three-hour taxi ride, and we were in Damascus in time for afternoon tea. Leaving our hotel, a beautifully renovated 17th-century building, we headed for the souk. It was bursting with silk, cotton, jewellery, spices, medicinal herbs and antiques. Everywhere there were big open-air restaurants where people would sit until 11 or 12 at night. We met Fadi and Ziad, brothers who became our drivers in Syria, Lebanon and Jordan.

Syria had always held a powerful interest for Sylvie and me. We had long wanted to visit the cities of Damascus and Aleppo, and historic sites like Palmyra, the Krak des Chevaliers and the Cardo Maximus in Apamea.

As a cadet journalist, I'd been greatly intrigued by the career of Syria's dictator Hafez al-Assad, public enemy number one of the West. Assad had come to infamy in 1982 when he'd ordered tanks to surround the town of Hama, a stronghold of the fundamentalist Muslim Brotherhood, and open fire, killing as many as 20,000 people.

His son, Bashar, had become the accidental dictator. His father had always wanted Bashar's brother, Basil, to succeed him. Major Basil al-Assad was an engineer and army officer who was leader of the Presidential Guards; he had been groomed for power and invited into the leader's inner circle. But his death in a car accident at 33 threw succession plans into disarray. Bashar, his younger brother, was training as an ophthalmologist in London. On the death of Basil, Bashar took over and quickly positioned himself as a reformer, but he soon came under the influence of the old military machine that had supported his father.

After we visited Hama, I asked the brothers about the brutality of Hafez al-Assad. They did not want to talk about this, but Ziad was positive about Bashar. He pointed out the many universities between Damascus and Jordan, all established by Bashar. He told us how different Bashar was from Hafez. 'His father was a hard man but Bashar is trying to make a future for young Syrians,' he said.

One thing that stood out for us was the number of images around Damascus of Bashar al-Assad with Sheikh Hassan Nasrallah, the head of Hezbollah in Lebanon. These were two of the main leaders in the Middle East aligned with Shia Islam. Syria had a majority of Sunni Muslims – about 60 per cent of the population – but was governed by an Alawite regime, which was an offshoot of Shia. The Alawites made up only 12 per cent of the population. What the number and prominence of the Shia images said to me was that the Assad regime wanted the image of the 'Shia brotherhood' of Assad and Nasrallah displayed for all to see. In every market, we noticed flags and posters of Nasrallah holding a machine gun, the symbol of Hezbollah. Some Syrians saw Nasrallah as the new Gamel Abdel Nasser (Egypt's second president): the face of pan-Arab 'resistance'.

Damascus was a particular stronghold of the Assads. The secret police had done a brilliant job of disguising the hard weaponry of the dictatorship, but I sensed there was a lot of underground opposition to the 40-year regime.

I did observe something interesting on this trip: while I was in an internet café trying to check my email, a couple of people in their 20s started talking about how restricted they were in terms of social media; they'd found themselves blocked by the regime. It was clear that there was much going on beneath the surface.

We travelled to Aleppo – a grand city, which had been at the crossroads of trade for centuries. One memorable event was a rooftop dinner under the Aleppo Citadel, brilliantly illuminated. The Madina Souk of Aleppo was breathtaking in its grandeur. It featured giant chandeliers leading to a maze of cobbled streets where one found antique coffee pots, wooden boxes inlaid with mother of pearl, olive oil soap and a great deal of cloth. Aleppo beamed wealth and confidence.

While travelling around with Fadi, we discussed the differences between Sunni and Shia Islam. We talked about the hostility between the two, and how it seemed to be escalating. So what, we asked Fadi, *were* the differences between the two branches of Islam?

'There are two important differences,' he replied. 'The first is that for us Shias, our Ramadan goes for 29 days.' And the second difference? 'When Shias pray we go like this,' he said, crossing his arms in front of him. 'But when Sunni pray they put their hands by their sides.' So that was it. Stripped of all the arguments since the Prophet Mohammed formed Islam in the seventh century, these were the main differences – according to Fadi.

*

We returned to Syria with Jack's older brother, Nicolas, then 24, an engineer living in Sydney, who joined us for our holiday. It was December, just a couple of days after Mohamed Bouazizi's self-immolation. This time we visited Palmyra – the spectacular ruins of an ancient city, including a monumental colonnaded street more than 1100 metres long and the great Temple of Ba'al.

Within months of this visit, the Sunni–Shia tensions in Syria would escalate to the point where civil war broke out on 15 March 2011. According to the Syrian Centre for Policy Research, over the following six years, more than 470,000 Syrians would die, and the war's economic cost would be US$255 billion – essentially wiping out the nation's entire wealth.

When Islamic State arrived in Palmyra in mid-2015, they would destroy the Temple of Ba'al and want to know where antiquities were hidden. Islamic State funds itself in part by selling antiquities. The professor who for 50 years had protected the city's relics, 84-year-old Khaled al-Asaad, refused to tell them, so they murdered him. Islamic State beheaded him, then hung his body from a pole in the town square, his head stuck between his legs.

*

From Syria, we went to Lebanon for Christmas. It's an extraordinary country. It only has 4 million people, and 1 million of those have come as refugees from Syria. The population is divided into religious groupings called 'confessions'. Under Lebanon's constitution, each confession is entitled to certain positions. The Prime Minister must be a Sunni Muslim, the Speaker of Parliament must be a Shia Muslim and the President a Maronite Christian. The Parliament has 128 seats – Muslims must get 64 and Christians 64. Sunni Muslims must get 27 seats, Shias 27, Druze (a monotheistic minority faith) eight and Alawites two. The system is designed to avoid the type of violence that tore Lebanon apart during its civil war from 1975 to 1990.

Memories of the trauma of that war meant that Lebanon would remain relatively stable throughout the Arab Spring. But the threat of violence was constant – as suggested by the national election I'd reported on in June 2009.

Most of our time in Lebanon was spent in Beirut, a remarkable city. Thirty minutes' drive from the luxury boutiques of central Beirut was the Shatila refugee camp. In 1982, Israeli soldiers who were fighting in Lebanon surrounded the Sabra and Shatila refugee camps on the outskirts of Beirut. Under the command of Ariel Sharon (who went on to become Prime Minister), the soldiers encircled the camps, while Phalangist Christian militia entered and conducted a massacre of between 762 and 3500 people. (According to the *New York Times* an Israeli investigative commission concluded in 1983 that Israeli leaders were 'indirectly responsible' for the killings and that Sharon bore 'personal responsibility' for failing to prevent the killings of at least 800 civilians.)[2]

Sylvie and I wanted to visit the camps for a possible story. We decided to take Jack with us because we were on a family holiday and we thought it would be interesting for him to see a refugee camp in Lebanon. We had not expected to find such poverty and misery 25 years after the famous massacre. Jack later described the camp in his diary:

The Lebanese will not let them [the Palestinians] have jobs outside of their camps, will not help them and does not care for them … It is just horrible to hear from some of the officials about the camp's struggles. 'We have the highest rate of breast cancer in the world,' said one of the surgeons, 'the highest rate of lung cancer and even one of the highest rates of anaemia in the world.' The worst part is that one in every 10 babies is born dead. Hold it right there: think about it, this is a space of about 25,000 people, compared to 7 billion people in the world and it has the highest rate of all of these sicknesses and diseases. It is just horrible.

*

Hezbollah was invisible in central Beirut, but no one should doubt its influence. Following an agreement in 2008, Hezbollah effectively controls the government of Lebanon: it has power of veto over major government decisions if it can muster two-thirds of the vote in parliament. This two-thirds support is automatic, because Hezbollah leads a coalition of Shia- and Syrian-aligned political groups.

The previous Lebanese Prime Minister, Fouad Siniora, tried to wind back Hezbollah's power: in 2008 he moved to close down its private communications network and to end its control over Beirut's airport. Hezbollah took to the streets to shoot at pro-government militia. The army was not prepared to confront the better-resourced Hezbollah. The government was forced to back down.

My first conversation with Hezbollah would be a disaster. Living in Israel, you realise that Hezbollah – meaning Party of

God – is one of the few military machines that Israel takes seriously. The Israelis feel little threat from Hamas in Gaza; a war with Gaza is like a training exercise. But Hezbollah is a different matter. The last war Israel had with Hezbollah, in 2006, proved extremely costly for Israel, and its own official inquiry into the war (the Winograd Commission) found its military seriously unprepared.

So, in April 2013, after speaking to several Israeli Army commanders about Hezbollah, I travelled to Lebanon to pay it a visit. As a visiting journalist, I knew I needed government accreditation, so I visited the press office in Beirut. Inside, a grumpy official who chain-smoked looked at my application. Finally, he stamped it.

But the Hezbollah office acts like the real government. I telephoned Dr Ibrahim Mousawi, Hezbollah's media officer. Mousawi has a PhD in Political Science from Birmingham University in the UK, and clearly likes to run his department like a military operation. Over the phone I requested a meeting.

'Busy now, call tomorrow at two,' he said.

I called the next day; it was two minutes past two.

'I told you two o'clock,' he snapped. 'It's two minutes past two. Try tomorrow.' He hung up.

Hezbollah had just hung up on me; things were not going well. The next day I rang at two o'clock.

'You rang on time,' Mousawi said. 'You can have 20 minutes with me tomorrow at three o'clock in my office.'

'Where's your office?' I asked.

'If you can't find out where Hezbollah's office is you shouldn't be doing what you're doing,' he said and hung up.

My journey into Hezbollah's stronghold, the southern suburbs, was fascinating. In the space of 30 minutes, I went from central Beirut, with its boutiques filled with millionaires from Saudi Arabia, into one of the Shia strongholds of the Middle East. The main road in this part of the city was lined with photos of 'martyrs' from the 2006 war with Israel. Journalists who pulled out a camera around here would often find Hezbollah police pulling up alongside them demanding Hezbollah media credentials.

I found the Hezbollah office in an old building. The previous office had been bombed by Israel, and apparently Hezbollah keeps moving so that the Israelis are never sure where they are. The only indication it was Hezbollah's office was a logo in the foyer: a clenched fist holding an AK-47.

Ibrahim Mousawi appeared and showed me into his office. On the walls were two huge posters: one of Ayatollah Khomenei and one of Ayatollah Khamanei. These are the two Supreme Leaders that Iran has had since the Shah was toppled in the 'Islamic Revolution' of 1979. It reflected the closeness between Hezbollah and Iran. 'Great leaders!' Mousawi said when he saw me looking at the posters.

I asked about a recent speech in which Nasrallah had vowed to 'change the face of the region'.

Mousawi replied: 'Israel has always been viewed as an army that cannot be defeated. Israel is looked upon now as the policeman of the region, the superpower, the one that can do what it wants. This will change.'

Mousawi tried to convince me that Hezbollah was stronger now than during the 2006 war. 'Hezbollah has been training thousands and thousands and thousands of people to defend their country. Hezbollah is ready,' said Mousawi. If there was another war, he said, 'we will do something that they will regret'.

Then came two bizarre moments. Firstly, Mousawi said he'd been misquoted in an American magazine. 'They quote me as saying that "Israel is a pimple on the face of the Middle East". What I said was: "The occupation is a pimple on the face of Israel." I'm going to send a letter to the editor because once a statement like that is out there it will be repeated by other journalists. But what if the editor refuses to run the letter?'

For me this was extraordinary: the spokesman for a fighting machine with an estimated 100,000 missiles in southern Lebanon felt powerless to force the editor of a foreign magazine to run a letter.

The second strange moment came when Mousawi wanted my advice. 'I've had a couple of speaking tours to the UK which have gone well except for a few demonstrations,' he said. 'I hear you have a powerful Israel lobby in Australia – do you think there would be many protests if I visit?'

At that instant I considered the fact that this office might well be monitored by the intelligence services of several countries, including the US, Lebanon, Israel and Jordan. The last thing I wanted to do was to give advice to Hezbollah. 'That's not for me to judge,' I said.

Suddenly, the ice-man of the phone call returned.

'Stop sitting on the fence,' Mousawi said. 'As an Australian you can tell me your assessment of the reaction I would get.'

'It's impossible for me to judge,' I said.

Clearly, Ibrahim Mousawi realised I wasn't going to bite. We shook hands, and as I was leaving he said: 'Keep in touch.'

*

The civil war in neighbouring Syria would give Hezbollah years of battlefield experience. However, it would also erode the organisation's credibility in the region, putting Hezbollah in a situation where it was killing other Muslims – Sunni Muslims.

The dominant battle in the Middle East today is the battle for Islam between Sunnis and Shias.

Added to that are foreign influences like the US and Russia. But at its heart this is a historical battle within Islam that has now become entrenched in politics. It was originally a dispute over who was going to succeed the Prophet Mohammed, and the two sides then broke into two groups. Islam was divided from Mohammed's death in the year 632. Iran, Syria and Hezbollah in Lebanon are trying to preserve a 'Shia crescent' amid a Sunni majority.

In the north of Lebanon, in Jabal Mohsen, about 50,000 Alawites – a version of Shia – live on a hill surrounded by about 500,000 Sunnis.

Sylvie and I travelled there in April 2013 to research why people from the Sunni area below regularly shot up the hill at the Alawites, and vice versa. Below, we met Sheikh Bilal Radwan, a Sunni cleric. He saw the hand of Iran behind it all. 'It is Iran which is supporting Syria,' he said. 'They are the big players who are giving orders to Hezbollah. And they in turn give orders to try to enslave all the people in Jabal Mohsen,' he said.

We met a Sunni barber, 27-year-old Ahmed Shaaban. 'They start shooting by snipers and then the battle starts,' he told us. 'I finish whatever haircut I'm doing and run and get my gun.'

We also spoke to Jihan Khodor, who lost her 21-year-old son in this war in Jabal Mohsen, a microcosm of the Sunni–Shia war. 'In the last battle he put on his uniform and was going to work and they shot him in the heart,' she explained. Mrs Khodor's building was covered in anti-Assad graffiti such as 'Bashar is an Infidel Pig'. She showed us bullet holes in the walls of her apartment.

I asked Mrs Khodor what the war was about: 'I really don't know,' she said. What message would she give the Alawites? 'May God not forgive you for making me lose my son. This area is unbearable but I have nowhere to go.'

Sylvie and I then drove up the hill to a world of Shia Islam. We met 10 men sitting in a café; not one had a job. A job would mean driving through Sunni areas, which they regarded as too dangerous. They rely on relatives who are able to work in the village or are prepared to cross the checkpoint.

One man, Mohammed Rabee, showed us a bullet-ridden children's bedroom. 'They have no mercy on us,' he said, looking down the hill. Like those below, nobody here knew why they were fighting – except that one lot were Sunni and the other lot were Shia.

*

On another occasion, I went alone with a fixer to southern Beirut to meet Abu Jihad, a gun dealer. We met in the home of my fixer's mother. When Abu Jihad walked in, he pulled out a gun; my fixer told me later he wanted to make it clear that I should not try anything silly.

Abu Jihad was a devotee of Hezbollah. His phone rang frequently with calls from people wanting weapons. He set up a laptop and showed me videos of himself giving weapons training to Hezbollah militia. He said the Lebanese police were looking for him – 'There are 46 warrants out for my arrest' – but he believed that they would not dare to come for him because they were afraid of Hezbollah. I asked Abu Jihad what he would do to anyone who criticised Shia Muslims. 'I would kill them,' he said. 'I *do* kill them.'

Two days later I interviewed someone at the opposite end of the spectrum, who would delight in killing Hassan Nasrallah. In an apartment in Tripoli, Lebanon, Sylvie and I met Abu Bari, a commander of the al-Farouq Brigades, a Sunni group. He'd just returned from Syria for medical treatment. He pulled out his computer – laptops are as much a part of modern warfare as guns – and began showing us videos. In Syria, the al-Farouq Brigades had been fighting the Assad army and Hezbollah, and he played us a video in which missiles were being fired towards Hezbollah fighters. Just before one missile was fired, his troops shouted: 'This one's for Nasrallah!'

Nearby, in a café, we met a recruiter for the Free Syrian Army. Like Abu Bari, he'd fought in Syria against the Assad regime, but was now wounded. He told us how one Australian man – a student from Sydney University – had contacted him and wanted to meet. But because he was recruiting Sunni fighters in Lebanon, a Shia-dominated country, he carefully vetted fighters. When the Australian came, the recruiter led him on a merry dance around Tripoli. The recruiter was watching as the Australian turned up at a café, but telephoned to send him to a different venue. They finally met, but then the recruiter drove around Tripoli, ensuring that no one was following. Finally, the recruiter gave the Australian instructions for who to meet once inside Syria. The Australian man went into Syria and the recruiter never heard from him again.

One day the Lebanese police had come to arrest the recruiter but he'd been able to quickly marshal a mob of Sunnis to surround the building. The last thing the police had wanted was an open confrontation with Sunni militia, so they'd departed.

Survival in Lebanon relies largely on how strong others perceive you to be. After 15 years of civil war, Lebanon is one of the most traumatised nations in the Middle East – which is saying something. So traumatised, in fact, that its people are prepared to go to almost any length to avoid another war.

CHAPTER 9

'I Think Egypt is Going to Blow'

30 January 2011

WHEN SYLVIE, JACK AND I TOOK OUR FIRST FAMILY TRIP TO Egypt – in July 2009 – the country had appeared to be stable. President Hosni Mubarak had ruled as dictator since 1981, having come to power after the previous president, Anwar Sadat, was shot dead by Islamic extremists at a military parade. There had been a state of emergency in Egypt for 35 years, which meant that the security forces had complete power. Yet the fundamentalist Muslim Brotherhood, banned in Egypt for more than 50 years, was becoming stronger. It seemed that change was in the air.

Our journey to Egypt had been memorable in itself. We took a bus south from Jerusalem to the border with Egypt, where we passed through the Taba Crossing. Once on the Egyptian side, we boarded another bus for Cairo; the interior was covered with shag-pile carpet, and as we set off across the Sinai an Egyptian soap opera began playing on the TV. The six-hour trip took us across the Sinai Peninsula – a barren, inhospitable strip of land that has become etched into history for its military battles between Israel and Egypt.

This was the place that sparked the decisive Six-Day War of 1967. Since the peace deal between Egypt and Israel in 1979, this slice of land had become a no-man's-land. Egypt had very few soldiers here, and was only allowed to increase the number with the approval of Israel.

The Sinai showed us how quickly things can change in the Middle East. Within a year of our trip, it deteriorated into a lawless zone. The proliferation of roaming Bedouin criminals and human trafficking gangs made it a no-go zone for tourists. We certainly decided that we would not take that trip again. While it was rarely reported, because few victims wanted to go public about it, there had been many instances in which Bedouin criminals had boarded a tourist bus, abducted two or three passengers and demanded large ransoms. Often the passengers had been Japanese or Korean, and their governments or families had paid.

But having safely crossed the Sinai, we drove along a stretch of the Suez Canal. For me, this place had an aura about it: the Suez Crisis of 1956, when British Prime Minister Anthony Eden publicly battled Egyptian President Gamal Abdel Nasser, has become one of the great landmarks of modern history. Before that the 150-kilometre canal had been a lifeline for the British Empire, carrying Britain's oil from the Mediterranean to the Red Sea. For an area that had played such a role in history, through the window of our bus it looked so bland; Egyptian soldiers stood every few hundred metres along the cement wall, against a backdrop of palm trees and desert.

After our arrival in Cairo, an old friend, Cheryl Porter, introduced us to Abbas Abbas Mahmoud, a leading Egyptian engineer. He invited us to join him for dinner at Café Riche, a historic establishment just off the famous Tahrir Square, which over the decades had been a meeting point for Egyptian writers, journalists, actors, politicians, spies and activists. Gamal Abdel Nasser would meet there in the early 1950s with his officers as they planned the downfall of King Farouk, which eventually led to Nasser becoming in 1956 Egyptian President.

During the day, Sylvie would go sightseeing with Jack and I'd break away to do research and meet people, catching up with professors or politicians. In the evenings, I would often sit with the owner of Café Riche, Magdi Abdel-Malak, and talk about Egypt. He offered me useful insights into how the non-religious sector of Egypt was feeling. He told me Egypt had become much more Islamically observant. 'Look out there,' he said, pointing to veiled women walking by. 'Thirty years ago you'd hardly see any women covered like that. I am losing my country.'

I saw his hostility when a religious couple – the woman was wearing a hijab – opened the café door. 'We serve beer here, go away!' he shouted.

'You were pretty strong with them,' I said.

'I have to be strong,' he replied. 'If the Muslim Brotherhood ever get power they are going to want me to live under sharia law.'

At the café Sylvie and I also met an investigative journalist who told us about the large number of women who wear the full hijab, not for religious reasons, but to protect their identities while they begged or worked in prostitution as poverty worsened.

On Fridays, Abdel-Malak hosted a lunch to which Sylvie and I were often invited when we visited Cairo. These events proved to be a boon in terms of contacts: we met Egyptian journalists, writers, diplomats, government officials and lawyers who felt alienated from the Mubarak regime but also wanted to stop the rise of the Muslim Brotherhood. Their fear of this group would turn out to be amply justified.

One night, Sylvie, Jack and I were walking near Tahrir Square. It was a typically hot Cairo evening, when families went out into the streets for relief from the heat of their apartments. Down a side street we saw a police vehicle, with about 10 policemen standing around it. This didn't look like normal crowd control. The police were looking anxiously up at the surrounding buildings. We would see this scene repeated around Cairo.

Back in Jerusalem, we met with two friends, a UN official and a French official. They began arguing about stability in Egypt. The UN official insisted that everything was fine. The French diplomat disagreed: 'I think Egypt is going to blow,' he said.

*

Fast-forward eighteen months and the diplomat's words looked prophetic. Egypt had become the next possible 'domino' in the line of governments falling in the Arab Spring. By travelling to Egypt to report on its protests, I would have my own personal encounter with one of the crumbling Arab dictatorships. My horror stretch in Cairo began on 30 January 2011 – less than two weeks before the fall of Mubarak. That night, the streets rang with the most extraordinary sound I've ever heard: the roar of anarchy. In the space of 24 hours, one of the world's great cities had become lawless.

Gangs roamed the city, looking for places to loot. Each street was only as strong as the force it could muster; neighbourhood groups armed with machetes, baseball bats and guns were hastily formed to keep the thugs away. In a final act of desperation, Mubarak ordered the release of psychiatric prisoners, in the hope that they would cause so much chaos that the iron fist with which he ruled would be appreciated.

One of the great allies of the United States and Israel was teetering – they had supported Mubarak in the past because he offered stability. He was a pillar of the peace agreement between Egypt and Israel that had ensured the two countries hadn't fired at each other since 1973. But tonight Cairo was imploding.

The previous night in Jerusalem, a Friday, I'd heard that Mubarak was in real trouble. Protesters were gathering across Egypt and I decided I should get down there quickly. Sylvie was away at the time and Jack had two friends sleeping over. At midnight I had to drive them back to their homes and find somewhere for Jack to stay.

Then I drove down to the border. It was a terribly wet night, and at one point, travelling beside the Dead Sea, I skidded across the road and slammed into the barrier at the side. Because it was so late on the evening of Shabbat, luckily there were no other vehicles around. It probably saved me. I'd knocked the headlights out and there was damage to the side of the car, but I could still drive it, so I kept going and then stayed the night with some Israeli friends right on the border.

The next morning, I caught a taxi van across the Sinai. By mid-afternoon, the road into Cairo was chaotic. The army was starting to panic and had set up roadblocks. I said to the driver, 'Let's find a back road into Cairo.' As a foreign journalist with a foreign passport, if I'd come to a checkpoint in that atmosphere I was likely to be detained and questioned.

Entering the city, I asked the driver to take me to my regular hotel, the Semiramis, right on Tahrir Square. I knew the hotel staff and there were always journalists staying there.

The driver said, 'I can't get you to the Semiramis. It's too dangerous.' There was shooting on the bridges we would normally cross and the crowds were refusing to leave Tahrir Square. The reality of Egyptian politics is that whoever controls Tahrir Square controls the city. It's a focal point that connects roads in all directions. I could feel my driver was feeling nervous. He said: 'The best I can do is get us to a small hotel where I know people.'

Cairo is a city of 21 million people and I didn't have any idea where we were. Because I'd left Israel in a hurry, I hadn't had time to get an Egyptian SIM card, and the hotel switchboard wasn't working. As evening fell, I was completely uncontactable. This was just the beginning of the worst night I've ever spent. At about 8pm I went to reception and discovered staff rolling up the carpets, taking the furniture and valuables away and barricading the doors. I asked: 'What's happening?'

They said, 'We think there could be trouble tonight.'

By now it was dark and I went up onto the rooftop to get an idea of what was going on. I came across an Egyptian tour guide. We stood looking over Cairo, listening to the shouting, horns honking and occasional gunfire in the distance. That growl of anger and chaos is something I'll never forget. The guide said he wanted to get his group to the airport; he told me his room number and said if things got 'really dangerous' and they evacuated I could join them.

I went back downstairs and all the staff were arming themselves with baseball bats, machetes and iron rods. Many were carrying knives and metal poles. They told me there were gangs at the end of the street wanting to loot the hotel.

I started thinking, what do I do if the gangs storm the hotel? I went down the back way through the kitchen. Staff there were brandishing weapons in case someone came in that way. 'Don't worry,' one said. 'We are here to protect the guests.'

Most guests were in their rooms, regarded as the safest place. The city's electricity had crashed and Cairo was in darkness, but I could hear all sorts of noises. I returned to my room on the first floor and from my balcony I could see the red glow of cigarettes. A group of staff from the hotel had taken up positions outside under a tree to try to deter looters. There were people at both ends of our street, I was told, who were going to try to stop the mobs from coming in. In one way the darkness was good. The gangs couldn't tell how many people were standing ready to defend our hotel.

I started to panic, thinking, what is my plan? I'm totally by myself, I have no phone communication.

Exhausted, I lay on my bed but heard gunshots. My mind began playing tricks on me.

Around midnight I decided to look for the tour guide. I ran up several flights and knocked on the guide's door. I shouted his name but there was no answer. I realised he and his group must have left.

I couldn't see a single person in the hotel. I become convinced that everyone but me had left. What if the staff had felt they were outnumbered and they, too, had fled?

I ran back down to my room and closed the door. I felt completely and utterly alone.

Because I couldn't contact anyone I had to rely on my wits. I could tell I was in adrenalin mode and somehow I needed to calm down. The only way I could think of to settle myself was to come up with a plan so that I felt at least that I had some control over what was going to happen, so that I didn't feel completely at the mercy of outside events.

As I listened to the anger on the streets, I decided my only chance of surviving if a gang entered the hotel was to hide in the room. I needed to make up the room as if no one was staying in it, in the hope that any mob would believe it was empty.

I put down the toilet seat and placed toilet paper across it – imitating the way many hotels present their bathrooms. I hid my toothbrush. I dried the washbasin. I made the bed as if no one had slept in it. In retrospect it seems like bizarre behaviour, but I was simply following my instincts.

I hid my bag behind the curtain. If they charged in, I'd hide myself behind the curtain too. I undid the chain across the door. A chain across the door would only confirm that there was someone in the room. Anyway, tonight that chain looked useless against the anger of Cairo.

With all these measures in place, I lay on the bed, ready to activate my survival plan. The gunfire continued outside. I wouldn't describe the next few hours as sleep, but I was so tired I dozed enough to forget my situation.

Dawn finally arrived. I ventured downstairs, to find staff still on alert in front of the hotel. They told me every time a mob had tried to move towards the hotel during the night, they'd fired at them.

By now I just wanted to get out of there – I knew no one in this neighbourhood. To my relief, I found my driver from the night before. 'Can you drive me to the Semiramis?' I asked him.

It was disconcerting to see the vibrant city I had known in chaos. As we drove across Cairo the streets were full of burning bins. There were army checkpoints everywhere. There had been riots along the bridges over the Nile River. We finally found our way to the Semiramis.

I caught up with a few of the other foreign correspondents, and heard plenty of reports of journalists and activists being taken away, and someone tortured at the Interior Ministry. Mark Corcoran from the ABC had been punched and kicked by pro-government supporters, and Peter Stefanovic from Channel Nine had been detained.

Because I was by myself and had no security people, I tended to work with a network of colleagues and friends. I would go with them into Tahrir Square. They had a fixer who was walking around the perimeter, keeping an eye on them and on one occasion when it was getting dangerous he came over to us and said, 'Let's get out of here.' One American female reporter from CBS was sexually abused in Tahrir Square around this time.

It had previously been a time of hope and optimism – the first time people felt change was possible. Egyptians who were 40 or 50 had known nothing but dictatorial, authoritarian regimes. This had created a sense of paralysis, a feeling of powerlessness, numbness. But suddenly the youth had a voice, a confidence, dreams and optimism. Even though the Arab Spring had not led to change, this was a movement that would probably percolate underground, almost certainly rising to the surface again in the future. But on this occasion, as quickly as it had appeared, it crashed.

Earlier in the uprising, the square had been a welcoming place where people would bring their children after work. The anti-Mubarak people at that point tended to be the students and the professionals, and they tended not to be intimidating or violent. But as the days went on it got nastier and nastier, to the point where the media became targets.

Two or three days after my night at the small hotel, there was a knock on my door at the Semiramis. I opened it to see five or six men in leather jackets. I didn't want to let them in so I said, 'Can you wait a moment?' I needed to think what to do next.

But they pushed the door in and said, 'No, now!' They didn't identify themselves but they went all over my room and bathroom and out onto the balcony – looking, as I found out later, for cameras and broadcasting equipment, because some media, such as Britain's Sky News, were broadcasting from the balconies, looking straight down onto Tahrir Square.

This was the Mubarak security apparatus trying to shut down the media. They had disabled the internet and confiscated a large amount of equipment. In fact, one of the men who came into my room was carrying several cameras he had seized.

The men left quickly. But because the internet had crashed, the only way I could file stories was by going to friends in the media, particularly Sky News, who had portable BGAN machines that hook up to a satellite; I subsequently got one of these for myself.

One night soon after, I went out to dinner at another hotel where a lot of the media were staying, with Jason Koutsoukis of Fairfax Media and two German journalists. Like me, Jason was based in Jerusalem and we'd become good friends. The two Germans, a man and a woman, were friends of his.

Mubarak had established an 8pm curfew when everyone was meant to be off the streets. The high state of tension was evident from the number of tanks and soldiers with machine guns.

At about 10pm, on our way home, many roads were blocked off, so our taxi driver was taking back roads to get us to our hotel. We came across a roadblock, where four plain-clothes policemen stopped the taxi and asked for our passports, which we handed to them. Sensing we had a problem, I rang Sylvie in Jerusalem and told her that if she didn't hear from me within an hour to call an official I knew in the Egyptian Foreign Ministry, whose number I gave her. She did this and was told by him that there was nothing he could do to help. She then rang Stephanie Schwabsky, the Australian Ambassador to Egypt, who began making efforts to find out what was happening to us. One of the German journalists also telephoned the security officer of the German Embassy in Cairo and told him the situation.

Meanwhile, we were made to get out of the taxi. While we were waiting, we saw a group of foreigners put in the back of an army vehicle about 100 metres up the street. In this atmosphere, foreigners had become easy targets.

We were driven to a police station, where an officer told us we would be taken for questioning by State security. He brought out blindfolds and asked another foreigner who had been detained to blindfold us. When it came to my turn, I had a physical reaction to the blindfold. I felt a violent urge to be sick. Until that moment, I'd never appreciated how much we rely on our eyes. They are our early warning system, and I was about to have mine disabled. The police then took thin electrical wire and tied our hands together. Then we were handed over to some soldiers.

The soldiers walked us out. We were taken into a vehicle; we found out later it was a bus. There were eight of us now: seven foreigners and one Egyptian. There were two Australians – me and Koutsoukis – two Germans, two French and a Belgian. After about 10 minutes, one of the German journalists who was sitting next to me and who knew Cairo well, whispered: 'It's good we're still driving – it means we're not going to the Interior Ministry.' The Interior Ministry was the place where many journalists and protesters were being tortured.

After about half an hour we reached our destination: an army base, I later discovered. Throughout the next two hours of interrogation, the engine of the bus was left running, perhaps to keep up a level of tension. Although we wore blindfolds, lights were shining into the bus. Out the corner of my eye I could see high, wide walls and our captors' army uniforms. All the bus's windows seemed to have been smashed. Interrogators walked around it shouting questions at us one by one.

'What are you doing in Cairo?'

'Who do you support in this situation?'

'Do you take photographs?'

'Have you been to demonstrations?'

It was hard to judge how the others were feeling because we all had to be quiet. But earlier on, when we were being detained, we four journalists had decided to admit to our occupation. We thought that would be much smarter than trying to bluff or lie and then being caught out. The only thing I didn't mention was that I lived in Israel: despite Egypt's peace agreement with Israel, it's not a smart thing to admit to in Egypt at one in the morning while wearing a blindfold and being held by the army.

I'd written about the brutality of the Mubarak regime, of its poor human rights record, the imprisonment of one editor for questioning Mubarak's health. I'd written about the men who had come into my hotel room. I'd written about how Mubarak's son, Gamal, had been given control of much of the tourism industry around the Red Sea. And once you start writing about the families of dictators it becomes a whole different thing.

My fear was that they would separate us. While we were in a group, I felt some comfort, but if we had been taken off one by one there would be no accountability and it might be the last we were heard of. Until an hour ago, Jason Koutsoukis and I had been competitors, but now we would share whatever fate these soldiers dealt us. This experience would bond us for life.

As foreigners in this highly charged atmosphere we needed to be very careful. We had the blindfolds and they had the guns.

The interrogators understood immediately what 'foreign journalist' was, but when the Belgian man behind us told them he was a museum curator, there was a pause. 'What's your job?' one shouted.

This will be interesting, I thought: a Belgian man speaking English and wearing a blindfold, trying to explain to Egyptian soldiers who speak Arabic what a curator does.

'I look out for interesting pieces of art then bring them together in exhibitions,' he replied.

The soldiers obviously decided it was easier to concentrate on the journalists. I remember thinking, somewhat bizarrely, that should I ever be kidnapped again I'd want to describe myself as a museum curator.

'You like Mubarak or you like opposition?' one asked me.

'I do not take sides, I just report what is in front of me,' I said.

There was no physical abuse of the foreigners, but the Egyptian in front of us – who had been caught taking photographs – was assaulted. He seemed to be going crazy. The soldiers shouted at him in Arabic and he shouted back. Each time he did, I heard a dreadful sound; I found out later they were bashing his forehead with the butts of their guns. He was in a completely different category from us and I felt a deep pity for him. We had a foreign government behind us, and that meant something; this man, being an Egyptian, was completely powerless.

About two hours into the questioning there was a dramatic change of tone. In the time since the German journalist called her embassy, German security services had managed to track us through our phones. Although the police had taken them, they had not removed the batteries – which meant the German Embassy had been able to track us and, through them, so had Australia's Department of Foreign Affairs and Trade. Australia's Foreign Minister, Kevin Rudd, told me later he personally intervened that night, phoning Egyptian officials and telling them: 'I say to you very clearly – no harm is to come to the Australian and German journalists your army is holding and you should release them immediately.'

The German and Australian intervention presumably explained why the aggressive tone of our interrogators had suddenly softened.

'You realise we have brought you here for your own safety?' one soldier said. 'Cairo is a dangerous place at the moment. As foreigners you are in particular danger. We've got you here to protect you.'

'Thank you for helping us,' I replied. It went against the grain but this was a time to be low-key, not angry.

The soldiers took off our blindfolds and electrical cord but left them on the Egyptian. I could now see he had blood all over his forehead.

Around 2am, we were driven back into Cairo. That was when I saw one of the worst things I've ever witnessed.

Approaching central Cairo, we drove down a side street blocked by a Mubarak mob carrying Mubarak posters and armed with machetes and baseball bats, who had set bins alight. Seeing our bus slow down, the mob ran towards us. The seven soldiers on the bus jumped off, holding their guns in the air. The mob backed away.

One of the soldiers then grabbed the Egyptian man by the back of the shirt and dragged him off the bus. He was bent over and still tied up and blindfolded. The soldier pushed him towards the mob. I couldn't hear what was said but I surmised that the soldier was telling them the man was anti-Mubarak. The soldier then pushed him into the crowd.

The last thing I saw as the bus drove off was the mob kicking the blindfolded man. Here was a man who had probably just been in the wrong place at the wrong time. He had absolutely no protection. He was probably killed within minutes. In Mubarak's Egypt, life and death could be that fickle.

My Australian colleague Hamish Macdonald – one of the best foreign correspondents I've seen in action – put the treatment of foreign journalists into sharp relief. 'The attacks on journalists these past days are probably just a small window into what this 30-year-old regime is capable of, and the kind of treatment that has been meted out for decades on Hosni Mubarak's own people,' he wrote in the *Sydney Morning Herald*.[1]

*

That night, I saw up close the ugliness and unpredictability of the Middle East. No one in Cairo was safe. The rule of law no longer existed – but it had got to the point where the critical mass of opposition and anger was so strong that it overwhelmed even the apparatus of a dictatorship. Thirty years of pent-up anger, frustration and fear were finding an outlet.

The soldiers took us into the centre of Cairo and dropped us off somewhere a few blocks from our hotel, saying, 'OK, you can go now.' I said to the soldiers, 'Could one of you escort us back to our hotel? You've been telling us how dangerous Cairo is and now you want us to walk the streets at 2am.'

Weirdly, one of the men who'd blindfolded us then escorted Jason and me several blocks back to the Semiramis.

Jason and I separately rang our editors in Australia, who said they wanted us to write the story of what had happened.

I stayed in Cairo for another few days after that. *The Australian*'s Managing Editor, Louise Evans, offered me a security escort, but I said to her, 'The last thing I want is a guy with a gun hanging around. There are enough guns here. It's not going to help.' In that situation, you're better off as a smaller target. The offer from my paper highlighted to me the different situation I was in compared to Egyptian journalists and citizens. Twelve journalists in Egypt had been killed since 1992, according to the Committee to Protect Journalists, and according to human rights groups scores of others were imprisoned and tortured during this period. I had the back-up of a newspaper and foreign government – they had nothing.

*

Within 12 days, Mubarak would step down, yet the popular protests that toppled him would cause a vacuum into which Mohamed Morsi and the Muslim Brotherhood would rush.

I would go back in October to cover the period leading up to the first elections Egypt had had for four decades. It was a very busy, vibrant atmosphere, and there was a sense of excitement among the public that they could finally vote.

But the newly reinstated Muslim Brotherhood was obviously well prepared and had very good networks, even though it had been banned for 50 years. It was very active in getting young people to vote. I went to a hospital where I interviewed a doctor who was one of the Muslim Brotherhood leaders. He told me that there would be a strong social welfare element, and that they would invest in schools and hospitals.

A lot of Egyptians were practising Muslims who felt that Mubarak hadn't been in any way religious. There was a strong sense we'd noticed even before the revolution of wanting to get back to Islamic traditions. Secular Egyptians obviously didn't like that. The Muslim Brotherhood candidate, Mohamed Morsi, ran on a platform that was a hybrid of democracy and sharia law.

There were plenty of Egyptians who didn't want an Islamic country, but the Brotherhood had a strong constituency and they won the election. Morsi was elected President in June 2012.

However, Morsi made some terrible judgments and that allowed the army to run a counter-campaign against him, backed by public demonstrations, and launch a coup that saw him deposed a year later. In Egypt, the army is all-powerful and if you alienate the army then you are in trouble. One of the triggers for the army to move against Morsi was that he allowed jihadist groups to go into the Sinai without providing strong enough backing for the army there. Some soldiers turned up to Morsi's office, kidnapped him at gunpoint, took him to an unknown location, and he has been in prison ever since. The Muslim Brotherhood was immediately declared a terrorist organisation.

Having launched a coup, the army then wanted to cloak its actions in legitimacy. By banning the largest political party – the Muslim Brotherhood – from running in elections, the victory of their candidate, army general Abdel Fattah el-Sisi, was guaranteed. In 2014, el-Sisi was elected the new President. It had been a masterclass in how the army retains power in a country such as Egypt. The crackdown on freedoms and human rights under el-Sisi was just as bad, if not worse, than it had been under Hosni Mubarak.

The more things change …

CHAPTER 10

Colonel Gaddafi's Gangster Regime

February 2011

WITHIN DAYS OF RETURNING TO ISRAEL AFTER MY ARMY interrogation in Cairo, I was off to cover the implosion of yet another Middle East dictatorship: the Gaddafi regime in Libya. Egypt's Mubarak regime had been appalling – but to me the Libyan one had an added element of cruelty to it.

Even in a region of bloodshed, Libya stood out under Colonel Muammar Gaddafi. He and his family ruled Libya – a small but extremely oil-rich country – for 42 years. Like many dictators, he put his sons into key positions. His second son, Saif al-Islam, was a playboy. But inside Libya the atrocities were extraordinary.

Gaddafi's reputation was as bad as that of Mubarak, so it was no surprise that any crackdown would be just as brutal. My Editor said to me: 'Libya looks like the next domino to fall, can you go there?'

It was very hard to fly in directly. So I flew into Cairo and then I got a public bus to near the border with Libya and stayed at a little hotel there. I met two Indian journalists who said they were driving into Libya the next day, so the three of us drove into Libya together.

There was no one at the border when we crossed. Gaddafi's border guards had all fled. No one could get into the capital, Tripoli, so most journalists, like us, were going in from Egypt and travelling via Tobruk to Benghazi, on Libya's northeast coast.

Benghazi is a historic seafarers' port with old markets. It was strongly fundamentalist. The eastern part of Libya had always been anti-Gaddafi and Bengahzi had become the capital of the uprising. Gaddafi had the view 'Benghazi hates me', therefore he starved it of money. Over time it had fuelled hatred and hostility.

Some of the people I talked to told stories about gunfights going on around Benghazi between Gaddafi's army and the anti-Gaddafi militia. In fact, the anti-Gaddafi forces had been so strong that they had forced the Gaddafi soldiers out of Benghazi.

At breakfast in my hotel, which was right on the water, one of the other journalists said to me, 'There's a body floating up onto the shore.' When I went back to my hotel room, I could see it.

Gaddafi began as a charismatic leader with enormous public support. Many Libyans were proud of how this nationalist stood up to the powerful United States. For a country of seven million people, Libya punched well above its weight. Gaddafi saw himself as a great Arab socialist who would share the spoils of Libya. During his first 10 or 15 years in power, he spent a lot of the money on schools and hospitals and aged-care centres. Libya today is almost Soviet in its appearance, full of Gaddafi architecture that resembles East Germany of the 1960s.

But then Gaddafi appeared to become delusional, even psychopathic – he would brutally dispense with his enemies without flinching. He banned English from being taught in schools and universities to hermetically seal off his little kingdom from contact with the outside world.

One incident showed me the cruelty of his regime.

It was 6 June 1984 and Gaddafi wanted to deliver a message to his opponents. About 6000 students aged from six to 18 were taken to a covered basketball stadium in Benghazi. A long, thin curtain hung from the roof.

In a scene broadcast live on State TV, seven judges appeared and put on trial 30-year-old Sadiq Shwehdi, accused of being disloyal to the regime. He was quickly found guilty and the curtain dropped to reveal a noose. Some in the crowd, sensing what was about to happen, shouted, 'No!'

The noose was put around Shwehdi's neck and the rope was pulled up until he was hanging. But without any trapdoor or sudden fall, it did not break his neck. One of Gaddafi's supporters, a woman called Huda Ben Amer, began swinging on his legs. Still this was not enough.

He was taken to a hospital where a doctor injected him with poison. Still he would not die. A doctor filled a sock with sand and pushed it down his throat while holding his nose. Finally, he died.

I learnt the details of this story from the man's brother, who joined the 2011 protests against Gaddafi. The brother himself is in a wheelchair, having had his legs broken by the regime.

This is just one of hundreds of stories that reveal the darkness of the Gaddafi years. People would tell many stories of opponents of the regime found around Benghazi, strung up from traffic lights or soccer goalposts. Wherever I travelled in Libya, I saw fear.

*

Like a lot of dictators in the region, Gaddafi didn't fall quickly. There was a strong rear-guard action.

The situation in Benghazi was volatile. The word had gone out that my hotel was full of foreign journalists and Gaddafi opponents. One morning when I got up, the glass in the foyer of the hotel had been smashed; someone had thrown a Molotov cocktail. Another time, two men with Kalashnikovs had come in during the night, knocked on the door and taken away a doctor at gunpoint, probably to go and tend a wounded fighter from one of the militia groups.

I vividly remember the night when we thought Gaddafi was coming to Benghazi. One of the security men from Sky News said to me, 'We're flying out tomorrow because we think the Gaddafi troops are moving in. If I were you I'd get out.' I could see foreign media crews preparing to leave.

I'd become friendly with various journalists, including a couple of reporters from Turkey. They said, 'We've got to get out of this hotel, it's become a real target.' So I asked, 'Can I come with you?'

We left together and tried to get into another hotel. We couldn't get into the hotel across the river, or any other hotel, and it was too dangerous to go travelling into the night. So they rang the Turkish Consul General in Benghazi who said they could stay there, and that I could stay as well.

The Consul General was welcoming and organised dinner for us. One of the Turkish journalists and I slept on the floor of his office under a huge portrait of Mustafa Kemal Ataturk. I remember lying there looking up at Ataturk as the sound of gunfire could be heard around Benghazi – the sound of civil war. I felt extremely grateful to the Turks. Gaddafi's supporters had indeed made their way into Benghazi and the city was probably within 48 hours of falling. On 17 March the UN authorised a no-fly zone over Libya, which had the effect of pushing back the Gaddafi forces and, in my view, almost certainly headed off a massacre in Benghazi.

The fighting was going to go on and on and there was no resolution in sight. I flew back to Israel.

*

Some regimes would survive the Arab Spring. In Saudi Arabia, King Abdullah used force and a lot of money: he gave out US$130 billion in salary increases and spending on religious institutions. In Jordan, another King Abdullah used moderate force and moderate money. In Morocco, King Mohammed VI gave more rights to the parliament. But Gaddafi had built up so much hatred that the number of people who wanted him gone was overwhelming.

The uprising in Libya would ultimately fail, however, for two main reasons: the opposition fractured and there were no alternative institutions to replace the dictatorship.

Disillusionment quickly set in. Many of the anti-Gaddafi units began using their weapons for criminal activities. One man who had fought against Gaddafi lamented: 'Gaddafi was horrible, but I never knew of him capturing the relative of somebody if they could not find the person they wanted.' The man added: 'After 42 years of Gaddafi mentality, there's a little Gaddafi in all Libyans.'

This situation – replicated around the country after Gaddafi – reflected Libya's crisis. Gaddafi had been replaced by warring tribes. From a gangster regime to a gang culture. The country will take many years to find stability.

The chaos has unleashed a massive new supply of weapons throughout the Middle East. According to a European diplomat who specialises in weapons, many of the arms from Libya flowed through Egypt into Gaza.

*

In August 2011, the net began closing on Muammar Gaddafi. He'd gone into hiding, but special forces intelligence teams from the US, Britain, Jordan and Qatar had joined the hunt. Expecting that he might be caught any moment, journalists from around the world – including me – scrambled to get back into the country.

The journey to Tripoli was eventful. For part of it I was accompanied by Hamish Macdonald from Network Ten, then later ABC America. After a couple of days Hamish went in a different direction and I continued with some French journalists towards Tripoli. There I was driving through the desert of Libya and watching tracer fire shoot across the night sky. The unnerving thing about tracer fire is that it's hard to tell how close the shooters are. Someone with obvious firepower could be five minutes away. Or the darkness might be playing tricks on you: they could be 50 kilometres from you.

It's interesting how we adapt to our environment: after a while the group I was travelling with – mainly French journalists – barely looked up when another burst of fire appeared overhead.

We were forced to stop in the middle of the desert with a flat tyre. I set up my laptop on the back of the car with my BGAN – the machine that connects you to a satellite and gives you internet. I filed a story for *The Australian* as tracer fire raced across the sky.

There was one moment of farce. I hadn't brought a flak jacket: travelling with one means you can spend hours being questioned by airport authorities. I prefer to be able to move quickly. But as we drove into Tripoli our driver warned us of snipers. The French journalists put on their flak jackets. All I had that was metallic was my MacBook Air. I had no idea whether, ballistically, a laptop would slow or deflect a bullet, but I clutched it in front of me and hoped for the best. This greatly amused the French journalists. Of all the ideas Steve Jobs had for the MacBook Air, this surely would not have been one of them.

Our humour ceased when we heard that a car driving along this road earlier had been stopped by armed men who'd shot the Libyan driver dead and abducted his passengers. The three Italian journalists would eventually be released – no doubt after handing over money.

*

In October, after Gaddfai was found and killed, I travelled to Libya again and stood in a queue with thousands, waiting to walk into a meat refrigerator in Misrata where Colonel Gaddafi lay with a bullet hole in his head. Excited Libyans crouched next to him taking 'selfies'. Gaddafi's opponents wanted as many people as possible to see the body, to prevent any conspiracy theories that he was still alive.

He'd been caught hiding in a drain before a mob of his own countrymen dragged him onto the bonnet of a Toyota pick-up truck and did unspeakable things to him. At that moment, all of the fear that his family's gangster regime had instilled into Libyans, and the Gaddafis' obscene wealth and power, counted for nothing. The man who'd been one of the Arab world's dominant figures for four decades lay on a slab of concrete.

As a cadet journalist in Melbourne in 1980, I'd watched television reports of Ronald Reagan preparing to bomb Gaddafi, his public enemy number one. He was seen as being behind the Lockerbie bombing in 1988. Yet here he was, the man who had obsessed the Reagan White House, lying in front of me like a big dead rat with a gold tooth covered in dried blood.

The Arab Spring had come to this.

CHAPTER 11

Frankenstein's Monster

Early 2011

MOST OF OUR FRIENDS WHO VISITED FROM AUSTRALIA wanted to go to the Dead Sea. They enjoyed caking themselves in mud, then floating on the water while looking over at Jordan. As a result, we found ourselves hopping into our Hyundai Getz and doing the 25-minute drive from Jerusalem to the Dead Sea frequently. Each time, we drove past a small structure that told the story of Israel's occupation, but for two years we didn't know it.

The structure was a little school made of truck tyres and mud, perched on a hill in the Palestinian Bedouin village of Khan al-Ahmar. The Israeli Army would not allow the village to build with anything permanent, such as steel or wood.

The children had not been allowed to attend the schools in neighbouring Israeli settlements, and the closest school they could attend was 14 kilometres away. Some children could not walk that far and for those who did, it meant crossing a four-lane highway. After four children were killed making the journey, the village decided to build its own school. In 2009, an Italian aid organisation offered to help, and working bees saw the school go up.

The Jahalin Bedouins of Khan al-Ahmar were expelled by the Israeli Army in 1952 from their traditional home in the Negev in southern Israel and forced to settle in this part of the West Bank. In Khan al-Ahmar there was little water and the desert mountains barely provided enough grass for the shepherds. The army regularly arrived, making it clear that they did not want the 150 villagers to feel they were permanent residents; soldiers even took away playground equipment and 20 solar panels which provided electricity.

In August 2012, Jack and I drove Sylvie to the village so she could sleep there overnight. She wanted to take dawn photographs to accompany a story I was writing on the village. The poverty of the village was obvious. Jack captured the moment in his diary:

As my mum was sleeping the night at the Bedouin camp
to take some photos for my dad's article we went to drop
her off. We brought some food for the head of the camp
who had invited us, we walked in and these kids were
all standing around looking at the food. We walked a bit
further and they started tugging at our food and didn't give
up but we still let them [have it] because we felt sorry for
them. My mother told me how the next day when she was
walking around the camp, with the daughter of Eid the
chief, the girl always stayed in my mum's shadow. When
my mum turned, she did too, so she was never in the sun,
always in the shadow.

The school was a major victory for the village. By using recycled tyres they had not breached any army prohibition. The 152 students appeared to be making good progress and many hoped to go to university. Above the village sits Kfar Adumim, one of the Israeli settlements that surround Jerusalem. Sometimes the settlers drove into the village of Khan al-Ahmar at night in trucks, spun in circles and screamed abuse.

Khan Al-Ahmar has for years, with the help of NGOs, been fighting in the courts against demolition of its village and school and the expulsion of its community. Around Israel an estimated 80,000 to 90,000 Bedouins are fighting against being forcibly displaced and dispossessed of their land.[1] The matter of Khan Al-Ahmar is still with the Supreme Court so its future is in limbo. One village lost its fight in the Supreme Court. The Bedouin village of Umm al Hiran will be replaced by the Jewish town of Hiran.

One day, though, teachers noticed an Israeli official taking measurements. He said Israel had decided to build a 35-kilometre-long sewerage pipe from Jerusalem to the Dead Sea. Every few kilometres, the pipe needed ventilation outlets – known in Australia as 'stink pipes'. Despite the teachers asking the official if the pipe could be located away from the school, it was built three metres from the main classroom – as close as was physically possible to the school. To me this suggested a level of nastiness – a nastiness that these days appears to characterise the Israeli occupation.

One incident I witnessed seemed to demonstrate this vividly. Journalists in Israel get constant alerts from human rights groups when Israel is demolishing Palestinian houses. I received an alert that Israeli police were demolishing a Palestinian home in the Old City. Because it was the school holidays – and Sylvie was coming with me to take photographs – we took Jack along. The house belonged to 80-year-old Sayara Fakhouri, whose family had lived there for nearly 100 years. The authorities claimed that an extension to the house was illegal, while the family argued that they had repeatedly been refused a permit, in contrast to the Jewish residents of the Old City who were allowed to expand their houses.

On this particular day, we arrived to find about 60 Israeli police supervising bulldozers demolishing the house. It was part of a plan by Israeli authorities to demolish 90 Palestinian homes in the area, increasing the Jewish presence and reducing the Palestinian presence, thereby re-weighting the demographic balance and 'Judaising' the Old City. Mrs Fakhouri sat on the footpath – most of the time looking at the ground but occasionally glancing at the bulldozers crushing her home. Once it was destroyed, the officer in charge walked across and whispered something to her. I was intrigued. I imagined the officer, at a personal level, might have expressed some sort of sympathy. After the police left I asked her what the officer said.

'For every day that you don't clean up the rubble you will be charged 600 shekels [AU$200],' she said. Not only had her house been demolished but she had to clean it up. (Word went out around the Old City and children arrived with buckets to begin picking up the pieces of Sayara Fakhouri's home.)

That night Jack wrote in his diary: 'I think that it was very unfair.'

Another reality which to me suggested cruelty rather than security was Israel's 'cemeteries by numbers'. These cemeteries are located in military bases and are filled with small metal headstones with numbers but no names. Each number accords with the name of a dead Palestinian. Often if a Palestinian prisoner dies before their sentence is finished, Israel keeps the remains in these cemeteries until the full term is completed – sometimes a burial can be delayed for 20 years.

Haaretz newspaper called for an end to the 'necrophilic farce which makes Israel look delusional', that is, Israel's retaining of the bodies of dead Palestinians. Noting that the Palestinian Authority was 'our only partner for resolving the bloody conflict', it argued that a refusal to transfer bodies back to the Palestinian Authority would only strengthen that body's rival, Hamas. 'We can sympathise with the bereaved [Israeli] families whose loved ones were murdered by some of the terrorists whose bodies are at issue, and who are upset that these murderers will presumably be given heroes' funerals ... A society that ascribes special importance to the dignity of the dead should not adopt the practices of terrorist organisations when it comes to enemy bodies.'[2]

The reality of the occupation is infinitely worse than the public realises. The more I saw of it, the more fascinated I grew. Each time I drove through the West Bank, I noticed it everywhere – Israeli Army jeeps encircling Palestinian villages, soldiers suddenly appearing in an olive grove in Bethlehem, the towering Israeli settlements on the hilltops. Hundreds of thousands of Israelis now live in the Palestinian Territories, protected by the best private security service in the world: the Israeli Army.

Controlling another people under occupation is not easy. Israel and its lobby groups who arrange trips play down the optics of occupation. Before Pope Benedict's tour in 2009, fake green grass was laid at the checkpoint between Jerusalem and Bethlehem.

Most occupations have ended because the occupiers grew tired of the violence against them. The Americans in Iraq paid such a high price in casualties that they couldn't wait to get out. The French realised they would never win over the Algerians, and withdrew. The Indonesians grew weary of the international criticism of their occupation of East Timor.

In the modern age, how does a country – Israel – run a military occupation for 50 years?

It was something that Sylvie witnessed at the checkpoint between Jerusalem and Bethlehem that pointed me towards part of the answer. She saw an old Palestinian man talking to a soldier. The man was coming from Bethlehem to visit his daughter in Jerusalem. He'd handed the soldier his permit. Palestinians often request such permits, and more often than not are refused. This man, however, had succeeded. He'd brought a pink bag containing hot food to have with his daughter.

But the soldier said he couldn't pass. A valid permit didn't make any difference: the soldier had decided no, and in a military occupation the soldier is the law. '*Mahar!*' the soldier told him – the Hebrew word for 'tomorrow'. By now Sylvie knew the place well enough to realise that if the old man came back tomorrow, another soldier – or even the same one – might tell him that his permit was for the previous day.

She watched the old man shuffle away with his pink bag.

This incident made me realise that the tyranny of the occupation comes through the power of 18- or 19-year-old soldiers. These checkpoints are daily incubators of hatred, generation after generation. As long as there is an occupation there will be hatred. And, in some cases, a desire for revenge.

And so, because of that old man whose name we never knew, I set about investigating Israel's permit system. The more I saw, the more I came to realise that it was a massive case of remote-controlled social engineering. Dr Yael Berda, from the Harvard Academy for International Studies who specialises in the permit system, said: 'The permit system is the world's largest and most developed mechanism for filtering, identifying and restricting movement of a large civilian population.'[3]

The most significant fact I discovered, which even most Israelis seemed not to realise, was that Israel has 101 different permits for Palestinians. Not one applies to Israeli settlers. The information about the permits was obtained by B'Tselem under Freedom of Information.[4]

There are business permits, permits for religious purposes and permits for spouses of Palestinians who live in Jerusalem. There are permits for hospital visits, permits that a doctor needs to travel and permits to escort sick people in an ambulance. There are permits to travel to a wedding and permits to attend a funeral, permits for work meetings and permits for court hearings. There are permits under which a Palestinian must leave Jerusalem by 9pm. On one occasion, a meeting of Israeli and Palestinian business leaders was organised to try to develop better relationships. At the end of the day, they all sat down for a dinner. But at 8pm, all the Palestinians stood up, explaining that if they were not out of Jerusalem by 9pm they could be imprisoned.

Israel's web of permits largely runs on auto-pilot. 'A population of two million people is dependent on the functioning and good will of sixteen clerks, said a major report by Israeli human rights group Machson Watch.'[5]

Nowhere is Israel's permit system better illustrated than in the Seam Zone. This is the Palestinian area that has been cut off from the rest of the West Bank by the wall. When building that wall, Israel cut into the West Bank, trapping these Palestinians between the Green Line – the armistice line that operated from 1948 until 1967 – and the wall.

For the Seam Zone, Israel has created 13 special permits. In 2003, the Seam Zone was declared a 'military zone'. This means that 11,400 Palestinians who live in 12 villages have to obtain permits to live in their own homes. B'Tselem reported that for the Seam Zone, Palestinians had to prove 'needs' and 'connections to the land'. A permanent resident certificate required documentary evidence to show they had a right to the house and land. If a piece of land was owned by two siblings, only one would be given a permit.

Research by other human rights groups documented the difficulties of living in the Seam Zone. 'Only those who live in the Seam Zone can enter, meaning that the women who have usually moved into the Seam Zone to live with their husbands, are isolated from their own families, friends and community … even for funerals, where family and friends would normally come to the home of the deceased to pay respects cannot take place as family members cannot cross into the Seam Zone.'[6] There is restricted access to health services and great overcrowding, as there have been virtually no building permits given and repairs are rarely allowed. The living conditions are dangerous, with zinc roofs and asbestos ceilings. Often the trucks to pick up the sewage are not allowed through the checkpoints and sewage overflows, causing skin and other diseases. The checkpoints are not regularly open and sometimes the men cannot make it home after work.

In March 2017, the regulations were further tightened to deny permits for agricultural plots of 330 square metres or less, which can eventually lead to dispossession. One illustration of life in the Seam Zone is the 'Lone House'. The Israeli wall goes straight through this family's land. The family now live hemmed in by the wall and barbed wire.

Human rights group HaMoked documented the case of SK and RK, a couple from Jenin in the West Bank who married in 2009. The distance between their homes was a few hundred metres, but Israel's wall separated them. They sought to make their new home in the wife's village. After the wedding, the husband updated his address to his wife's address and applied for a 'new seam zone resident certificate'. In Israel's Orwellian permit system, the application was rejected on the basis that the applicant was 'not a permanent resident'. To see his new wife, he requested a permit to visit the Seam Zone. The military issued 'a personal needs permit' that allowed him to visit his wife for three days over three months, and only during the day.[7]

The genius of the permit system – from Israel's point of view – is that it is silent and mostly invisible. The lives of Palestinians are being made difficult by a brilliantly masterminded bureaucracy. A lot of thought by a lot of very clever people has gone into this system, which is why, after 50 years, the occupation is more entrenched than ever. Israel says its permit system is for 'security reasons', but over time I realised that the security justification is the default position – sometimes justified, but often completely without foundation.

If you are a settler, your life is free of regulations; you have the complete protection of Israel's civil law code. If you are Palestinian, you live under Israeli military law. There are many roads on which Palestinians are not allowed, but on those where they are permitted to drive they must have a permit. If they do not, they can be taken for interrogation. This can mean remaining in prison, without charge, if an Israeli soldier says he believes they are a 'security risk'. In 2010, Israel passed a military order that any Palestinian without an army permit in the West Bank was 'an infiltrator' and liable to seven years' imprisonment. Palestinians are also liable to pay the cost of their own imprisonment and can be deported from the West Bank to Gaza.

American journalist Richard Ben Cramer has written that the cost of maintaining this permit system is 'mind-numbing'. 'No one in the developed world can truly understand what these numbers mean', he wrote in *How Israel Lost*.[8] In 2016, the International Monetary Fund estimated that Palestinian GDP would be between 40 and 130 per cent higher if the West Bank and Gaza had not yet years of political uncertainty and restrictions on the movement of people and goods. Israeli analyst Bradley Burston says the settlement movement has cost Israel some $100 billion in the past 40 years.[9] The Israeli human rights group Hamoked concluded: 'Violations caused by the permit regime have a destructive effect. They lead to creeping dispossession of West Bank residents from their land under the cover of a bureaucracy that operates pursuant to military law with the Israeli Supreme Court's seal of approval, yet in breach of a number of norms accepted in both Israeli and International law.'[10]

Israel uses the permit system to recruit informants. One source close to Israeli security told me there are about 20,000 Palestinians in the West Bank and East Jerusalem paid to inform. Payment often means giving informers permits so they can travel to Jerusalem for work. Palestinians who are approached to be informants but who refuse are often blacklisted, meaning they cannot get permits. Referring to them as 'invisible prisoners', Israeli group Machsom Watch has estimated that 180,000 Palestinians are 'security blacklisted'. Most have never been in prison and have no idea why they are blacklisted. According to Machsom Watch, the majority are victims of a system that aims to maintain 'a big pool' of potential collaborators. It says blacklisting helps to keep the population 'frightened, hungry, vulnerable and in continuous uncertainty', and hampers social cohesion by fostering suspicion about who might be informing.[11]

*

Israel has also established a network of secret units to infiltrate the Palestinian population. As early as 1950, Mossad set up 'Ulysses', whose purpose was to plant 'deep agents' among Palestinians. Yasser Arafat held his first meeting to plan the downfall of Israel in the apartment of an undercover Mossad agent.

Known in Hebrew as 'Mista'arvim', these units include the Dovdevan, who dress as Palestinians. Often they are Sephardic Jews or Druze, both of whom speak Arabic. They blend in with protesters, sometimes even going to Friday prayers. Once a protest starts, they pounce on the Palestinians. Part of their training is to go from complete calm to complete violence within seconds. Because the Dovdevan go into crowds of protesting Palestinians, Israel gives them *Rishaon laheshel* – licence to kill. To minimise the risk of infiltration, Palestinians now insist that those who join protests tie their shirts above their waists to reveal they are carrying no weapons.

Well-placed sources say that Israeli security services recruit from Palestinian crime groups. They sometimes approach crime gangs and tell them they are aware of their activities but will not prosecute them on two conditions: that they never sell drugs to Jewish Israelis and that they become informers for Shin Bet.

*

It was 8 September 2014, and as I walked up several flights of stairs in an old Bauhaus-style building in Tel Aviv, I felt enormous excitement. It's a sensation that – every so often – journalism presented. I didn't know who I was about to meet but what I did know was that the people waiting in the apartment had been working at the heart of Israel's military intelligence. They knew many of the country's deepest secrets. And they were prepared to talk to me.

The meeting had been months in the making. The process began when an Israeli military contact came to our apartment – he wanted to meet privately. He explained that there could soon be major defections from Israel's most elite military intelligence unit, Unit 8200, Israel's equivalent of the US National Security Agency. Unit 8200's main role, he said, was electronic surveillance of the 2.9 million Palestinians in the West Bank to monitor any security threats and to gather material that could be used to blackmail them into becoming informants.

Israel's electronic capability is brilliant. Israeli journalist Shimon Shiffer gave an insight into it when he recalled a visit to the Defence Ministry in Tel Aviv. 'Trying to impress me with the depth of the intelligence blanket that covers Gaza, an aide to the minister opened a map on a screen and offered me a tour of a specific street in Khan Yunis,' Shiffer wrote. 'In seconds, we had a close-up view of the goings-on in the street.'

The contact who visited our apartment stressed that the defectors would be branded as enemies of Israel and might even be sent to jail. He said that in a couple of months a selected group of journalists would be given access to some of the defectors and I would be one of them.

Months went by. Finally, I found myself walking up four levels in this old apartment building. My contact introduced me to four men – reservists from Unit 8200. They had put their names to a letter to Prime Minister Netanyahu signed by 43 members of the unit. But with us they asked to be known as Nadav, 'A', Daniel, and the fourth said he would prefer not to speak.

Before telling us what their letter concerned, they gave us some background to their action. 'We know what's happening inside,' said Nadav. 'We've been there and we are the ones who did those things. We are in favour of Israel defending itself. However, the occupation is a choice; when it lasts for almost 50 years it's not self-defence.'

Daniel said: 'We realise the occupation is detrimental to the safety of Israel because it's perpetuating a cycle of violence. We were a part of this cycle of violence and we think it would be better for both Palestinians and Israelis if this situation, this occupation, would end.'

Aspects of 8200's operations that disturbed several of the letter's signatories were the use of blackmail against gays or those who needed medical treatment for their children. Palestinian society, whether Muslim or Christian, is conservative, and homosexuality is something people often try to hide. One officer said: 'If you're homosexual and know someone who knows a wanted person – and we need to know about it – Israel will make your life miserable. If you need emergency medical treatment in Israel, the West Bank or abroad – we searched for you. The State of Israel will allow you to die before we let you leave for treatment without giving information on your wanted cousin.'

One-third of Unit 8200 were women and it had a large number of gay officers who each year held a concert where one of the men is crowned 'Miss 8200'. The targeting of gay Palestinians by the unit added to the anger that many of the officers felt. Nadav said: 'An 18-year-old soldier sitting in the intelligence forces can say who is a target and who is not a target. In this way every Palestinian basically can be a target ... Every country has its military intelligence and it's legitimate because it's against other countries. But the Palestinians do not have a country. They are under our military regime. It's not another country that can protect itself. They're like citizens of Israel except with no rights like the citizens of Israel.'

According to one of the defectors, there is no limit on the information-gathering; Israel's aim is to strengthen its grasp on 'every aspect of Palestinian life'.

The use of Palestinian informants is a daily fact of the occupation, said AFP journalist Philippe Agret. 'I don't like to make a moral judgment on collaborators – I would not, as a French person who knows French history. Palestinians have been under occupation since 1967. It's a tragic story and a human story: you live in Gaza, you send your wife to the hospital and she's going to die because she has cancer, and you're asked to collaborate with Israel if you want her to be treated in Israel. It's part of a daily, grim reality. It's a major story.'

The most secret – and feared – of Israel's intelligence machines is Mossad. Its motto says: 'By way of deception, thou shalt do war.'

The most extensive information about Mossad has come from Victor Ostrovsky, who worked as a secret agent for four years but became disillusioned. In *By Way of Deception* he wrote:

The [first] intifada and resultant breakdown of moral order and humanity are a direct result of the kind of megalomania that characterizes the operation of the Mossad ... This thing is uncontrollable. In Israel, they're still beating Palestinians, and [Prime Minister Yitzhak] Shamir says, 'They're making us become cruel. They're forcing us to hit children. Aren't they terrible?' This is what happens after years and years of secrecy; of 'we're right, let's be right, no matter what'; of keeping the officials deliberately misinformed; of justifying violence and inhumanity through deceit, or, as the Mossad logo says: 'by way of deception.' It's a disease that began with the Mossad and has spread through government and down through much of Israeli society ... The strongest curse inside the Mossad that one katsa [agent] can throw at another is the simple wish: 'May I read about you in the paper.' It might be the only way to turn things around.[12]

*

The longevity of Israel's occupation could not have been achieved without settlers.

In a settlement deep inside the West Bank, Daniella Weiss is Queen of Greater Israel. In December 2012 this matriarch of the settlements made Sylvie and me a cup of tea and gave us a tour of her home and its collection of Judaica – this home could have been on the leafy north shore of Sydney.

But when the conversation turned to Palestinians, her warmth evaporated. She had a clear message for Palestinians: you will never have your own State.

Daniella Weiss had been one of Israel's first settlers. In the early 1970s, she and her husband had moved to Kedumim in the West Bank, where they put up tents on Palestinian land. By the time their children were born they'd put up caravans and eventually they built a permanent brick home. The local Palestinians were not game to try to force them off, as the Israeli Army was always close by to intervene should the Weisses call for it.

As well as having an army on call, Daniella Weiss developed a close relationship with Ariel Sharon, then Minister of Housing. She told us: 'With my work with Ariel Sharon, there was a clear understanding, a very clear planning of spreading the communities, the Jewish communities, in the way that there will be no option for a Palestinian State in Judea and Samaria.'

For Daniella Weiss, the vote by the United Nations in 1947 to divide Palestine into a Jewish and an Arab State was irrelevant. 'We came to a land where there were other people living, but this land was promised to the Jewish nation by God,' she said. 'And if the Palestinians behave themselves then they can stay. As long as they are good guests. This is the only way I see it, so those who accept it live nicely. Those who do not accept it encounter confrontations.'

We asked Weiss, as a grandmother, what message she had for young Palestinians. 'It's true that in the course of history Arabs came to this area from all over, but the promise of God is more important than the changes in history and the political changes. That is why you have to put it deep, deep into your mind, that you do not have any chance whatsoever in any point of history, neither you nor any of your offspring, to ever have an independent State of your own here.'

She continued: 'The settler leadership should not by any means criticise any element of settler behaviour, no matter how extreme it is. The Arabs keep threatening our lives every day and every night. I very much believe in creating a situation where the Arabs are afraid of what we do.'

In February 2014, after Sylvie and I had done two years of research, I would present a report for the ABC's *Four Corners*, on the trials of Palestinian children in the Israeli military court in the West Bank. It would be my use of Daniella Weiss in that report that most angered the Israeli lobby in Australia. To have an Israeli saying that the settlements had been deliberately planned to ensure there could be no Palestinian State was far more confronting for the lobby than to have an Australian lawyer, Gerard Horton, talking about abuses by the Israeli Army of Palestinian children.

Weiss took Sylvie and me to visit the Hilltop Youth, a group of Jewish youth who target a hilltop or piece of land – often privately owned by Palestinians – and, heavily armed, take it over. Like Daniella Weiss, they believe they are entitled to take such land because of a biblical mandate from God. The owners of the land know that if they try to take it back they are likely to be met with gunfire. The Hilltop Youth are usually armed, but if not they know that they can call on the army should they get into a confrontation. Videos abound in which the Hilltop Youth attack Palestinians while soldiers stand by.

In the West Bank, the settlers have become the law enforcers. When you spend time with people out here – both Israeli settlers and Palestinians – it becomes clear that the settlers are in total control. Each settlement has a security committee that is able to summon the army at any time. Former Israeli soldiers say these committees are able to give orders to the army. Over several months in late 2013, I researched a case in which one complaint from a settler in Hebron led to the arrest of a five-year-old Palestinian boy by six soldiers. When the boy's father intervened – peacefully – the soldiers blindfolded him. The settler had been able to activate the army within minutes of one unsubstantiated allegation that the boy had thrown a stone.

Once a small settlement is established the army will often come and set up a 'monitoring point' and have two or three soldiers staying there, and if it becomes big enough, they will form a small army base. This suits the settlers because they are being returned the land they claim God gave them; it suits the army because it gives them more bases throughout the Palestinian Territories and it means that they can enforce the occupation and have army bases 'looking out' across Jordan and towards the Arab world should they come under attack.

Given the power of the settlers, it would be a brave, or naïve, soldier who countermanded a settler security chief. 'I saw one settler threatening a colonel in the Israeli army,' Israeli journalist Gideon Levy told me. 'The settler stood with a gun and told the colonel, "If you do one more step I'm shooting you," and the colonel went away.'

In addition, settlers are often armed with weapons the army gives them; this is official Israeli policy if settlers say they feel threatened. Sylvie and I visited a firing range attached to the settlement of Gush Etzion where Israelis are trained in how to use hand and machine guns. A significant number of settlers has become heavily armed gangsters who roam the West Bank taking over Palestinian houses and destroying property and – sometimes – lives.

Many of the settlers I spoke to had come from the US originally. They loved the pioneer spirit, they were fanatical about how God had 'given' them this land, and they felt they had an obligation to take it and protect it.

But why are the settlers so powerful? Israeli journalist Gideon Levy said: 'They are the only group in society which is ready to do something for collective reasons. There's no other group in Israeli society today which is ready to sacrifice, to fight for something collective. Israel is totally individualistic now – people here would not go on the street for anything. Settlers would. They care about something. This must be appreciated – they are fighting for an idea. From day one they were very powerful. They can blackmail any government here.'

On 25 February 1994, US-born doctor Baruch Goldstein left his settlement of Kiryat Arba and drove to nearby Hebron, where he entered the Ibrahimi mosque and shot dead 29 people as they prayed. Goldstein's tomb carries the epitaph 'He gave his life for the people of Israel, its Torah and land. His hands are clean and his heart good.' In 1999, the Israeli Government passed a law outlawing monuments to terrorists. After pressure to dismantle Goldstein's tomb, the army took down the shrine but left the tombstone. Israel's District Court ruled that 'lauding' Goldstein does not constitute incitement. The BBC covered the sixth anniversary of Goldstein's massacre, when settlers dressed up as Goldstein, wearing doctors' coats and fake beards.[13]

*

In this war for land, the settlers are the advance unit. The most common way that Israel takes Palestinian land is for armed settlers to take it in the first instance. Because Palestinians are not allowed to carry weapons, the land is taken relatively easily. If a settler kills a Palestinian, they will not be prosecuted if they say that they *believed* they were in danger. The only complication is if someone captures it on video and it is clear the settler killed the Palestinian in cold blood – though, based on statistics, the settler still has a high chance of being found not guilty. Data from the Israeli human rights group Yesh Din indicates that there is only a 1.9 per cent chance that a complaint filed by a Palestinian will result in a conviction of the perpetrators.[14]

Yehuda Shaul is a former Israeli Army commander who founded human rights group Breaking the Silence, which has collected the testimonies of more than 1000 current and former Israeli combat soldiers. 'The Israeli occupation of the West Bank has certain checks and balances,' Shaul told me:

but there is one thing about which Israel is ruthless and
for which there are no checks and balances: land. With
everything else there are boundaries. Today, rather
than the assumption being that it is Palestinian land and
Israel needs to prove a claim, it is the exact opposite: the
assumption is that it is Israel's land and Palestinians are
the ones who have to prove it is their land. This is the way
it works: a Palestinian comes to cultivate his land and the
settlers who have moved in come and beat him up. There is
no point calling the army or police because you know which

side they will support. Then the Palestinian comes back
to try again to work his land, and he gets beaten up again.
Without farming he has no money so finally, after a number
of beatings, he decides to leave and move to the closest
town, Yatta, to look for a job. He moves on with his life,
which means moving off the land. The settlers then control
the land with no opposition from the owners.

The settlers then farm the land for 10 years – which means that
legally it becomes theirs. As Yehuda Shaul told me: 'The less land
the Palestinians have to farm means the less chance they have of
surviving.'

When their land is taken, Palestinians often appeal to the
Israeli Army. The army often tells the Palestinians that it is not
up to them, but the Supreme Court, to decide the ownership.
Appeals to the Supreme Court can take up to 15 years, during
which time settlers build houses, schools and synagogues on the
land. Once enough time has elapsed, Israeli authorities sometimes
say it is too late to reverse the decision. Even if the Supreme
Court makes a ruling that it is private Palestinian land, the army
will not enforce that or, if it does, the settlers ignore the ruling. It
surprised me how often that happened. The Palestinians rarely
get their land back. This is a pattern that has been occurring
since Israel began its occupation in 1967.

Israel uses a range of laws and devices to take private
Palestinian land. One of these is to apply a 'state of emergency'
law. Until I lived in Israel, I had no idea that it was still operating
under a state of emergency The law is renewed by the Knesset
every three or six months, and gives it almost total power
regarding Palestinians.

The legislation is called the Defence (Emergency) Regulations and began under the British Mandate in 1945. According to Israeli human rights group B'Tselem, it means the Israeli Army can imprison someone indefinitely, demolish and seal homes, impose indefinite curfews and deport residents. In 2011, the Knesset Foreign Affairs and Defence Committee extended the powers to cover enterprises by Palestinians including ice-cream production, selling tickets for artistic performances and conducting amniocentesis tests for pregnant women – such enterprises can be shut down.

One emergency power that has had an enormous impact on Palestinians is the Absentee Property law. Award-winning British journalist Jonathan Cook, who lives in Nazareth, has reported that since this law was established in 1950 Israel has used it to transfer millions of acres of privately owned Palestinian land, as well as thousands of homes, bank accounts and other properties, from the 800,000 or so Palestinian refugees. Essentially, the law says Israel is entitled to seize any Palestinian house or property that was vacant in 1948. Cook said:

By the early 1950s, Israel's rural economy depended on the plundering of Palestinian refugees' farmlands, whether olives trees, vineyards or Jaffa orange groves … no compensation was, or ever has been, offered to the refugees or the millions of their descendants, many of whom today languish in poverty in refugee camps across the Middle East. Nor has Israel settled accounts with the absentees who live inside the Jewish State. A quarter of a million Arab citizens of Israel are today deprived of all rights to their original property, having been declared, in truly Orwellian language, 'present absentees' [present in Israel but absent from their property for a day or more in 1948].[15]

Another way Israel takes over private Palestinian land is to invoke an old Ottoman law. Under the Ottoman Empire, in order to farm land the owner had to pay a high registration cost. If someone stopped farming their land for three years, the sultan could declare it dead land and give it to someone else to farm. Importantly for today's occupation, the sultan decided that if someone farmed unregistered land for 10 years it became theirs. The Israeli Army often prevents Palestinians from gaining access to their land while settlers are permitted to use it. The settlers then need only go to the Supreme Court to show that for 10 years they have been caring for this 'abandoned' land. The Palestinian ownership is then cancelled. Although the Israeli Supreme Court overturned this law in 2012, it still influences decisions of the court.

I regularly witnessed the court's endorsement of discrimination. 'Most of the cases we deal with involve a twisted interpretation of the law,' Yariv Mohar from Rabbis for Human Rights told me. 'Mostly the government tries not to bluntly disobey the law but they try to make it confusing so that it always serves the interests of the settlers. They will say that they are considering a claim by settlers under Ottoman law but then the Israeli courts will give it an interpretation that has never been made in the past. What they do is invent new interpretations of the law without inventing new laws themselves.'[16]

Israel has also claimed land through 'security buffer zones'. There are 12 settlements in the West Bank that have formal buffer zones, and any Palestinian who enters one of these areas is liable to be shot.

Sylvie and I had an opportunity to meet Dror Etkes, Israel's foremost expert on land in the West Bank, soon after he finished a report on the amount of agricultural land taken over by settlements. He had also investigated 'closed areas' in the West Bank. More than 50 per cent of the West Bank land controlled by Israel has been closed for military activities, even though 78 per cent of it is not used for manoeuvres. These closed military zones are not accessible to Palestinians, but some of them have been built on by settlers.

This is how Etkes described the creation of Greater Israel: 'From audacious fraud and forgery to military seizures for "security needs" and "the public good" to dusting off antiquated Ottoman laws, the Israeli settlement enterprise has no shortage of tools for taking over Palestinian land in the West Bank ... What we are actually witnessing is the rule of law disappearing before our eyes.'[17]

Simply counting the number of settlers in the West Bank does not give an accurate picture of settlement growth, said Etkes. The fastest growth now is through agricultural rather than residential settlements, through gaining more land rather than simply more settlers. The growth of commercial areas is also substantial. In addition to commercial centres inside settlements, there are approximately 20 Israeli-administered industrial zones in the West Bank, according to Human Rights Watch.[18]

Dror Etkes also found that in the last decade there had been a decline of about one-third in cultivated Palestinian agricultural lands in the West Bank. One factor behind this was the ongoing expansion of Israeli agricultural areas. This expansion included de facto appropriation of actively cultivated private lands whose Palestinian owners – individuals or entire communities – had been expelled, whether by the settlers or by the Israeli military.

Etkes found that Israeli agricultural lands in the West Bank covered about 93,000 dunams (Ottoman acres) – about one and a half times the total built-up area of the settlements, not including East Jerusalem. This showed that 'settlement growth' covered more than residential areas. This is important because Israel's lobby groups, including AIJAC in Australia, often point to residential settlements to argue that they only account for a small area of the West Bank. According to Ektes, Israel's system was set up for 'a land grab' such as this. 'There's no rule of law,' he told me. 'The rule of law is a dead letter in the West Bank.'

I'd arrived in Israel with the belief that, whatever the country's problems, it adhered to the rule of law. But the more I researched the reality in the West Bank the more I came to the gradual realisation that the manipulation of the rule of law was used in the quest for Greater Israel. There was one occasion, for example, when a regulation was changed for 24 hours by the Defence Ministry's Civil Administration to allow 250 settlement houses to be approved. Israelis from the settlement of Ofra retroactively requested a permit for 200 houses that had been built and 50 planned houses. Most of the 200 houses had been built illegally on private Palestinian land. But there was a problem: the houses were 80 metres from the main road and the army regulation was that no house could be built within 120 metres of the road. So for 24 hours the Civil Administration reduced the limit from 120 metres to 80 metres, which meant all settlements houses could be approved. The next day, a Palestinian family in the village of Beit Ummar, hearing of the changed law for the neighbouring settlement, also retroactively requested a permit for a house that had received a demolition order. The Defence Ministry rejected the application, saying that the rule was that a house could not be within 120 metres of a road.[19]

*

Israel's settlements began with guns and a lie. Soon after Israel took the West Bank in 1967, hardline religious elements decided to 'reclaim Judea and Samaria'. Prime Minister Levi Eshkol made no official ruling on whether settlements could proceed, but Rabbi Moshe Levinger, a leader of the pro-settlement national religious supporters, took the initiative. A firebrand who today would fit the US State Department's definition of a terrorist, Levinger and his supporters travelled to Hebron in the West Bank for Passover in 1968. They checked into the Park Hotel saying they were Swiss tourists. And they hid their weapons. The Park Hotel would become a base from which they formed a militia to seize central Hebron and force out Palestinians. A secret document from 1970 confirms the deception the government engaged in to help those first settlers: 250 new housing units were to be built, but 'all the building will be done by the Defence Ministry and will be presented as construction for the IDF's needs'.[20]

What began as Israel's 'settlement enterprise' has, 50 years later, become Frankenstein's Monster.

One myth perpetuated by many of Israel's supporters is that the occupation came as a surprise – but the ambition of taking over the West Bank as part of Greater Israel was clear before the country won the Six Day War of 1967. In the documentary *The Law in These Parts*, former Supreme Court president Meir Shamgar states that laws for the West Bank were written in the early 1950s.

The master plan for Israel to take over the West Bank was formed by Yigal Alon when he was Minister of Labour in the early 1960s. The strategy was that controlling most of the West Bank would effectively push Israel's border to Jordan. It gave Israel a security buffer against Jordan, Syria and Iraq. The Alon plan also meant Jordan and the West Bank could never form any political or military entity against Israel.

Another result was the fragmentation of Palestinian towns, according to British journalist Jonathan Cook who has studied Israel's methodology in Nazareth, where he lives. Cook's view is that a neighbouring Jewish city of Upper Nazareth, built in the 1950s, was the prototype for Israel's settlement movement. He told me that is where Israel first tested the model of encirclement, isolation and containment of Palestinian communities. Today, Upper Nazareth encircles the Palestinian community in Nazareth, leaving it unable to expand, while also isolating it from Palestinian villages nearby. This is similar to the way many Israeli settlements in the West Bank have encircled Palestinian villages.

Under the Oslo Accords, the West Bank is divided into three areas: Area A, which is 18 per cent of the West Bank and is under the control of the Palestinian Authority; Area B, 21 per cent, is under civil control of the Palestinian Authority, and Israel retains control of security; Area C, 61 per cent, is totally under Israeli control. This is where all the settlements are. But even in Areas A and B, the Israeli Army can enter anytime and has complete authority if it claims there is a security issue. It enters parts of Areas A and B most nights.

Oslo was intended to be an interim agreement of five years to allow both parties to move to a final agreement under which a Palestinian State could be formed. But Israel has entrenched its control over Area C.[21] There were 110,000 settlers in the West Bank when Oslo was signed in 1993. Today there are 394,000. In a time of peace, the number of settlers has surged.

'One of the things that killed Oslo was as a result of Oslo,' Yehuda Shaul said. 'The system of bypass roads that it led to.' At Oslo the Israelis won the right to build bypass roads in the West Bank – they argued this was necessary for security. Before Oslo, many settlers would need to drive through Palestinian towns to get to and from their settlements. The US mediators should have realised that if Israel wanted to build a network of roads they were not thinking of leaving after five years. 'It [Oslo] was fatal for the Palestinians,' Israeli journalist Gideon Levy told me. 'All the big settlements came after Oslo. If the Israelis did not evacuate one house in the settlements from Oslo it shows they had no intention.'

The by-pass roads entrenched the settlements. After building these roads, Israel banned Palestinians from using many of them. Israel had used Oslo to make a Palestinian State more difficult.

'It gives them absolute control over Palestinians' movements,' said Yehuda Shaul. 'The way the dual infrastructure of roads and permits has been set up by Israel means less restrictions but absolute control. In 15 minutes, 300 army jeeps can shut down the West Bank's entire road system. We have absolute control over what roads you can use and at any moment we can block them.'

It also made access to the settlements from Israel easier, effectively turning them into commuter suburbs. Yehuda Shaul explained: 'Because of that system, settlers could say, "When I drove out here I saw Palestinians and had to drive through Palestinian towns. Now I see modern highways, I see no Palestinians and I'm safe."' Crucially, settlements went from being a pioneering and messianic experience to a suburban, middle-class one.

Israel's largest-selling newspaper, *Yedioth Ahronoth*, reported in 2003: 'When most of the Israeli public, and maybe most of the world too, think about the Jewish settlements in what used to be called "the territories", they envision mainly a handful of wind-swept sheds and beat-up old trailers. But the current state of affairs is completely different. The Jewish population in the 1967 territories is already equal to half of the Palestinian population there, and it is in the midst of one of the largest demographic surges in the world.'[22]

New York Times journalist Jodi Rudoren agreed. 'One thing people are totally shocked by is how big and established the settlements are and who lives there,' she told me. 'You come and have this notion it's bearded, gun-toting [people] and caravans and you go to Ariel or Maale Adumim or Efrat and it's full of people who are mostly middle-class people. First of all, sometimes you meet non-ideological people and their view is "My government gave me tax breaks to move here and I moved here because I wanted a backyard and I didn't mean to oppress anybody and by the way I do think it's mine."'

Since Israel began its occupation it has provided financial incentives for Israelis to move to settlements. You get tax concessions, you get private security, you get good schools and hospitals, and most of all you get cheap housing. House and land packages are much cheaper when you don't have to pay for the land part. This has been a major attraction – my Hebrew teacher could afford a much bigger apartment in Har Homa than he could in Jerusalem. Some people distinguish between economic and religious settlements, but in the end they amount to the same thing: ever more land for Israel.

Some secular Israelis may be moving to the settlements, but other Israelis think the settler movement is not worth it: Israel takes so much punishment in the Western world because the settlements are always the running sore for the international community. Some in the centre or on the centre left of politics are contemptuous of the settlers. However, the majority of Israeli opinion now would be: 'We're there and it's ours. The Palestinians should find somewhere else to live.'

For Israel today, there are three main reasons why the settlements are important. The first is religious: the references to Judea and Samaria in the Bible. The second is security: having a large number of the hilltops looking east towards the Muslim and Arab world allows the best defence. And the third is economic: the Jordan Valley's agriculture is lucrative and the settlements alleviate housing pressures in Israel. The dominant view is that if Israel can keep increasing the number of settlers in the West Bank, then eventually it can argue that there are more Israelis there than Palestinians so it's logical to annex it – or at least Area C. This would leave Areas A and B for an independent, although tiny, Palestinian State.

According to the *Washington Post*, 39 per cent of the land used for settlements is privately owned Palestinian land.[23] There are 131 settlements, including three very large ones – Maale Adumim, Gush Etzion and Ariel. There are also 99 outposts – small communities that attach themselves to settlements but which even under Israeli law are illegal. Even the outposts have military protection, cameras, mailboxes, public transport and electricity. This is despite the fact that connecting electricity to an unauthorised location is illegal. Once they have electricity and water from the settlements, they begin lobbying to be made official. Israel's human rights group Yesh Din researched how Israel retrospectively makes these outposts 'authorised settlements'. They found: 'Approximately a quarter of the 100 outposts that currently exist have been approved or are at various stages of the approval process ... Simultaneously, the [Government of Israel] consistently denies the status of these outposts, established without official permission and in violation of Israeli (as well as international) law, as settlements.'[24]

'The strategy with the outposts is to fill in the gaps between the settlements,' former Israeli commander Yehuda Shaul told me. 'The intention was that the settlements and outposts would duplicate themselves – that every settlement would break out of its borders and duplicate itself. Every Palestinian village in the West Bank is encircled. With Bethlehem, for example, on one side are the settlements of Nokdim and Tekoa, one side a military base and nature reserve. We've worked it all out. We've taken Bethlehem as a test case. This is a strategy of fragmentation.'

In 2005, the Israeli Army commissioned a comprehensive database of Israel's settlements to give legal ammunition to the State to defend any claims of loss of ownership by Palestinians. In 2009, when Defence Minister Ehud Barak received the report and saw the result, he decided that it should not be published because 'publication could endanger state security or harm Israel's foreign relations'.

But someone leaked the report to Israeli newspaper *Haaretz*. It revealed that in about 75 per cent of settlements, construction – sometimes on a large scale – had been carried out without the appropriate permits or contrary to the permits that were issued.

The database also showed that in more than 30 settlements extensive construction of buildings and infrastructure – roads, schools, synagogues, yeshivas and even police stations – had been carried out on private land belonging to Palestinians. Put simply, the settlement construction had been conducted illegally.[25]

Sarit Michaeli from human rights group B'Tselem told me:

Everything has been incremental but 50 years later you
have half a million Israelis living in an occupied area
that's not part of Israel's sovereign territory – except East
Jerusalem which was annexed, therefore Israel views it
as its own – you have 120 so-called legal settlements and
another 100 so-called illegal settlements that are all illegal
under international law, you have two legal systems that
apply to Israelis and Palestinians in parallel, you have
Israeli democracy in tatters because of all the problems that
stem from such a long-term occupation. Everything is legal
because they found various legal excuses to justify it but of
course it's not legal. Clearly it's a complete farce.

*

The settlers have established deep roots in Israel's political and military establishments: an estimated 12 per cent of the commanders of the IDF themselves live in settlements. Even Avigdor Lieberman lives in the illegal settlement of Nokdim: the only defence minister in the world who does not live inside his country's borders. The task of the IDF in vacating settlers – including many of their own commanders – would be extraordinarily difficult.

The *New York Times*'s Jodi Rudoren thinks that 'among left-wing people or critics of settlements or the occupation there's a view that undoing it would be simple. When people come here they realise it would not be simple.'

According to Dror Etkes:

> If you applied the law tomorrow you would have to evict thousands of Israeli settlers. You have entire settlements which are constructed on private Palestinian property. What would you do with Ofra, with half of Beit El? You have thousands of families and tens of thousands of dunams of agricultural land which you would have to uproot. You would have to break roads in settlements which are passing through Palestinian property. The entire system in the West Bank is built on breach of law. Two neighbourhoods in the same settlement – in between them is a valley which used to be cultivated in the '80s by Palestinians, then the settlement took over and there is a road which joins the two. How do you deal with that? There is no way a settlement could function if the law was applied.

When Israel evicted 8000 settlers from the Gaza Strip in 2005, the settlers put up considerable resistance. The removal of more than 600,000 settlers in the West Bank and East Jerusalem would be much more difficult – though not, in my view, impossible. The way to do it would be for Israel to offer financial incentives for settlers to move back into Israel – but there is no political will to do this and insufficient pressure from the international community.

As successive Israeli governments encourage settlements, the chances of a Palestinian State recede. In addition to this the settlements have been strategically located to make a contiguous Palestinian State impossible.

At this stage, the best the Palestinians can hope for are the equivalent of Bantustans – the disconnected black communities built by apartheid South Africa, allowing the government to claim it was giving blacks some autonomy. The Israeli Government likewise claims that under the Palestinian Authority, Palestinians have autonomy.

The Israelis have two major problems in terms of their occupation. The first is international opinion, which, as will be seen, is increasingly hostile. The second is a growing Palestinian population. When Israel took over the West Bank in 1967, there were 1 million Palestinians. Now there are 2.9 million, and by 2020 there are likely to be 3.5 million. Palestinians do not want to live under occupation, and their number is growing.

Australian lawyer Gerard Horton of Military Court Watch told me: 'Imagine if the US put 600,000 Americans into Afghanistan and the army was told they had to guarantee their protection. Any military given that mission has three options: it can kill all the locals, deport them or intimidate and terrorise them. It's essentially the third option employed by the Israeli military at the friction points in the West Bank.'

French journalist Philippe Agret said if this was Israel's strategy it would not work. 'I don't think the Palestinians will leave. The Israelis want to show who's in charge – they are the boss, they are in charge and you shut up. One can be shocked by this never-ending occupation, the sheer brutality of it. Comparison is not reason but France was occupied for four years, they [the Palestinians] have been occupied for 50 years. Fifty years of occupation, so yes it's shocking, the repression is shocking.'

Much international law has been written from practical experience. The legal order established at the end of the Second World War drew on the horrors of war to try to prevent another. Its foundation was that most wars begin over territory disputes. The key legal principle is the non-acquisition of territory through aggression, even if acting in self-defence (Article 2 of the UN Charter and numerous Security Council resolutions).

Israel argues that it was acting in self-defence when it occupied the West Bank, but even so this does not give it any rights of *permanent* possession. On top of that, Article 49 of the Fourth Geneva Convention prohibits an occupying power from transferring its civilian population into occupied territory. This is precisely what Israel is doing.

For the international community, an important principle is at play. If it allows Israel to continue to breach the Geneva Convention, does that mean every country can do so? When Russia annexes Crimea, can the world object? When China begins colonising the South China Sea, can the world object?

Either international law applies across the board, or international politics is a free-for-all survival of the fittest.

*

One of the images of the occupation I will never forget is a crushed car in a water cistern.

The Supreme Court had ruled that everyone in the West Bank was entitled to be supplied with water – but not necessarily where they lived. In the remote Bedouin village of Susiya, water was available, but the villagers had to travel many kilometres to collect it.

For the Palestinians of Susiya, who had farmed their land since the days of the Ottoman Empire, life had become a daily battle with the Israeli settlers across the hill. In 1982, the whole village of Susiya was expelled and two Palestinians were murdered by settlers. However, some Palestinians returned. But in 1991, said Yehuda Shaul, the army came and put the villagers into trucks and took them away again. On this occasion a settler was murdered by Palestinians, and the army's response was ruthless. 'The IDF erased the village,' said Yehuda Shaul. 'My [army] company took part in it.' Some Palestinians again resumed living in their village. In 2001, they won an important victory: the Supreme Court ruled that the village had been demolished illegally. Two months after the villagers returned, the IDF showed up with a demolition order for the whole village. The army said the tents the Palestinians were living in did not have building permits. 'The strategy works,' Yehuda Shaul told me. 'There used to be 100 families in Susiya, now it's down to 30. Every time there is a demolition of the village fewer and fewer families come back. Some decide it's just too hard.'

The army and settlers had tried various ways to cut off the water supply of the Palestinians. Thirty of their 36 cisterns had become part of a 'security buffer zone', and any Palestinian who entered the zone was liable to be shot. The army had then brought in bulldozers to push rocks into the six cisterns that remained. Yet still the Palestinians were able to place hoses through the rocks to draw water.

Finally, the IDF came up with another idea. As a former army officer, Yehuda Shaul is ashamed of what his army did next. 'The army crushed a car and pushed it into one of the water cisterns so it would poison the water and make it undrinkable.'

On 1 May 2013, I drove to Susiya, about an hour from Jerusalem. I wanted to see for myself the car that had been crushed into a cistern. In a place already so tough, where water was gold, I found it an almost unspeakably cruel thing to do. It was an unforgiving place: no greenery and unrelenting heat. The village leader, Nasser Nawaja, told me: 'We are on the edge of the desert so we don't have much rain. [Not having access to our water] makes our lives very hard and makes it very difficult to do our farming. It drains you.'

I stood there looking at the rusted old vehicle in the well and tried to reconcile this with the constant refrain of the Israeli lobby: that this is the most moral army in the world.

*

The battle to achieve Greater Israel is timeless.

If the messianic campaign to colonise the West Bank takes decades, so be it. God has ordained that the Jewish people should have 'Judea and Samaria', the settlers argue, and they are obliged to make sure that his wish is observed. If the fight for Greater Israel needs to be done house by house, room by room, water cistern by water cistern, then so be it.

In the Old City of Hebron, each floor of shared apartment buildings where Jews replace Palestinians is a triumph. Some settlers moved next door to Palestinians in the main street, Shuhada Street. One day, when the Palestinians were not there, the settlers smashed down the connecting wall and moved in. They were heavily armed, so the Palestinians knew it would be a massacre to try to re-enter. One more house on the road to Greater Israel.

Today, settlers live in that house and taunt foreigners or Israeli human rights workers who walk past. (Palestinians are not allowed to walk on that street.) I've been on a tour with Yehuda Shaul, while a young settler boy walked alongside him shouting 'Kelev!' – 'Dog!'

As I discovered when researching the eviction of Nasser Jaber, much of the battle over property in Jerusalem goes on in the Old City. This is not just the world's slowest war, it is also the world's quietest war. Pilgrims and other tourists bargain over Armenian pottery, rent crucifixes for their stations of the cross or sip coffee while, in courtrooms a kilometre away, the battle over ownership goes on.

We also saw this battle in the East Jerusalem suburb of Sheikh Jarrah. First came the Hebrew names to replace the Arab ones, then came the Israeli settlers. In our first six months in Jerusalem, Sylvie and I would go sometimes to Sheikh Jarrah to cover the weekly protests as Palestinians were removed from houses they were resettled into according to an agreement between Jordan and the UN in 1967. After the Six Day War, these people had been evacuated from Jaffa or East Jerusalem, where their houses had been taken over by newly arrived European Jews.

A year or so after one of these evictions, I drove back down there to see how it was all going. I saw a distressed old Palestinian man in a dressing gown. He told me his water supply had been turned off. Two young Jewish settlers standing nearby admitted they had done it. They said they meant to turn off their own water but accidentally turned off the old man's water. I asked them: why would you want to turn off your own water? They had no answer.

This old man looked like he was close to breaking point. I realised he was a bit player in a big, historic drama. History will probably never know his name, but he was a small part of the march towards Greater Israel.

This is a long game. One day the army pushes a rusted car into a water cistern in the Hebron Hills. The next some settlers in East Jerusalem turn off the water of an old man.

This is how Israel works in this seemingly endless occupation.

CHAPTER 12

Coffee with the
Israeli Army

9 December 2011

WHEN THE MOST POWERFUL ARMY IN THE MIDDLE EAST
wants to meet for coffee, something is happening. Captain Arye
Shalicar, who'd been my guide on 'children's day' at the West
Bank military court, phoned to say the army was unhappy with
my story about the visit.

We agreed to meet. Just before he hung up, he said: 'I'll be
bringing my wife.'

By this point I'd been in Israel almost three years – long
enough to be suspicious of the IDF. I was worried that Captain
Shalicar might later misquote something I said then produce his
wife as a witness. I mentioned my concern to Sylvie. 'Then I can
come along too,' she said.

So, on 2 December, Sylvie and I walked into Masaryk Café
in the German Colony. Over the next hour, we would take part

Jerusalem.

John, Sylvie, Jack and elder son Nicolas at Qala'at ibn Maan Castle, overlooking Palmyra, Syria.

On camels, just outside Cairo in 2009. Once the internal unrest in Egypt began, tourism virtually died.

Sylvie and Jack in Cairo in front of street art depicting fallen Egyptian dictator Hosni Mubarak.

Palestinians in the Old City of Hebron have erected a metal covering to protect themselves from bricks, chairs, rotting chickens and dirty nappies which the settlers throw onto them.

Sylvie and Jack having a day out in the Old City of Jerusalem.

John and his editor, Paul Whittaker, in Hebron. 'Like Dresden after the bombing,' said Paul.

Israeli soldiers walk through the Palestinian market of the Old City of Hebron.

John joins the Israeli Army for the weekly clash with Palestinians at the wall in Bil'in.

Every Saturday afternoon Israeli soldiers escort settlers, who sometimes destroy Palestinian goods, through the market in Hebron.

Border police check the IDs of Palestinians who want to enter the Old City of Jerusalem for Friday prayers. Males aged five to 50 are sometimes refused entry.

HOUSE OF WISDOM

بيت الحكمة

Gaza, 2010: John interviewing Ahmed Yusef, a member of the Hamas executive.

Gaza 2014: two children stand between a bombed water tower and mosque.

The long walk into Gaza: through Erez Crossing then for one kilometre along this caged corridor.

Transporting by donkey a fridge smuggled via a tunnel into Gaza from Egypt.

The wall in Shuafat refugee camp in Jerusalem. Palestinians who cannot get a permit sometimes resort to climbing ladders to get into Jerusalem for work.

Jack building a Lego 'wall of Bethlehem'.

Israeli police demolished the house Mrs Fakhouri's family lived in for decades.

Police in Jerusalem clash with ultra-orthodox Jews trying to shut down the Mamilla shopping centre car park during the Sabbath.

An elderly Palestinian man asking his Jewish neighbours why they have turned off his water.

John asking the same.
They said it was an accident.

Christian Zionists from around the world travelled to the West Bank to celebrate the end of a 10-month settlement freeze.

John with Yehuda Shaul, the founder of Breaking the Silence, a group of more than 1000 current and former Israeli combat soldiers trying to end the occupation.

Palestinians clash with the Israeli Army at the Shuafat refugee camp.

John with settler spokesman David Ha'ivri. He was born in America as David Axelrod and changed his name to David Ha'ivri, meaning David the Hebrew.

Four Palestinian youths appear before an army judge in the Israeli Military Court in the West Bank. Children as young as 12 can be taken from their homes at night and are not permitted to have a parent or lawyer present for questioning.

John talking to fellow Melburnian Mark Regev who moved to Israel and became the spokesman for Prime Minister Benjamin Netanyahu.

Former prime minister Ehud Olmert talking with John at a dinner in Jerusalem.

Doing research in the West Bank with prominent US journalist Peter Beinart.

On the Jerusalem balcony: (left to right) friend Hamish Wyatt; John; and founders of Military Court Watch Salwa Duaibis and Australian lawyer Gerard Horton.

in a very strange conversation. But it would also prove to be illuminating in terms of how Israel views international opinion.

Captain Shalicar pulled from his pocket the article I'd written for the *Weekend Australian Magazine* on 26 November 2011, entitled 'Stone Cold Justice'.

'We have a problem with this,' he said.

'Are there any factual mistakes in it?' I asked.

'No,' he said, 'we're not challenging the accuracy, but our concern is that it's been published outside Israel. If this had appeared in Israel, in *Haaretz* or *Yedioth* [*Ahronoth*], we could live with it. This sort of thing appears quite a lot. But this appeared in Australia.'

I told him I didn't understand his point.

He explained: 'People in Israel are committed to the State of Israel. Either they have moved here because they are committed to Israel or have remained here because they are. So when they read a story about Israeli soldiers and Palestinian children they read it in the context that whatever they read, it is not going to shake their commitment. But people in Australia may not have the same commitment. So when they read a story like this they may question their support for Israel. If I was sitting in Australia reading this I would think that Israeli soldiers were brutally treating Palestinian children.'

He paused. I said nothing. He continued. 'A story like this may damage the view that Australians have of Israel and they don't have the commitment to Israel to go along with that.'

Captain Shalicar was articulating a view that is widespread among Israelis: they don't mind if something is printed in Israel, but when it is published more widely they react badly. But to hear these words from an IDF media officer was extraordinary.

I'd faced this mindset ever since I filed my story on the tractor incident during the 2009 Gaza War. I'd endured an even worse barrage from Noga Tarnopolsky following my story about Nasser Jaber. Frequently in the Israeli media I'd read stories about various abuses by the Israeli Army, but the moment I reported them in Australia I was attacked.

When Jewish leaders in Australia complained I asked them: 'Are you saying Australians should not be able to read what Israelis read?' I resented the pressure not to report what I saw; I was covering the Middle East as an Australian journalist in the belief that events should be reported as you find them.

As one Australian who moved to Israel told me: 'The reason some people in the Jewish community in Melbourne don't want you writing stories about the treatment of Palestinian children is not that they think they're untrue but because they think that by appearing outside Israel they give Israel's enemies a weapon.'

Captain Shalicar's response wouldn't be the last criticism my story received. In mid-2012, Australian Foreign Minister Bob Carr would run into an old friend from the Labor Party, Mary Easson, in the Qantas lounge in Sydney. She was eager to show him something: she had been copied in on an email from Michael Danby, the federal Labor member for Melbourne Ports, to Gerard Henderson, the Executive Director of the Sydney Institute and columnist with my newspaper. By then I'd written several articles about the plight of Palestinian children in the Israeli military court. I had recently written an update about how Carr as Foreign Minister had raised concerns about the plight of Palestinian children in Israeli jails. Danby's email to Henderson on 28 July 2012 said he was not impressed with Bob Carr's 'fawning over John Lyons's attempts at self justification'.

When Carr read it he was outraged that one of his Labor colleagues would send this to a newspaper columnist and saw it as an attempt to portray his interest in the issue as 'a cook up' between him and me. Carr rang Danby, giving him what he now describes as 'a shot across the bows'. As Carr recalled: 'I told him that I have seen this [email] and I don't think that it is very loyal behaviour, especially given that you have not raised the matter with me ... I have not had any involvement with Lyons's stories.'

Carr and I had had dealings when I was editor of the *Sydney Morning Herald* and he was premier of New South Wales – often about stories he had not liked – but we hadn't spoken for a decade – the idea that Carr was 'fawning' over anything I'd written was ludicrous.

For me, one of the most bizarre aspects of being a correspondent in Israel was that while criticism coming from the Jewish leadership in Melbourne seemed continuous, from Israeli publications the response was much more reasonable. In fact, one of Israel's leading news websites even referred to the same article that Danby had used to attack me to praise me for my fairness. *The Times of Israel* website carried a blog post about me entitled 'An objective journalist – the unicorn of the Middle East'. Of the article about Bob Carr and the Palestinian children in the *Weekend Australian*, the writer said: 'I could imagine the pro-Israel lobbyists spitting out their Corn Flakes across the paper. What an anti-Israel, Iran-sympathising terrorist puppet! Why does he care so much about what's happening in Israel – look at Syria! He probably donates to the New Israel Fund. Shudder.'

The blog post then went on to note that in the very same edition of the paper I had a story about how Hamas was demolishing Palestinian homes in Gaza to sell their land and corruptly take profits. I had reported how when I rang the United Nations for comment they refused to condemn the creation of these new Palestinian refugees. 'The story was great journalism,' *The Times of Israel* item said.

> This is the kind of stuff pro-Israel media watchdogs exist
> for. House demolitions, quite rightly, draw much fire from
> the Western media when carried out, or threatened to be,
> by Israel. Identical events undertaken by Hamas, however,
> apparently do not. This journalist is the exception …
> Drawing fire from all sides is a signpost of good journalism
> in the Middle East. Here, this journalist had written two
> articles that described, in sober but firm terms, violations of
> what are considered international rights and norms by both
> Israel and Hamas. In isolation, each article could be viewed
> by partisans as bias in the extreme. Together, they leave the
> reader with the impression that both sides do bad stuff. It's
> up to the reader from thereon.[1]

In 2014, when I presented a television report for *Four Corners* based on my articles in *The Australian*, it was attacked by hardline Israeli activists in Australia before it even went to air. Some even circulated the link by which viewers could make a formal complaint to the ABC. Being a government broadcaster, the ABC was duty-bound to investigate each complaint, but the accusations proved groundless.

While the program faced a fierce attack by a small group, it was well received by the Australian public. Even the Israeli Government took the report in its stride.

France's leading current affairs program, *Envoyé Special* on France 2, decided they also wanted to cover the story, and contacted Sylvie, the co-producer of the *Four Corners* program. She put six weeks' research into it – people who could be interviewed were lined up and France 2 in Paris booked accommodation for the team. But two days before filming was due to start, France 2 pulled out. The explanation? The Israeli Army had said it would not give access. Separately, a journalist from Britain's *Daily Mail* told me: 'Your story about Palestinian children is a strong story but there's no way we could get that into our paper because of the influence of the lobby in the UK.'

*

Worse still was a media conference held by UNICEF, the UN's children's fund, on 6 March 2013, to launch a report on the same topic; Sylvie and I were invited because of the articles we had done together. The conference had been postponed several times, and one UNICEF official I knew had told me: 'You won't believe the pressure that has been put on us [by Israel] to cancel this press conference.' Another UNICEF official had said: 'We were limited [by Israel] in the number of journalists we could invite.'

Sylvie had brought her video camera, but as the briefing began UNICEF's Jerusalem chief, Jean Gough, announced that only the first five minutes could be filmed. 'And we ask that you don't quote us [by name].'

In the first five minutes, Ms Gough praised Israel. 'I want to thank them,' she said, referring to their cooperation with UNICEF. Then she ordered that filming stop.

With the cameras off, UNICEF began to tell the real story. One official said the ill-treatment of Palestinian children was 'widespread, systematic and institutionalised'; another told how children were sometimes told they would be raped or killed if they did not confess. Another said there was 'a systemic pattern of abuse and torture'. For the next 90 minutes UNICEF painted a picture of widespread abuse.

I'd never experienced such a schizophrenic press conference. I found it appalling that UNICEF was trying to use us to create a false impression. I sat there wondering how to report such an event. I decided to write both what Ms Gough said in the first five minutes and then what the UNICEF officials said in the next 90 minutes – readers could make up their own minds.

It confirmed for me how cleverly the Israel image-makers play the media. Had UNICEF officials said on camera what was in their report, the story would have echoed around the world. The Israelis had effectively killed any television coverage. And UNICEF had played along.

I discovered that to soften any criticism of Israel, rather than use the word 'torture' the UNICEF report had substituted the word 'duress'. The report admitted that the evidence examined included about 200 documented cases from Defence for Children International (DCI). The DCI cases included a boy who had had his hands tied behind his back for 19 hours; a boy whose handcuffs were so tight that flesh came off; a boy who said he was hit in his testicles; and a boy whose head was slammed against a wall. But these were not in the final UNICEF report. Jean Gough conceded that UNICEF 'took advice from Israeli lawyers'. I asked if those Israeli lawyers saw the final draft. 'Of course,' Ms Gough said. 'We had discussions on it. That is about ensuring we have a dialogue.'

For me, the final twist came when I emailed Yigal Palmor, the spokesman for Israel's Ministry of Foreign Affairs, asking for a response. Palmor replied: 'This year Israel has joined the UNICEF board and our working relations and collaboration with the organisation are appreciated by the international community.' How extraordinary – and, from Israel's point of view, brilliant. They had joined a board that should be holding them to account over their treatment of children. No other country has as many children under military occupation as Israel: in the West Bank, hundreds of thousands, and that number is growing. Being on the board means Israel can be forewarned of any UNICEF criticisms.

*

Why do the supporters of Israel want to prevent stories like this one from spreading overseas?

When we arrived in Israel we did not realise the prize that it coveted. It was only by living among Israelis, mixing with them at the local sports club or over a Shabbat dinner, that we came to understand the endgame: formalising the occupation into official annexation and achieving Greater Israel. Scores of foreign journalists, diplomats and businesspeople who have lived in Israel long enough have come to this same conclusion.

For Israel, the prize of Greater Israel far outweighs any criticism it receives. To take this path, the Israeli public have had to convince themselves that 'the world hates us anyway' and would criticise anything Israel did. That is, the world is becoming increasingly anti-Semitic.

For Israel to continue pursuing its endgame – annexing the West Bank – it cannot allow the international community to form the view that the occupation is unacceptable. Israel tries to minimise reports of its brutality in the West Bank so that international opinion does not turn against it.

As long as Israel insists on maintaining an occupation there will be tensions between journalists reflecting the values of their host countries and Israelis who want to maintain the occupation. To maintain the course towards Greater Israel, Israel needs to be seen to want a peace agreement. Israel's problem is that the media sometimes reports the reality: that it is relentlessly growing settlements, encouraged by financial incentives and a free security service, the IDF.

The only way for Israel to manage this is to attack the media. As long as the media is seen as biased, anti-Israel or anti-Semitic, then Israel is not at fault.

There are three battles in the Israeli–Palestinian conflict: the military battle, the settlements battle and the public relations battle. Clearly, Israel has already won the military battle. While it regards Hezbollah in Lebanon as a formidable enemy – backed by the power of Iran's funding and military assistance – Israel can crush Hamas in Gaza with little effort. Israel has also won the settlements battle. As discussed, settlements and the military bases that go with them are liberally located across the West Bank, strategically placed to prevent a viable Palestinian State.

But the third battle the Israelis have still not won, and in fact are losing: the battle for international public opinion. The challenge for Israel, through its embassies and lobby groups, is how to make sure that foreign journalists do not stop the creeping annexation of the West Bank from continuing. Israel needs to portray itself as the vulnerable one, even though it has the most powerful military in the Middle East, with an arsenal that includes at least 220 nuclear warheads.

We live at a time when more people are trying to shape reality than report it. The collapse of the traditional newspaper model means there are more people in public relations than journalism, and Israel operates one of the most effective public relations machines in the world. There's a Hebrew word for it: *hasbara*, or 'propaganda'. Hasbara is even the name of a government unit. Because Israel so brilliantly manages its reality, many people – tourists, diplomats and journalists (me included) – are shocked when they come to Israel and see the occupation up close. Philippe Agret, the former Jerusalem bureau chief of Agence France Press, arrived in the Middle East 'with a completely free mind'. 'I bought, to a certain extent, this story of "plucky Israel" fighting against a hostile world. I had some admiration for the building of the State of Israel, what they'd done since 1948. I was 50–50.' But the reality Agret encountered was very different.

Britain's Sky News correspondent Dominic Waghorn said that in managing their message the Israelis are 'peerless'. Yet despite its massive spending on *hasbara*, Israel has failed to convince the world to accept its settlements.

Philippe Agret said: 'At the end it doesn't work, it cannot work, because the cause is wrong. When I mean the "cause" I mean occupation, colonisation, discrimination. You might have the best *hasbara* in the world, the best propaganda machine in the world, but you still have the root of the problem: occupation. The injustice is there and you cannot fight a fact of injustice even with the best propaganda machine. Look what happened to the Americans in Vietnam. It's a bit similar – they lost the propaganda war because the cause was wrong.'

Agret said he was shocked by what he found in Israel. 'For me the best example is the one you see the first time and which you see every day – it is young Israeli soldiers, new migrants, "Boris and Galina" coming from, say, Russia and Ukraine, checking, body searching and taking the identity cards of Khaled and Ahmed who have been farming in Nablus for many generations. This is the basic proof, the daily evidence that there is something wrong. Why are Galina and Boris checking, pestering and humiliating Ahmed and Khaled whose fathers and grandfathers have been in this place for centuries? There is something wrong.'

Reuters' Crispian Balmer agreed: 'However much PR you throw at it, you're never going to make this thing look good. The occupation is an absolute fucking disaster for this country. I see it as a growth on the State of Israel that they have to remove but they can't bring themselves to remove it and it might well be too late to remove it.'

Balmer added: 'For Israel, which has done and achieved astonishing things in its [70] years, there's no denying it – if you look at where this country has come from, there can be few others that have achieved as much – it's morally corrosive and politically and diplomatically devastating to be clinging on to huge swathes of territory. If they were saying "We will annex it all and everybody will be a citizen with equal rights, equal access to airports, everything," that's a different thing. But they're not saying that. You cannot justify subjugating a people indefinitely.'

New technologies are worsening the situation for Israel. Smartphones mean that more people than ever can capture images of brutality committed by the occupier. The mobile phone has been damaging for Israel's reputation. Crispian Balmer said: 'Incidents that stick in my mind include when the soldier rammed his gun into a guy's face. There was a bike protest and they were trying to cycle one way [in the West Bank] and this guy for no reason just smacked him in the face. Without that image that incident wouldn't have been an incident. The mobile phone has the potential to turn these incidents into global stories because they're everywhere.'

Balmer's four years in Israel coincided with the rise of social media: 'When I came here I didn't really know what Twitter was about. I saw some people who used it but I had no real concept, I didn't have it myself. That has opened up a whole new direct front in the dialogue.'

Perhaps the biggest threat to the occupation is the internet. Anyone can visit the website of *Haaretz* and read the material that many supporters of Israel want to keep from foreigners.

This is one of the longest military occupations in history, with 2017 marking its 50th year. It is one of the few left. The world today does not like occupations, and few are able to endure.

In Europe in particular, opinion is increasingly hostile. Up until the occupation began, countries such as France considered Israel a close friend. Those friendships have steadily crumbled as the European public finds it increasingly difficult to condone the occupation.

So deeply has Israel alienated Europe that even in Germany – which has been reluctant to criticise Israel since the Second World War – attitudes are changing. Gil Yaron, correspondent for Germany's influential *Die Welt* newspaper, said Chancellor Angela Merkel 'hates' Netanyahu, as do many Germans. 'They feel lied to and have no understanding of his policy of settlement constructions.' Yaron said Netanyahu could be 'mesmerising' when he assures German politicians he wants peace. 'I think they are exasperated with his talk about peace, they just do not believe him.' Yaron said criticism in Germany of Israel's settlements is 'still muted but I'm not sure they are going to remain that way. People who are 15 to 20 years will have completely different commitments to Israel than those who are in power now.'

Things are very different in the US. Dominic Waghorn said television networks there had 'caved in'. Reuters' Crispian Balmer concurred: 'I think most criticism [of the media] would come from America, most of it from pro-Netanyahu Zionist organisations.'

During my years in the Middle East, Judi Rudoren held what is, without doubt, the most sensitive position in international journalism: Jerusalem Bureau Chief of the *New York Times*. The US is Israel's most important ally, and this is the newspaper that matters to the American elite. The job has left incumbent after incumbent battered, bruised and sometimes bitter.

Veteran *New York Times* Jerusalem correspondent Clyde Haberman – himself Jewish, like Rudoren – has said every NYT correspondent has been subjected to 'non-stop assault' and therefore few on the paper want the job. 'We've had decades of correspondents that, no matter how different they've been one from the other, no matter how talented they are or how many Pulitzer Prizes they have to their name, always end up being accused of being either anti-Semites or self-hating Jews. At some point, this seeps into the DNA of the newspaper. This is what you can expect if you go there – to have your integrity hurled back in your face every single day.' But, said Haberman dryly, he finally discovered how to placate Israeli hardliners: 'If I didn't want to be accused of hating Israel, I should start every story with: "50 years after 6 million Jews died in the Holocaust, Israel yesterday did one thing or the other."'[2]

Jodi Rudoren has taken hits from all sides. Rudoren and I became friends by spending time on the road together, including two assignments in Gaza. 'Americans by and large accept that Israel is a different type of place,' she says. 'They don't apply their standards, they buy this idea of Israel as a Jewish State created out of the worst moment of history and that it may be an anomalous ethnocracy that they are willing to accept, even though they don't think ethnocracies are a great idea, but to be an ethnocracy that has fairness and justice and whatever. They simply buy this Jewish–Israeli consensus notion of a Jewish and democratic State.'

Ultimately, though, there is pressure on all foreign journalists to sugar-coat their reporting. As Gil Yaron said: 'There are two societies at war and you cannot expect either one to be comfortable with equal reporting, because when you are at war you are looking for allies, you are not looking for a judge.'

Jodi Rudoren admitted to 'defensive writing' about Israel; *Die Welt* requires as a condition of employment that its journalists 'support the vital rights of the people of Israel'; Reuters has a special rule book for what wording must be used.

*

The Guardian's Chris McGreal agreed that some journalists provided a flattering portrayal of Israel because they did not want to have to defend tougher reporting. 'I think there are newspapers which steer clear of controversy on Israel. I think that has less to do with the reporters on the ground who see the situation for themselves than senior editors trying to avoid controversy. It's evidence that the harassment can work if not resisted.'

The pressures on a journalist, said Crispian Balmer, meant that reporting could become 'unbelievably dull, a ping-pong of "he said, she said". Every fact is disputed and there is a binary narrative like train tracks that never meet. There is no simple story that you can write in a fluid and fluent fashion because every other line is "But the other side says no." There's a danger that people working here do stick to certain formula[e] because they know it's gone through before and they know they can defend it.'

I also noticed a pattern where Israel would delay any confirmation of serious allegations until the media lost interest. If it is reported without official confirmation, only those who are staunchly anti-Israel will believe it. One case I became aware of was in Gaza during the 2009 war. Doctors there were saying, 'People are coming into our hospitals and we believe that they have been exposed to white phosphorus.' White phosphorus can be used in the desert to highlight army targets but also burns the skin, and it is considered a war crime to drop it onto a populated area. I rang the IDF's spokeswoman Avital Leibovich to get her response to that and she said, 'How dare you accuse us of doing something like that! It's offensive and outrageous that you would buy that sort of propaganda.' Several months later, the army quietly admitted that it *had* used 'limited' white phosphorus. By then, though, no one wanted to follow it up.

Uffe Taudal from *Berlingske*, a conservative Danish newspaper supportive of Israel, said every word in Israel was politicised, 'so if you write Jerusalem [as the capital] it means you accept the annexation, if you write "Israelis think" then 20 per cent of the population – Palestinians living in Israel as Israeli citizens – are excluded from the political life.'

Most correspondents I knew in Israel said that pressure came from self-appointed pro-Israel groups rather than the Israeli Government. I believe the government effectively 'outsources' that pressure, which allows it to maintain workable relations with correspondents on the spot while the pressure is applied on the journalist's editors. This was certainly what I found with the Australian pro-Israel lobby.

Journalists based in Israel often faced a backlash back home. 'I did not get many complaints from the Israeli Government, very few actually, but a fair lot from pressure groups outside Israel,' says Philippe Agret, who believes the aim was partly to exhaust journalists.

'The biggest message you'll get from me,' said Jodi Rudoren, 'is that all of this noise and activism is based on a very strange set of criteria that have nothing to do with how we actually operate ...

> I really have come to see that it's not a tiny number
> of people but it's a finite number of people mostly
> talking to each other and it's really not journalistic in
> its understanding, its assessments, its goals. It's political
> and you just have to try as hard as you can to turn back
> to people who share your values, who ask journalistic
> questions about the story and what you've written and who
> you can trust as to whether you're tilting in one direction or
> another ... anybody who knows anything about journalism
> or politics or the situation knows that articles aren't critical
> of Israel or somebody else. Most articles are probably both,

most sentences are probably both and most of it probably
depends who's reading it, how they view something ...
Good for the Jews, bad for the Jews – that's not how I'm
writing. Most things that happen here are not that simple.

Often Western countries argue that the status quo is preferable to
a further deterioration in the situation. Taudal says: 'There are
600,000 settlers and more all the time ... The idea of status quo
is another smokescreen.'

According to Jodi Rudoren, the fact that the occupation has
gone on for so long has meant it has started to look 'a lot like
apartheid'. And it is not just the reality of Palestinians in the West
Bank which looks like apartheid, said Rudoren, but for those in
Israel also. 'I actually think the issue of apartheid is more relevant
to how Arab Israelis are treated within the framework of the
country,' she said.

Yet Crispian Balmer said: 'I suspect that the public around
the world by and large sees what it wants to see because it's such
a polarised story.'

For Taudal, the gap between the reality and the international
perception means a media failure: 'In many ways we in the media
have collectively failed in our reporting of Israel. There was a
Danish TV journalist who came here, he was not used to being
here, and he did a story about Israeli settlers in Hebron spitting
at Palestinians and it made a huge fuss in Denmark but that's an
everyday occurrence. But [when] he put it on TV it was like "Is
this going on?" Nobody in the West believes what's going on here
unless they see it with their own eyes because there are so many
people back home saying it's not true.' Because the reality of what
Israel is doing is only occasionally glimpsed, when violence breaks

out many people around the world assume this is just the reaction of Palestinians who will never accept Israel's existence.

*

Colin Rubenstein is the man who runs AIJAC and is hugely influential in shaping the opinion of the Australian Jewish community, and Australian politicians and journalists. I would only fully appreciate his views when I read on AIJAC's website a speech he made in Melbourne during the 2014 Gaza War. Rubenstein told the audience on the steps of the Victorian Parliament: 'Israel does more than any other country to avoid killing civilians.'

It revealed something to me about AIJAC. In effect, Rubenstein was saying that he believed that the Israeli Army acted according to higher moral values than other countries, including his own.

I've always had the view as a journalist that each story, each government and each country should be judged on its merits. Countries, armies and governments can change; they can improve or deteriorate. To make a blanket statement like 'Israel does more than any other country to avoid killing civilians' flies in the face of logic. The media regularly place the US, Australian and other armies under scrutiny and sometimes find their behaviour unacceptable. Yet somehow the Israeli Army is better than these armies.

During the 'golden period' soon after my arrival in Israel, I got invited to lunch by an American-born Israeli who runs a Jerusalem-based lobby group designed to influence foreign media and closely aligned with the Israeli Government. He wanted to convince me of several things. One of them was the special status of the Israeli Army.

I asked him why the Israeli Army had higher moral standards than the Australian Army.

He talked about the codes of conduct of the Israeli Army. I replied that while I didn't unconditionally defend the Australian Army – that they had sometimes been involved in bad behaviour – they also had a strict code of behaviour.

Finally, the lobbyist came to the point. 'Because the Israeli Army has Jewish values,' he said.

I asked prominent Israeli journalist Gideon Levy what he thought of the idea that the Israeli Army has higher values because they are Jewish values.

'It's like claiming it's the most moral army in the world,' he responded. 'Most Israelis surely believe in that ... the denial and self-cheating [are] so deep that it doesn't matter that there are 2200 or whatever civilians killed, that half of Gaza is destroyed, they're all terrorists and not human beings.'

I pointed out that if someone claimed the Australian or US Army was the most moral in the world, no one would believe it, so why could people get away with saying it about Israel?

Levy answered: 'Because it is the chosen people. I tell you "the chosen people" is a key thing here. It explains a lot.'

He told me that 'the notion that we are the chosen people is very deep-rooted in this place, much more than people tend to see. Most Israelis are deeply convinced that they stand for the chosen people – most Israelis are deeply convinced that after the Holocaust the Jews have the right to do whatever they want. Most Israelis are deeply convinced that international law applies to any country in the world except Israel because Israel is special. These are all things you get here from childhood.'

Levy said the sense of being 'the chosen people' was taught to Israeli children in many ways.

'You don't have to call it the chosen people but you may call it "Israel is something else".'

Since the occupation began, the messianic right of Israeli politics has convinced the public that 'Judea and Samaria' were given to them by God. And for non-religious Israelis, the mantra for an endless occupation has been security – a claim that can be debunked with the simple question: if the West Bank is so dangerous, why has Israel given financial incentives to more than 600,000 citizens to move there since 1967?

Both the right and the centre of Israeli politics are now hooked on occupation. For the right, it represents a completion of the biblical circle in which they have finally returned home. For the centre, it represents cheap housing. If Israel were ever forced to end the occupation it would not be a security crisis it would have to deal with – no other country better knows how to deal with security – but a housing crisis. Suddenly, 600,000 Israelis would have to be housed in Israel.

To understand the mindset of Israelis, one needs to consider their view of the international community. They argue that when the Nazis were engaging in their State-sponsored campaign to kill Jews, the world did nothing. They watched as trainloads of their fellow Jews were being taken to concentration camps. They watched as, in the heart of Europe, their people were almost extinguished. Israelis frequently ask: do we trust the international community?

Israeli land expert Dror Etkes said:

We have to understand the human drama in this story.

Think about Israel in 1967. This is 22 years after Auschwitz

was liberated and Holocaust survivors were still in Israel.
The vision of the Jewish Israeli leadership was still very
much shaped by the Second World War and of course 1948
and the huge events and demographic transitions that took
place in historic Palestine in 1948, 1949 and 1950. There
were Palestinians who became refugees who vanished in
18 months – it had never happened in the history of Islam
that this amount of people had been transferred in such
an efficient and compressed period of time out of their
country. The minute this encounter between modern Israel
and the West Bank occurred there was almost an inevitable
explosion of emotions and ideological aspirations [by Jews]
which could not be fulfilled.

Legendary *New York Times* journalist Clyde Haberman wrote
that the verbal attacks on successive NYT correspondents have
been because 'Jews still don't believe that the world won't turn on
them. It's hardwired into their systems. They can't accept that the
Holocaust is a distant memory for most of the world's population
and they get upset when they are not perceived as perennial
victims, even though they hardly look like victims anymore.'[3]

Israeli journalist Akiva Eldar said: 'Ezer Weizman, our former
President, used to say, "The Jews left the ghetto but the ghetto did
not leave the Jews." The ghetto mentality is inside us … We love
to be victims and we will not give the Palestinians even the benefit
of the doubt that they are victims. If you listen to people from the
left they will tell you that we are also victims of the occupation.
The occupier is the victim of the occupation also.'

Israeli-French journalist Sylvain Cypel wrote: '"Them against
us" is the mode of mental functioning that explains why so many

Israelis know deep down or perceive privately that crimes against the Palestinians are committed in their name yet refuse to admit this, at least publicly, in front of the "others", since this would mean betraying the fundamental affiliation and running the risk of expulsion from the cocoon that ensures their loved ones' solidarity ... the IDF, its leaders keep repeating, remain the most moral army in the world.[4]

The majority of Israelis today were either born into the occupation or migrated into it. Israelis now entering the army at 18 were born a generation after the occupation began. Unlike their grandparents, who often had relationships with Palestinians, the only Palestinians young Israelis know are those they have met at checkpoints, or those that they have read about as terrorists. They have been educated to believe that they are the victims rather than the occupiers. Famous Israeli historian Benny Morris has echoed this sentiment: 'We are the greater victims in the course of history and we are also the greater potential victim. Even though we are oppressing the Palestinians, we are the weaker side here.'[5]

'I think the real danger in this country,' said Crispian Balmer, 'is that if you arrived in Tel Aviv and that's where you stay then this country is a great country.

> Who wouldn't want to live down there by comparison to anywhere else in the Middle East? It's fantastic. But most people have no idea that 60 kilometres away there's some [Israeli soldier] kid at a checkpoint humiliating a little old [Palestinian] lady – I've seen it happen – getting a little old lady out of a car to stand there ... That is just a half-hour drive from the beaches of Tel Aviv. I think one of the

problems of modern-day Israel is that most people have absolutely no contact with Palestinians whatsoever so a lot of people are in total denial with what's going on, they bury their heads in the sand and assume it's not so bad. They say, 'Well, it's much worse in Syria.' They're right – who wouldn't prefer to live in Ramallah [in the West Bank] than Damascus? – but that's not the point. The point is there's a continuous occupation for which there's no end in sight and you have a political class here that really has no vision, no united vision whatsoever, as to how to end this occupation.

*

We weren't prepared for the amount of racism we encountered in Israel. It seemed particularly entrenched among younger Israelis. One poll found that 56 per cent say that their fellow citizens who are Arabs should not be allowed to vote in Israel's national democratic elections; 52 per cent of schoolchildren say that Arabs should be banned from the Knesset; and 48 per cent of Israeli Jews want Arabs transferred out of the country.[6]

Often leading rabbis drive racism. *The King's Torah*, a 2009 book written by two prominent rabbis, told Israelis that 'there is justification for killing [Palestinian] babies if it is clear that they will grow up to harm us [Jews]'. A year after we arrived in Jerusalem, 50 leading rabbis signed a letter urging Jews not to rent apartments to Arabs, which would be bad for property prices. It said: 'Among [Gentiles] are those who are bitter and hateful toward us and who meddle into our lives to the point where they are a danger.' Any Jew who did rent to an Arab should be ostracised: 'The neighbours and acquaintances must distance themselves from the Jew, refrain from doing business with him, deny him the right to read from the Torah and similarly [ostracise] him.' All 50 rabbis were government-paid, but not one was reprimanded.

In Israel's *Yellow Pages* phone directory, some companies advertise 'Avodah Ivrit' – 'Hebrew Labour'. A Tel Aviv cleaning company offers its customers different hourly rates according to the race of its cleaners – African, Eastern European or Western European; Arab workers are not offered.[7] Many carers for elderly Israelis are Filipinas who talk to each other in Tagalog. Even though there are hundreds of young Palestinian women in the villages of the West Bank, Israelis would rather spend thousands of dollars arranging visas for Filipinas.[8]

I've always loved sport. As a boy in Melbourne I'd go with my father on Saturdays to watch our AFL team, Fitzroy. To me sport is something you throw yourself into. In early 2013 I went to a game of soccer in Jerusalem involving Beitar Jerusalem, which had just recruited two Muslim players from Chechnya. When one of the Muslims got the ball, the crowd jeered. So angry were some supporters that police had to take them away. Israeli media reported that at one game on the day the players were signed, fans of the club displayed a banner bearing the words 'Beitar – pure forever' and 'chanted anti-Arab slogans', leading to four arrests. On 8 February 2013, two fans set fire to the club's offices, apparently in response to the new players from Chechnya. On 3 March, one of them scored his first goal for Beitar, prompting hundreds of the team's fans to leave the stadium. At the game I attended I asked one Beitar supporter: 'If the score was level, would you prefer one of the Muslim players to score a goal or for your team to lose?'

'That's a hard one,' he said.

But of all the discrimination we saw in Jerusalem, there was one situation that appalled me every time: soldiers at checkpoints making Palestinian ambulances wait. In contrast, Israeli ambulances were always waved straight through. I'd often see soldiers smoking or on their phones, as Palestinian ambulances, their lights flashing, just sat there. The Israeli media reported how on one occasion soldiers sat around eating pizza while a Palestinian boy who urgently needed dialysis was made to wait. Journalist Gideon Levy told me about a story he wrote of a Bedouin woman in labour who was rejected at one checkpoint after another, and finally lost her baby giving birth in the car. The reaction was a public scandal.

A report by Physicians for Human Rights in 2015 found infant mortality in the occupied territories was 18.8 per 1000 births compared with 3.7 in Israel. The maternal death rate in the occupied territories was 28 per 100,000 births in contrast with seven in Israel. The average life expectancy was 10 years lower and the gap had increased in recent years. The major factor was the Israeli limitation on the freedom of movement of patients, medical professionals, ambulances and medications.[9]

For years, leaders of the Australian Jewish community kept telling me the Israeli Supreme Court was a stronghold of justice. Living in Israel soon dispelled this myth. While Israelis become used to stories of legal disparities, they stood out for us. One case involved an Israeli woman and Palestinian man who had consensual sex. Sabbar Kashur, a 30-year-old Palestinian from East Jerusalem, was a delivery man for a legal firm. He met a Jewish woman while doing his rounds and they agreed to adjourn somewhere for sex. The woman apparently assumed he was Jewish, but later discovered he was an Arab. Six weeks later the police placed him under house arrest and eventually he was sentenced to 18 months' jail.

Kashur later told the media: 'If I were Jewish, they wouldn't have even questioned me.' But the judges were steadfast: 'The court is obliged to protect the public interest from sophisticated, smooth-tongued criminals who can deceive innocent victims at an unbearable price – the sanctity of their bodies and souls. When the very basis of trust between human beings drops, especially when matters at hand are so intimate, sensitive and fateful, the court is required to stand firmly at the side of the victims – actual and potential – to protect their wellbeing.' The judges acknowledged the sex was consensual, but they found Kashur guilty of 'rape by deception'.

Israeli journalist Gideon Levy said: 'Do the eminent judges understand the social and racist meaning of their florid verdict? Don't they realise that their verdict has the uncomfortable smell of racial purity, of "Don't touch our daughters?" The court had established a precedent for rape by deception based on race.'

Living in Israel, I saw discrimination everywhere. One of the reasons I thought it best to leave after six years was that daily humiliation against Palestinians almost became unremarkable – at that point I think a foreign correspondent faces the danger of 'going native' and can fail to notice the extraordinariness of events around them.

Gideon Levy has been writing about the occupation for 30 years. He has noticed that while some Israelis used to feel a sense of injustice at the treatment of Palestinians, this has largely dissipated. In 2012 he wrote a story revealing how Israeli military officials had calculated the minimum number of calories a Palestinian in Gaza needed so as not to starve: 2279 per day. After its calculation, the army added another 34 tons of food a day as a charity to ensure toddlers did not starve. Israel has a naval blockade around Gaza and decides which goods come in and out. They allow virtually no goods to leave for export and only limited goods to enter. Levy wrote: 'Who came up with the idea of calculating the caloric intake for 1.5 million people under siege? What train of thought even gives Israel the right to enter the mouths and invade the stomachs of the people living under its jackboots? So now it's not just their bedrooms that are brutally broken into every night; now it's also their digestive system.'

The document was prepared by the Coordinator of Government Activities in the Territories, who said it was just a 'working paper'. Levy wrote:

> The very fact that such a document was composed, whether
> it was used or not, points to a satanic way of thinking. But
> the reason the army didn't want this document made public
> had nothing to do with its diabolical content. Nor did it
> fear a public storm [in Israel], which it knew wasn't likely
> to happen in a country afflicted with blindness. The reason
> the Israeli Defence Forces was reluctant to publicise this
> document was because it would make Israel look even worse
> in world opinion than it already does. It's a matter of image,
> you know: the goyim [non-Jews] shouldn't find out. It's not
> nice for the goyim to know how low Israeli racism could
> sink.[10]

Israelis now regard it as normal that their army practices on real Palestinians. For training purposes, Israeli soldiers storm into the houses of Palestinians at two or three in the morning, throwing stun grenades and shouting. Terrified residents, including children, have no idea what is going on. One Israeli newspaper accompanied Israeli soldiers on such an exercise in Bir Zeit, a Palestinian village near Jerusalem, which is home to the largest Palestinian university. The journalist reported that for the exercise the army needed to land at a nearby Jewish settlement, Beit Arye. When an attack helicopter landed without prior warning, the public relations man from the settlement angrily complained to the army, saying that it 'woke up children and caused panic among the inhabitants'. The army apologised and explained that the helicopter was meant to have landed next to a nearby Palestinian village. The reporter noted: 'After almost 48 years of occupation, it seems that only an outsider is taken aback by situations the IDF blithely accepts ... the Palestinian residents become extras who are not asked whether they want to take part in the dress rehearsal and receive no warning of what is about to take place. Their homes are targets for night visits, searches and the family's coerced awakening.'[11]

One case of racism in the Israeli Army suggested a culture that had been allowed to develop. It involved Colonel Itai Virov who, when defending one of his soldiers for assaulting Palestinians, explained that 'a slap, sometimes a blow to the neck or chest or sometimes choking to calm down [a suspect] is reasonable'. Such violence, he said, was sometimes necessary for 'completing the mission'.

The response to Virov's statements was typical of what often happens in Israel – publicly, he was rebuked and a criminal investigation launched against him. Privately, his career went from strength to strength – the criminal case was dismissed for 'lack of evidence', even though his own words had condoned the use of violence. Two years later Itai Virov was promoted to brigadier general and made commander of the Gaza Division – responsible for the behaviour of Israeli soldiers in Gaza.

This contrasted with the treatment of Shachar Berrin, a 19-year-old Australian-born soldier who, in a public forum on the subject 'The Occupation is Destroying Israel', said: 'I serve in the Jordan Valley and we see every day how soldiers ... look at these people [Palestinians] not as human beings, not as someone who is equal, but someone who is less than them. And to think that we can just leave the racism and xenophobia – that they will only be racist when they humiliate Palestinians – of course not ... I think that once you are conditioned to think something, you bring it back with you [to Israel] and that it deeply affects Israeli society and causes, as our President [Reuven Rivlin] says, to be more racist.'

Within 12 hours of speaking those words, Berrin was ordered back to his barracks, tried, convicted and sent to a military prison.[12]

One ruling in the Jerusalem District Court highlighted the way racism is often a factor in court decisions. Judge Moshe Drori heard the case of Itamar Biton, who did not want to pay 18 shekels for his parking ticket as he left a car park. On 1 January 2006, when the attendant, Ethiopian-born Noga Zoraish, insisted he pay, he rammed her. She screamed but he kept driving, so fast that she fell from the car's bonnet and was seriously injured. He drove off. Biton pleaded guilty but Judge Drori acquitted him – he said he did not want to give Biton a criminal record and harm his chance of becoming a rabbinical court judge. While publicly the system acted – the Supreme Court in August 2009 overturned the verdict. The Supreme Court issued a suspended sentence. Biton did not serve a day in prison.[13]

The Supreme Court's verdict in the case of an apartment block in Jaffa, near Tel Aviv, was also revealing. A property developer had marketed apartments for Jews only. The marketing was clearly discriminatory, something that technically is illegal in Israel. The residents had conclusive evidence – the marketing brochures. The Supreme Court agreed the marketing was discriminatory. The President of the court, Dorit Beinisch, said the project was 'wrongful discrimination'. However, the Supreme Court allowed it. The marketing project was too far advanced to be stopped – it was 'a done deal', the court ruled, so any suggestion of taking the land off the developer was 'theoretical', Beinisch ruled. The fact that the Supreme Court had allowed an illegal deal to proceed meant a precedent had been established – if a Jewish-only development could become advanced enough before anyone appealed then developers could argue that the Supreme Court had set a precedent.

While the Supreme Court rhetorically argues against discrimination and sometimes makes decisions that entrench it, some Israeli leaders are open about their racism. The chairman of the Knesset's Constitution, Law and Justice Committee, David Rotem, has said: 'In my opinion, every Jewish town needs at least one Arab. What would happen if my refrigerator stopped working on a Saturday?'[14]

The case of 19-year-old Maysam Abu Alqian demonstrates how shocking the racism can be. To earn money, he worked at two jobs in Tel Aviv – one at Burger King and one at the Super Yuda supermarket. On 22 May 2016, while working at the supermarket, he took some rubbish outside. Two men – one dressed in shorts –

demanded Alqian's ID. According to eyewitness Erez Krispin, Alqian replied: 'The ID is inside, who are you?' Krispin says: 'Before he even finishes speaking, he's being beaten senseless, a beating like you've never seen, teeth flying through the air. The Arab is crushed.'

Krispin said that an elderly woman tried to intervene, but one of the men yelled: 'Fuck off before we finish you too!' Krispin said police arrived and joined in – there were five men beating Alqian. The store manager, Kobi Cohen, said other employees who intervened were also hit. 'They hit him mercilessly until he was incapacitated,' Cohen said. 'Everyone is shocked by what happened. And there's only one reason for it – the guy was Arab.'[15]

Despite the existence of videos and eyewitness accounts, the head of the Israeli Police media department, Chief Inspector Sharon Yamincha, called for a boycott of the supermarket on Facebook. 'I don't shop at a supermarket whose employees beat cops,' he wrote. Yamincha's post drew support from other police.[16]

Israeli writer Ari Shavit wrote in *Haaretz* newspaper:

An evil wind is blowing in this country. First it was the rabbis who prohibited the renting of apartments to Arabs. Then it was Jewish youths who attacked Arab passersby ... A series of incidents that are ostensibly unrelated, and aren't even similar, have created a new atmosphere of xenophobia. They have turned Israel into a country that exudes a xenophobic stench. What's happening to us? Why have dark forces that always bubbled beneath the surface suddenly erupted into the city square? Why has racism reared its head ... Instead of arguing about the foreigners who surround us, we're arguing about the foreigners who live among us.[17]

In *Haaretz* newspaper, under the headline 'Berlin 1933, Jerusalem 2014', Israeli journalist Chemi Shalev wrote that as the son of parents who lost their families in the Second World War he needed no convincing that the Holocaust was a crime unique in its evil. 'But I am a Jew … and when I saw the videos and pictures of gangs of right-wing Jewish racists running through the streets of Jerusalem chanting "Death to the Arabs", hunting for random Arabs, picking them out by their appearance or by their accents, chasing them in broad daylight, drooling like hysterical beasts and then beating them up before the police could arrive, the historical association was automatic', he wrote. This public racism was 'growing by the day, encompassing ever-larger segments of Israeli society, nurtured in a public environment of resentment, insularity and victimhood, fostered and fed by politicians and pundits – some cynical, some sincere – who have grown weary of democracy and its foibles and who long for an Israel, not to put too fine a point on it, of one state, one nation and, somewhere down the line, one leader.'[18]

*

Despite my first bizarre meeting with Captain Shalicar at the café in the German Colony, the Israeli Army did not give up trying to pressure me. That first meeting was friendly, but a few months later Captain Shalicar phoned me again

'John, I want to let you know the IDF is considering banning you.'

'Banning me?' I replied. 'What does that mean?'

'It would mean you would not have access to the IDF.'

Over 35 years in journalism, I'd upset some powerful people, but this was the crudest attempt at intimidation I'd experienced.

'Arye, could you please let me know when you do ban me?'

Shalicar seemed surprised by my response. 'Why do you want to know?' he asked.

'Because I think I can get a page one story out of this.'

'You wouldn't actually write about being banned, would you?' he asked.

'Of course,' I said. 'When we met at that café in the German Colony you told me you had no problems with the facts of my reporting. You still have not indicated you have any problem with that. My editors would not appreciate us being banned for doing nothing wrong.'

Shalicar quickly changed tack: 'We're not going to ban you, but we've been talking about it.'

Through my six years in the Middle East I'd come under constant pressure from Israeli Army lobby groups to pull my punches. I realised from many discussions with other foreign journalists that this pressure was applied in many countries around the world. Essentially, the Israeli Government, Army and lobby groups did not want the reality of the occupation reported. Of the many hours of discussions I had with my colleagues in the foreign media, one comment shocked me. It was when I asked Philippe Agret, the bureau chief of Agence France Press, a question. AFP is one of the most powerful news agencies in the world. It is highly regarded as credible and independent. It is famous for resisting pressure in whichever country it operates. Agret and I were discussing how some media groups censored their reporting out of Israel in a way that they did in no other country. I asked him who he thought was self-censoring out of Israel. Without hesitation, he replied: 'Everybody.'

CHAPTER 13

Walking into Syria

March 2012

FROM THE OUTSIDE, IT LOOKED LIKE A TYPICAL SUBURBAN house, painted white and nestled in a small village in southeast Turkey. But after some time in this 'safe house' of the Free Syrian Army, we realised what it was: a place where everyone wanted to bring down the Syrian dictator Bashar al-Assad.

There was something suggestive of the old IRA about this place: a nondescript house in which men in their 30s and 40s sat on the floor drinking coffee. Boxes of 'blood stoppers' – medical goods used in emergencies – lay on the floor. There was no furniture, just piles of mattresses and blankets. Between dozing or talking, the men were on their mobile phones, quietly coordinating one side of a war.

I was with Australian video journalist Ed Giles in Antakya, or Antioch, and from this house we could look across a valley into Syria, which was about a kilometre away. Suspicion levels in this area were high. This village had a long history of trading across the border – weapons, cigarettes, alcohol, anything. But if goods could cross a border so too could fighters and spies, and this part of the border had become crucial for the movement of weapons and supplies into Syria.

On a later trip to this border, without my knowledge, my fixer started asking a shopkeeper about how much it would cost to take weapons across the border. The shopkeeper even offered a valet service where your weapons would be waiting for you on the other side after you crossed. There were youths at illegal crossings who would help you cross if you gave them US$30. A whole industry had grown up based on the war just on the other side of the hill.

Ed Giles and I wanted to come to this border to try to work out the role that Turkey was playing in the Syrian conflict. Turkey was trying to give the impression that it was not helping the rebels to fight the regime of Bashar al-Assad, and I thought that by spending time along the border we could observe whether in fact there was tacit support being given to the rebels by allowing easy transit of supplies and fighters from Turkey into Syria. Syria had become unpredictable, and we'd figured our best chance of getting in – and out – was with the Free Syrian Army. For now, they were the government's main opposition. But within a year, their uprising against Assad would collapse amid divisions and distrust.

We visited the safe house three days in a row, trying to get to know the commander, who told us he might be able to get some of his fighters to escort us across into Syria. The commander, a former Syrian Army officer, expressed anger at the role Russia was playing in this war, selling weapons to both sides. He said the price he had to pay for bullets had gone from US25c to US$3 in recent months as the Russians profiteered.

I asked the commander what strategies he was employing, given that the Assad regime had a serious advantage in terms of firepower. 'Shoot and hide,' he replied. 'We are snipers. We shoot, we run, we hide.' He said his fighters were under instructions to attack only Syrian soldiers who were not backed up by tanks, and if they killed them it was their chance to take weapons. The commander was overseeing a guerrilla movement, some of whose fighters were teenagers.

On our fourth day in the safe house, the commander finally gave approval for one of his fighters to take us across the border. The three of us headed down the valley and walked through a field of Turkish orchids. A red sign about 200 metres from a Turkish Army tower warned us that we were entering a Turkish military zone. We had no idea where we were going.

We walked through the military zone and along a deserted road. We were now entering Syria.

We walked down a mountain track. Ahead, through a forest, we heard voices.

Our guide said, 'Don't worry, they are our people. I won't put you in a situation where you are in any danger.'

We walked another 50 metres and came across tents, barbed wire, trenches, guns and a campfire, around which about 50 fighters sat chatting and drinking tea. They showed us a command post they had built on the hill.

From the lookout, we could see across the valley to where soldiers were walking around houses taken by the Syrian Army the night before. The fighters that Ed and I were with knew that they could be the targets of an attack. To try to defend themselves, they'd erected a wall of canvas so that anyone attacking would not be able to tell how many fighters were behind it. And if any attackers got this far, there was a final line of defence. 'Look here,' one of the fighters said, pushing aside some bushes. Underneath was an explosive device which, he told us, would be detonated from further up the hill if the army attacked.

The location of the camp was instructive. It was about 100 metres inside the Syrian border, between two Turkish military towers. It was clear that it had Turkish approval: Turkish soldiers in the towers watched us come and go. Not only could these Free Syrian Army fighters cross in and out of Turkey freely, but they could bring ammunition and supplies in too.

It was clearly a case of plausible deniability: the Turks could still deny accusations that their soil was being used, but at the same time could undermine Assad. It would also be difficult for the Syrians to shell this camp, as they would risk hitting the Turkish Army towers. Because of the relative sizes of the two armed forces – Turkey's army is the second largest in NATO, and dwarfs the Assad army – Syria did not want a war with its neighbour.

But on this day, the fighters from the Free Syrian Army made one thing clear to us: they were being beaten. 'We are exhausted and depressed,' one said. 'We don't have enough weapons to defend ourselves.' He, too, was critical of the way Russia 'has been playing both sides'. Russia's exports of weapons into the Middle East were believed to have increased 20 per cent in the first year of the Arab Spring. Profits from this conflict might have been one reason why Russia would repeatedly oppose any UN resolution calling for Assad to step down.

We departed with a clear sense that as long as Russia and China opposed any meaningful intervention, Bashar al-Assad would be free to turn Syria into a killing field.

*

The last time I'd been to Syria with Sylvie and Jack, two years earlier, it had been a beautiful place. Then the conflict started in March 2011 in the southern city of Daraa, where a peaceful protest had escalated when President Assad sent in his security forces.

Assad had seen what had been happening in Egypt and Libya, and his thinking would have been that he could not let a small group of protesters become a large group, and that he should crack down early, and hard. Mubarak had allowed the protesters to build up in the streets of Cairo. Millions massed in the streets for 18 days, crippling the economy: the unions refusing to work, massive national strikes. The message to Assad would have been: 'Crack down, be ruthless, and you have more chance of toughing your way through this.'

So Assad sent troops in to break up the protests, and instead of just the usual tear gas, they used live ammunition and shot several protesters dead. Assad's brutality added a new dimension to an already highly stressed population which had endured a harsh drought. Researchers from NASA and the University of Arizona estimated that it had been the worst drought in 500 years, according to media agency Vice News. It reported that between 2006 and 2011, the drought caused 75 per cent of the country's crops to fail, forcing as many as 1.5 million people off the land and into the cities where they were unable to find jobs.

Assad had thought that it would end things, but the crackdown was so brutal that it created a sudden welling up of anger across Syria and induced others to come onto the streets. The more security forces Assad threw at the uprising, the more people pushed back – and out of this the Free Syrian Army was formed.

At Damascus University at the start of 2012, about a year into the violence, Assad gave a speech that had a big build-up. It was his first public speech in months, and there were expectations that he was going to either resign or say something historic that would signal genuine reform.

Instead, Assad decided that he was digging in. He blamed the West and took no responsibility himself. He had done what the hard men around him urged him to do. The same hard men who had urged his father to slaughter 20,000 people in Hama. He went against his own instincts, which were more liberal. He agreed to go down the hard road of brutality.

Thus he signed the death warrant of any chance of peace in Syria. It was a historic decision. The country was at a crossroads and the President took the wrong road. And now hundreds of thousands of people have paid the price, either by losing their lives or by becoming refugees.

The Free Syrian Army had been a moderate group that wanted democracy. But a significant portion of the population was against the revolution. The civil war continued because some people benefited from the status quo and didn't want to lose their power.

The rise of the Free Syrian Army was quickly derailed by an extraordinary number of outside influences, waging proxy wars. Syria soon became Jihadist Central. The civil war broadened to also become a war against the West.

With the help of Alawite militia, Assad's army was involved in a series of massacres of the regime's opponents. Russia supported Assad from the beginning. Syria hosts a huge Russian naval base on the Mediterranean and Assad is Russia's major ally in the Middle East. Later, Hezbollah forces came across the border from Lebanon and started to help Assad, and were involved in some decisive battles.

By my count, 10 distinct outside forces would come to have identifiable roles in Syria, some occasionally and some permanently: Russia, the US and its allies (such as Australia), Saudi Arabia, Qatar, Iran, Hezbollah, Turkey, Israel, Jordan and Kurdish fighters. US intelligence would later estimate that there were about 1500 different rebel groups operating in Syria.

*

There was something different about the six Australians waiting near a border checkpoint between Turkey and Syria. By now – two years after I'd walked across the border with the Free Syrian Army – thousands of foreigners had ventured into Syria. But for the owner of a café about 50 metres from the Turkish border, this group, on 28 April 2014, was different.

'It was clear they were not rookies,' he told me. 'They seemed to know what they were doing.'

The owner was struck by several things. Firstly, only one of the men spoke Arabic. He seemed to be their leader, and looked to be in his 40s, while the others were younger. Secondly, they were supremely confident, well resourced and well dressed: they were wearing new walking boots and had backpacks packed to the brim, a contrast with many of the bedraggled jihadists who departed from this café to join the battle for Islam. They were physically very large and were wearing crocheted caps, popular with some Muslim men. All were 'very beardy', one local said. They all had Australian passports. The fact that most of them were not Arabic speakers suggested that they were second- or third-generation Australians.

The café owner drove them to an illegal crossing a few kilometres away. The most likely reason they didn't want to cross through the checkpoint was that they didn't want anyone – particularly the Australian Government – to know they were going to fight. That way they would leave no paper trail showing they had been in Syria.

As the car arrived at the crossing spot, the café owner saw three Syrian men waiting – all with handguns. He watched the men walk across fields into Syria.

Six more Australians had just gone to the war, joining the scores who had travelled there since the conflict began in March 2011.

I asked the café owner to drive me to the spot he had taken them. There was no fence. Further along, where there was a fence, I found a hole that had been stretched so you could walk in and out. I did a piece to camera to illustrate how easy it was to get from one country to the other.

The Australians reflected the new world created by Syria's war. It's a conflict increasingly drawing in foreigners, who will return home – if they survive – with new skills, including bomb-making. The ease with which the six Australians were able to join the war highlights the reality: there is, in effect, an open border for jihadists into Syria.

*

War in the Middle East can sometimes become a spectator sport. On the border between Turkey and Syria, it had become an outing for the whole family.

It was September 2014, and I arrived at the border to see a crowd spread across the hill watching Islamic State trying to take the Syrian town of Kobane. The Kurds in Kobane were trying to defend it. Kobane was a prize Islamic State wanted because strategically it would give them an entry point into Turkey. But the Kurds were the toughest opponents they had faced. As the battle of Kobane escalated, I'd flown from Tel Aviv to Ankara, then on to Gazientep, the closest airport to Kobane. Then, with a fixer, I'd driven to the hill overlooking the besieged town.

The crowd was barracking for the Kurds: each time a missile was fired towards the hills where Islamic State was positioned, they let out a roar. Every so often, though, when a stray missile from either the Kurds or Islamic State came our way, there was a very different sound – part excitement, part fear.

Hundreds of people would go along there on a Saturday afternoon and sit drinking coffee. They would check out the war for an hour and then go back to their towns in Turkey.

Islamic State fired three mortar shells into Turkey. Turkish tanks near us did not respond. But Turkey had retaliated with significant firepower two years earlier, when Syria's army fired mortar shells – it claimed accidentally – into Turkey. On that occasion, five Turkish civilians had been killed by the shells, and Turkey had responded by pounding Syrian Army installations.

It was revealing that Turkey responded to fire from the Syrian Army but not from Islamic State. Turkey had always been conflicted about Islamic State. It had been reluctant to allow the US-led coalition to use its air bases to launch attacks into Syria against Islamic State. While Ankara was revolted by Islamic State's tactics such as beheading, the Kurds, one of

Islamic State's main targets, were bitter enemies of the Turkish Government. In the Middle East, the enemy of my enemy is my friend.

Of all the groups I'd reported on in the Middle East, Islamic State was different. They could not be negotiated with. Beheading became their signature, and they were killing indiscriminately. They were showing no mercy in their crazed effort to establish a caliphate, or Islamic State, across the Levant, the ancient region covering what is today Iraq, Syria, Jordan, Gaza, Israel, the West Bank and Lebanon. Along the border, I saw the Islamic State flag flying in many towns on the Syrian side; Islamic State's list of conquests was growing by the day. They would just decide someone wasn't a real Muslim and shoot them. There was no discussion. They locked out Western media in terms of access. And we saw too many videos of people in orange jumpsuits being beheaded to even want to try to get near them.

About that time the Americans came into the war and were bombing Islamic State around that area, but we could tell it was making little difference. We could see the Islamic State fighters, spread out in groups of two or three, so it was almost impossible for the Americans to bomb them in large numbers. The reason that fighting them is so problematic is that they don't act like a conventional army. From talking to Syrians who had fled to Turkey, I learnt they don't use military vehicles, but commandeer civilian cars, and stay in civilian houses. So the Americans and their allies don't know who they are – similar to the way the Vietcong would blend into villages during the Vietnam War. That was why in the end the US coalition concentrated on the cities of Raqqa in Syria and Mosul in northern Iraq, because they could see identifiable headquarters.

As a journalist in the Middle East, I knew that they were one group that I did not want to get near. But on one occasion I got too close to Islamic State for comfort. My fixer worked with me for a few days, but then had to leave. Unable to find a new one, I decided to go to the border with one of the authorised drivers from my hotel. I figured I'd be safe with him – and I was – but I encountered a different problem altogether. The driver spoke only Turkish.

He took me to the border, where we could see the battle for Kobane. I indicated that I wanted to see the hill where Islamic State fighters had gathered. We headed off along the border, on the Turkish side. We drove through a small village, but there was nothing to delineate the border and barely anyone around. There was a house or two every so often along the border. I tried to tell the driver that I wanted to go back, but he kept saying 'Daesh' – the Arabic acronym for Islamic State – and pointing up ahead. I realised that I'd broken my own rules: always make sure you can communicate and don't become isolated.

On the hill ahead I could see Islamic State fighters in groups of two or three, separated from each other by a few hundred metres. This was as close as I wanted to get to them – but the driver kept going. Finally he got the message and we headed back.

Along the Turkey–Syria border, it wasn't just mortars from Syria that were spilling into Turkey. I came across thousands of refugees who were fleeing from Islamic State. I'll never forget the fear I saw in their eyes.

I interviewed a family of 10 who had fled across the border. One of them was a boy aged about 17, who told me that when they heard that Islamic State was coming, they immediately packed up all their belongings and got ready to flee. A neighbour was a quadriplegic, in a wheelchair, and no one could carry him so they were forced to flee without him. Horrible stories were circulating about what Islamic State had done in other villages that might or might not have been true. But it made me realise that fear had become Islamic State's biggest weapon. Even if people just heard a rumour that Islamic State were coming, they would flee. It meant Islamic State could just come into a village that was essentially abandoned and break into the bank, take money, live in houses full of food, stay there for a few days and then move on somewhere else, raising the Islamic flag as they went. They often met no resistance.

Hamad Mohammed, 36, sat with his family in a disused shop in Turkey. 'They are savage beasts,' he told me. 'I saw a head cut off from a body.'

Mustafa Kurdo, 49, stood with his nine children. 'Look at this one,' he said, picking up his one-year-old son. 'Islamic State want to cut his head off. Who *are* these savages? It is one thing for men to fight men, but what do these women and children have to do with this war?'

The situation in Syria is now a stalemate, with neither side gaining much ground. They have found each other's measure and they have carved off their areas and they are holding them. But at a tragic, and ongoing, cost.

CHAPTER 14

The American Factor

March 2013

WHEN BARACK OBAMA WALKED ON STAGE TO SPEAK TO hundreds of Israeli university students, he received a rock-star welcome. It was Thursday, 20 March 2013 and Obama was clearly thrilled by the reception on his first presidential visit to Israel. Before a bank of American and Israeli flags, Obama gave a speech that delighted Israelis. He reaffirmed the bonds between the two countries. He said in his two days in Israel he had 'borne witness to the history of the Jewish people'. And 'I have seen Israel's shining future in your scientists and entrepreneurs'.

But then President Obama said something that took Israelis by surprise – it was certainly something they had not heard before from a US president. He referred to the Israeli Army as 'a foreign army' when it came to the West Bank. The Palestinian people's right to self-determination and justice must be recognised, he said. 'Put yourself in their shoes; look at the world through their eyes. It is not fair that a Palestinian child cannot grow up in a state of their own, living their entire lives with the presence of a foreign army that controls the movement of not just those young people, but their parents and their grandparents every single day ... Neither occupation nor expulsion is the answer.'[1]

Obama's words would stun Israelis. The reference to the IDF as 'a foreign army' hit Israeli leaders like a thunderbolt.

In the US, due to the power of the pro-Israel lobby, Israel is regarded as a domestic issue. In the lead-up to his election in 2009, Obama had competed with Hillary Clinton, his Democratic rival for the party's nomination, as to who supported Israel more. Their two speeches to the annual American Israel Public Affairs Committee (AIPAC) conference had shown the competition between them to win support from the Jewish.

But upon his election it became clear what Obama really thought: that Israel's relentless growth in settlements was disastrous. Barack Obama was a shock to Israel's system.

From the beginning of his presidency the Israeli media were gunning for Obama; they would frequently refer to him using his Arabic middle name, Hussein. The government seemed pleased to let this undermining occur, especially as Obama's stocks at home deteriorated. The view in Israel was that Obama was a one-term president, allowing them to stall on peace talks until another president was elected.

But Obama got his healthcare package through Congress and for a while his political stocks went up. In the Israeli media the dogs were called off. In the headlines he became 'Barack' once again, rather than 'Hussein'.

New York Times journalist Thomas Friedman is regarded as America's most influential writer on Israel. He has long been supportive of Israel. But in a feisty interview on Israeli television he would declare 'Shame on you, Israel' for trying to portray Obama as 'a Jew hater'.

Yet not even Obama could stop the settlements. Friedman went on to say that in the battle between President Obama and Prime Minister Netanyahu, 'Bibi won'.[2] Thanks to the successful campaign by the Israeli lobby to achieve soft media treatment for Israel, Obama and other senior members of his administration would find themselves engaging in the same kind of self-censoring as other US politicians before them.

When Secretary of State John Kerry walked into the Mandarin Oriental Hotel in Washington on 25 April 2014, he could not have anticipated the coming storm. At a closed meeting, he spoke about his frustration that he'd made no progress after three years of negotiations with Israel and the Palestinians. Unaware that someone was recording him, he nominated the growth of Israeli settlements as a key reason. 'There is a fundamental confrontation and it is over settlements,' he said. 'Fourteen thousand new settlement units announced since we began negotiations.' He warned of possible violence: 'People grow so frustrated with their lot in life that they begin to take other choices and go to dark places they've been before, which forces confrontation.' But then he added: 'A two-state solution will be clearly underscored as the only real alternative. Because a unitary state winds up either being an apartheid State with second-class citizens – or it ends up being a State that destroys the capacity of Israel to be a Jewish State.'[3]

In Israel, the media often reported warnings that Israel might become an apartheid state. Israel's most decorated soldier and former Prime Minister, Ehud Barak, had warned about apartheid. So had another former Prime Minister, Ehud Olmert: 'If the day comes when the two-State solution collapses and we have a South Africa-style struggle for equal voting rights then as soon as that happens, the State of Israel is finished.'

But three Purple Hearts were not enough to save John Kerry. America's powerful pro-Israel lobby unleashed an attack.

However, rather than argue his case, Kerry retreated. 'I do not believe, nor have I ever stated, publicly or privately, that Israel is an apartheid State or that it intends to become one,' Kerry said. 'If I could rewind the tape I would have chosen a different word to describe my firm belief that the only way in the long term to have a Jewish State and two nations and two people living side by side in peace and security is through a two-State solution.' But in a hint of defiance, Kerry added: 'While Justice Minister Livni, former Prime Ministers Barak and Olmert have all invoked the spectre of apartheid to underscore the dangers of a unitary State, for the future it is a word best left out of the debate here at home.'[4]

'Apartheid' is the one word that the supporters of Greater Israel resent. The *New York Times*'s Jodi Rudoren told me: 'I think that's what John Kerry was basically saying: "I lost ground on convincing people by using a word that people put me into a box that I'm one of those people who thinks it's apartheid and they think they can ignore me."'

This was not the only time Kerry had retreated. Some months later, Israel stated that the reason it had initiated the 2014 Gaza War was to target Hamas tunnels. But Palestinian civilian casualties had quickly spiralled – with an assault by fighter jets, helicopters, tanks and ships on the 365 square kilometre enclave, Israel had wreaked devastation.

Before an interview on Fox News, Kerry was caught mocking Israel's claim of a targeted operation: 'It's a hell of a pin-point operation!' The host, Chris Wallace, decided to put these comments to Kerry on air. Kerry took a much softer position. 'It's very difficult in these situations,' he said.[5]

President Obama's one-time Chief of Staff, Rahm Emanuel – now Mayor of Chicago – has also self-censored. Emanuel is regarded as a straight talker. Yet in an interview with *New Republic* magazine in April 2014, he insisted on going off the record when asked about Israel. The only thing he would say on the record was that he was 'optimistic' about a peace deal; it is quite possible that when he went off the record he said the exact opposite.[6]

Even US Ambassador to Israel Dan Shapiro – who is Jewish and regarded by Israelis as 'a close friend' – came under fire for describing reality. 'Too much vigilantism in the West Bank goes on unchecked ... There seem to be two standards,' he said in 2016, stating the fact that Israel's settlers live under Israeli civilian law while Palestinians next door live under Israeli military law. Prime Minister Netanyahu called Shapiro's comments 'unacceptable and wrong'. He summoned Shapiro to discuss them.[7]

Thomas Friedman said the sensitivity of discussing Israel for public figures in the US had reached the point where an ambitious young diplomat would not publicly state official US policy: that Israeli settlements are an obstacle to peace. On Washington's policy of condoning Israel's construction of settlements, Friedman said, 'That particular policy is a source for me of great distress.'[8]

What this sort of self-censorship by the Obama administration meant was that rarely did Americans hear the truth about Israel. The mild resistance of Washington during the Obama years – 'the settlements are unhelpful' – was not enough to stop the number of settlers from growing.

Yet the haste with which Israel escalated its settlement expansion upon the inauguration of Donald Trump in 2017 was extraordinary. Trump had made a campaign promise that he would lead the most pro-Israel administration 'of all time'. His election to the presidency was a godsend to Netanyahu and his government. Trump appointed his son-in-law, Jared Kushner, as a senior adviser with oversight of the Middle East. Kushner's family foundation, of which he is a director, has donated funds to various settlements in the West Bank. According to US tax records obtained by the *New York Post*, the family donated $US58,500 between 2011 and 2013. This included donations to Yitzhar, a settlement with a well-known history of violence. Settlers from there are regularly caught on camera attacking Palestinians and property in nearby villages, often as the Israeli Army stands by and watches. The *Washington Post* also reported that the man Trump chose to be the US Ambassador to Israel, David Friedman, is on the record as having opposed a two-State solution, and has been the President of Beit El Institutions, which financially supports Beit El and other settlements.[9]

Trump made clear during Prime Minister Netanyahu's first meeting with him as President in February 2017 that he would be dramatically changing US policy. Standing next to Netanyahu, Trump appeared to abandon Washington's long commitment to a two-State solution. 'I'm looking at two-State and one-State, and I like the one that both parties like,' he said.[10]

The editorial board of the *New York Times*, traditionally a strong supporter of Israel, noted after the meeting: 'There is no conceivable one-state solution that both parties will like. Smiling by Mr Trump's side, Mr Netanyahu, who has steadily undermined the prospect of a Palestinian state, clearly believed his vision was the one the new American President had in mind. The two leaders seemed almost giddy in their first official meeting, which was intended to show how Mr Trump can be a better friend to Israel than President Barack Obama was, even though Mr Obama completed a new 10-year, $38 billion defence agreement with Israel.'[11]

*

Former Deputy Prime Minister of Australia Tim Fischer believes you cannot understand Israel's power in the United States without studying an event that occurred on 8 June 1967, the fourth day of the Six Day War. On that day Israeli jets attacked one of the US's most important naval intelligence ships, the USS *Liberty*, killing 34 sailors.

The US decided not to attack the attackers but made a strategic retreat, having been mauled by the Israeli Air Force. To use the word of Tim Fischer, the US ship 'limped' back to Malta.

Files about the incident – specifically, whether the attack was deliberate – have been sealed. Whether the attack was intentional, or accidental as Israel claimed, one thing is not disputed: the US reaction was almost nonexistent.

In the ensuing years, several US officials questioned why the US had not protested at the attack. Senator James Abourezk said: 'The shame of the USS *Liberty* incident is that our sailors were treated as though they were enemies, rather than the patriots and heroes that they were. There is no other incident … that shows the power of the Israeli lobby by being able to silence successive American governments. Allowing the lies told by the Israelis and their minions in the US is disheartening to all of us who are proud of our servicemen.'[12]

Many became convinced that the attack was deliberate. Former congressman Paul Findley would write in 1985: 'The attack was no accident. The *Liberty* was assaulted in broad daylight by Israeli forces who knew the ship's identity ... the President of the US led a cover-up so thorough that years after he left office, the episode was still largely unknown to the public – and the men who suffered and died have gone largely unhonoured.'[13]

Former Senator Adlai Stevenson III said in a 1980 interview: 'Those sailors who were wounded, who were eyewitnesses, have not been heard from by the American public ... [Their story] leaves no doubt but that this was a premeditated, carefully-reconnoitered attack by Israeli aircraft against our ship.'[14] The deputy head of the US Mission in Cairo at the time, David Nes, said: 'I don't think that there's any doubt that it was deliberate ... [It is] one of the great cover-ups of our military history.'[15]

Tim Fischer has made a study of the USS *Liberty* incident and believes it has shaped US–Israeli relations. He told me it must have been 'one of the lowest points in US military history' to have left one of its ships on its own. 'It flies in the face of the general military code to go in and help which is why the US military establishment have hushed it up ... The US military have air-brushed it out of history because they are acutely embarrassed by it. Had the attackers been Chinese or Russian it would have been war.'

Mr Fischer added: 'Israel's attack on the USS *Liberty* and the non-reaction by America meant from then on Israel could do anything with impunity ... If President Johnson was not going to send fighter jets in to protect one of his ships they were not going to do anything else. What happened to the *Liberty* may have changed the face of the Middle East. Little young Israel could do anything and get away with it. It could start building the atomic bomb on a scale and they knew the US would do nothing – they had these friends in Washington and that was enough.'

George Ball, Under-Secretary of State at the time, would write in 1992: 'If American leaders did not have the courage to punish Israel for the blatant murder of American citizens, it seemed clear that their American friends would let them get away with almost anything.'[16]

History confirmed these words only too clearly. A letter from the US Ambassador to Israel, Kenneth Keating, to the State Department, dated 25 July 1974, made it clear that the US was in on the plan to build settlements in the West Bank from the beginning. Keating wrote it the day after meeting Yigal Alon, the Israeli Minister of Foreign Affairs. He wrote: 'I raised US concern over Israeli press stories on plans to establish new settlements in occupied territories and adverse effect these stories could have upon [peace] negotiations. Alon responded sympathetically to my remarks and said that he would make additional efforts to keep stories on this subject out of the press.'

The US–Israeli strategy was clear: to try to keep stories about settlements out of the media rather than to stop them.

'For the last 40 years, a succession of Israeli governments has misled, manipulated or persuaded naïve US presidents that since Israel was negotiating to give up significant territory, there was no need to fight over "insignificant" settlements on some territory', wrote Thomas Friedman. 'Behind the charade, Israeli settlers bit more and more of the West Bank, creating a huge moral, security and economic burden for Israel and its friends.'[17]

*

At first I assumed he was a real journalist. Indeed, the way he introduced himself was impressive. 'I work in the White House Press Corps,' he told me. It was 16 December 2009 and I was in the West Bank settlement of Ariel for a conference about how the rest of the world viewed Israel. We'd just sat down to lunch. The man's name was William Koenig, and he introduced himself as the White House correspondent for Koenig International News.

But the conversation took an odd turn when he told me that many of America's natural disasters had followed criticism. He listed various disasters and attributed them to US criticism or 'weakness' relating to Israel. Criticise Israel and God will be angry. I quickly realised that William Koenig was no ordinary reporter. I discovered that he was a leader of the Christian Zionist movement, which ensures Israel has enough support in the Congress to expand its occupation.

Koenig has written *Eye to Eye*, a book that shows the links between 57 'major catastrophes and events' and the 'anti-Israel' comments that caused them. Koenig argued that a 'very large majority' of President George W Bush's political problems and the many natural catastrophes during his time in office 'have a direct connection to his involvement with the Israeli–Palestinian peace process'. Koenig wrote: 'Many world leaders believe that Israel is the key to peace when in reality the continued pressure upon Israel and the subsequent events will rapidly lead the world into the final battle: the battle of Armageddon – the battle for Jerusalem. We hope and pray this book helps you become better aware of why the world is rapidly moving into her final days and nearing the return of the Messiah to Jerusalem.'[18]

Koenig argued that 'eleven of the twelve costliest hurricanes in US history have a direct tie-in to US-Israeli peace efforts'.

Hurricane Katrina, for example, which at US$80 billion was the most expensive disaster in US history, was retribution for the fact that President George W Bush expressed pleasure at Israel's withdrawal of Israeli settlements from Gaza; Hurricane Andrew came during the Madrid peace talks; Hurricane Charley came as the George W Bush Administration pressured Israel to withdraw from unauthorised outposts; Hurricane Wilma came as the US froze Israel's financial aid in response to settlement construction and Bush hosted Palestinian leader Mahmoud Abbas at the White House; Hurricane Ivan came as the 'Bush administration continued pressure on Israel'; Hurricane Rita was retribution for Bush's hosting of Jordan's King Abdullah at the White House.

William Koenig even linked the September 11, 2001 attacks to US policy on Israel. He writes:

> In August and September of 2001, President Bush worked
> with Prince Bandar – the Saudi Ambassador to the US –
> Secretary of State Colin Powell and Daniel Kurtzer, the
> US Ambassador to Israel, to develop a comprehensive
> peace plan that Abdullah [of Saudi Arabia] would approve.
> Powell was to deliver the Bush plan to the UN General
> Assembly on September 24, 2001. The plan divided Israel
> and created a Palestinian state, in return for 'peace and
> security' guarantees to Israel. The plan's completion and
> presentation were disrupted by the September 11, 2001,
> terror events. For a brief moment, the God of Israel lifted
> His protection as evil people attacked America.

Politically, what is important for Israel is that the US continues to support its settlement expansion – or, at least, never does anything more than issue statements that new settlements are 'unhelpful'. For this reason, people like William Koenig are crucial.

He explained to me how he tried to ensure that Israel was not criticised. 'We have eyes everywhere,' he said. 'We have eyes in the US, in Europe, in Australia. With the internet it is all so much easier. The moment one of our people sees something negative about Israel we jump. Someone hits back quickly.'

Aspiring members of Congress who challenge the Christian Zionist movement do so at their own peril. Christian Zionists argue against a Palestinian State. 'We think Israel should have all the land out here,' Koenig told me. The view that anyone who criticises Israel risks apocalyptic revenge has entered US mainstream politics. Even one-time Republican presidential candidate Michelle Bachmann echoed this outlook. Responding to pictures of floods in South Carolina, she tweeted: 'US turns back on Israel, disasters follow.'

Though the US has turned a blind eye to the settlements from the beginning of Israel's occupation, occasionally an administration has expressed some resistance. Jimmy Carter was the only president to brand the settlements 'illegal', and from that moment the pro-Israel lobby in the US ran a campaign against him. When Carter announced, at 90, that he had cancer that had spread to his brain, this was seen by some as punishment for his views on Israel. As a Jewish website reported: 'For some Jews (and evangelical Christians), the cause apparently is obvious. No, it's not his genetic make-up, or the spread of a mass from his liver to his brain. It's divine punishment for his behavior toward the Jews.'[19] George Bush Senior threatened to stop the US from guaranteeing loans to Israel if it did not curtail settlements, and likewise the pro-Israel lobby ran a campaign against him. After

George W Bush threatened loan guarantees to Israel if they continued settlements, the Republican Party received a backlash from pro-Israel supporters in the US, including the Christian Zionists.

Koenig described himself as 'an evangelical' and was scathing of some church groups which, he said, had made matters worse by supporting the peace process. 'It's all in the Bible. This land belongs to Israel. If Christian groups like the World Council of Churches and the Vatican had supported Israel for the last 40 years the whole situation wouldn't be in the mess it's in.'

In *Eye to Eye* Koenig explains Israel has a right to the West Bank 'because God said so'. Supporting this, he quotes from the Bible, Genesis 13:14–17: 'The Lord said to Abram, "Lift up now your eyes, and look from the place where you are northward, and southward, and eastward and westward: for all the land which you see, to you will I give it, and to your seed forever."' Koenig argues that 'God specifically declared "No Peace Deals", citing Exodus 32: "'Thou shalt make no covenant with them, nor with their gods. They shall not dwell in thy land, lest they make thee sin against Me."'

I asked Koenig what should happen to the Palestinians. 'I don't know,' he said. 'They just will become part of a larger Israel.'

*

A key link in the Christian Zionist chain is the International Christian Embassy in Jerusalem – the contact point in Israel for Christian Zionists. The day I met David Parsons, the head of the embassy, in October 2014, he had just come from a meeting with the Israeli Government.

Parsons once worked as a lobbyist in Washington. 'We have a strong branch in the US but our strongest branch is in Europe,' he said. 'We have branch offices established in 80 countries, including in some Muslim majority countries that we really can't name to protect them, but Christians there who support Israel. Our magazine goes to 140 countries, our email list to 150, our TV show is in probably 190 countries.'

Parsons said his followers had 'a predisposition' to support Israel. 'We're not anti-Arab, it's just that we see the animosity towards Israel, and we say, "Hey Christians, especially in Europe where there's so much history of Christian anti-Semitism, our churches made these mistakes for centuries, and we see the rest of the world buying into the lies now against the Jews in the form of the Jewish State, and it was a mistake to do it and it's a mistake for you to do it."'

So what is the goal of Christian Zionists, according to David Parsons? 'There's an effort to try to give fairness to the whole debate over Israel because of the way the Jews were so unfairly treated in the Christian world for centuries. It's a basic faith principle that the way we read the Bible it says God loves the whole world but to reach the whole world with his redemptive plan he chose a certain vessel to do this through and that was the Jewish people.'

As a leader of the movement, did Parsons think there should be a Palestinian State? 'I still believe that the Jewish claim to the entire land is superior historically and that the claim of Palestinian national identity is of more modern origin,' he told me.

He said the support of Christians in the US reflected the community as a whole. 'When you look at the polls in America concerning Israel it's always been high 60s into the high 70s of support for Israel, generally. The evangelical community tracks just a little ahead of that, we're the strongest but still not that far off from the general view in the US because a lot of it is based on shared values, shared democratic Judaeo-Christian values and traditions and such and they see Israel as a solid ally ... There's always been this Arabist bloc in the State Department that has tried to present the Arab point of view and the White House is always in between those two. This is Washington. The different White Houses over time and how they play that off and navigate that has always been interesting.'

Parsons rejected the notion that there was not a genuine discussion in Congress about Israel. 'I think they voice the concerns of the people and they're concerned about the Iranian threat, not just the threat to Israel but others in the region ... [pro-Israel lobby] AIPAC is viewed as powerful but it's just effective.' AIPAC, he said, 'knows how to speak to Americans and elected American officials.'

*

Jodi Rudoren from the *New York Times* has closely observed Israel and its influence in the US, particularly through its most powerful lobby group, AIPAC. She told me: 'AIPAC and the related groups long ago built a system in which they operate in every congressional district, they raise enough money and mobilise enough small donors to influence every single congressional district.'

I asked Rudoren whether this was unhealthy for US democracy: 'I don't think there's a very healthy debate in America over Israeli policy. There's very much this notion that you're with us or against us – betrayal, all that stuff.'

I asked Israeli journalist Akiva Eldar: does AIPAC distort the discussion of Israel? 'I think they are an obstacle to the two-State solution which is the very idea of Zionism,' he replied. 'Without the two-State solution Zionism is kaput. As to why AIPAC is opposed to a two-State solution, the cynical answer would be that if there is peace and no embargoes on Israel there will be no need for those people and there are hundreds of people who make a living from the current situation. It's similar to the weapons industry and the military lobby – if there is peace who needs to have such a big army in Israel, and so many arms dealers?'

I asked Eldar if American politicians were scared of Israel. He said:

They're scared of AIPAC. And they're scared for a very good reason. AIPAC has many dead heads on their belt – skeletons – of congressmen who dared not to vote against Israel but who didn't have a completely positive record on votes when it was about Israel or Iran.

I wrote a book called *The Jerusalem Capital Ambush* on how AIPAC was manipulating the Congress to pass a bill to move the [US] embassy to Jerusalem, embarrassing both Bill Clinton and Yitzhak Rabin. And how did they do this? By playing Republicans and Democrats. There was a story in the *New York Times* about how they got rid of an incumbent congresswoman from a district that hardly saw a Jew there by pouring money into the political action committee. It was an African American against an African American and they decided to get rid of the incumbent because she didn't have a clean record on Israel. AIPAC is considered to be one of the leading lobbies after the unions and gun lobby.

Eldar and other Israeli analysts believe that even though competition to AIPAC has emerged in recent years through groups more prepared to accommodate a two-State solution, such as J-Street, AIPAC still remains the Israel-related lobby group that US lawmakers fear.

*

It is impossible to examine the US factor in Israel without looking at the role of Sheldon Adelson, the Las Vegas casino billionaire who is one of America's wealthiest men. Adelson supports a Greater Israel under which settlers take the West Bank and leave no possibility for a Palestinian State. An address he gave to the Israeli–American Council on 9 November 2014 offered an idea of his views: 'I don't think the Bible says anything about democracy ... God talked about all sorts of good things in life. He didn't talk about Israel remaining a democratic state, and if Israel isn't going to be a democratic state – so what?'

Adelson is a major backer of Benjamin Netanyahu through his free newspaper *Israel Today*, the most-read newspaper in Israel. Ehud Olmert told me over dinner in August 2012 that he believed Adelson had founded the paper in response to Olmert's peace offer to the Palestinians.

The billionaire funds the Birthright – or Taglit – program under which hundreds of thousands of young diaspora Jews visit Israel, and gives financial backing to both American and Israeli politicians whose view of Israel fits with his. Adelson is famous for anointing with a huge financial donation the most 'pro-Israel' candidate in each presidential election.

Jodi Rudoren said Adelson was largely perceived in both the US and Israel as 'a bit of a clown, an old rich guy who doesn't care what anybody thinks of him'. She added: 'He's got more money than God and he's willing to spend it. It didn't work: he spent $100 million on Mitt Romney and he lost. But anyone who's going to spend $100 million on anything everyone is going to take seriously.'

Adelson is by no means the only wealthy American funding Israel's settlement push. In 2015 *Haaretz* newspaper found that between 2009 and 2013, private US donors used a network of tax-exempt non-profit organisations to funnel more than US$220 million to Israeli communities in the West Bank. 'The funding is being used for anything from buying air conditioners to supporting the families of convicted Jewish terrorists, and comes from tax-deductible donations made to around 50 US-based groups', the paper said. 'Thanks to their status as non-profits, these organisations are not taxed on their income and donations made to them are tax deductible – meaning the US Government is incentivizing and indirectly supporting the Israeli settlement movement, even though it has been consistently opposed by every US administration for the past 48 years.'[20]

One important American donor has been millionaire doctor Irving Moskowitz, who made his fortune in the US by buying and selling hospitals. Dr Moskowitz died in 2016 at the age of 88. According to his foundation's website, in 1988 the City of Hawaiian Gardens in California licensed his foundation to operate The Bingo Club as a charitable, non-profit organisation. The *Guardian*'s Chris McGreal did a major investigation of the club. He found: 'Each dollar spent on bingo by the mostly Latino residents of Hawaiian Gardens, on the outskirts of Los Angeles, helps fund Jewish settlements on Palestinian land in some of the most sensitive areas of occupied East Jerusalem, particularly the Muslim quarter of the Old City, and West Bank towns such as Hebron where the Israeli military has forced Arabs out of their properties in their thousands.' McGreal quoted local rabbi Haim Dov Beliak, who said, 'Moskowitz is taking millions from the poorest towns in California and sending it to the settlements.'[22]

*

The US remains one of the few countries unconditionally supporting Israel. Israeli journalist Gideon Levy told me that the notion that the US is an honest broker between Israel and the Palestinians as 'grotesque'. 'If the US decided now to stop supplying the Israeli Air Force with one screw [the occupation] is finished. No Israeli prime minister could say a word after that. The dependence is total ... Any country the size of Israel cannot live without trade. The Jewish community in the US is the key to everything ... I think the Jewish lobby is more powerful in America than the Christian Zionists, but those, together with the arms industry, are crucial.'

The US could force an end to the occupation 'within days,' said Levy. 'Israel doesn't exist without the US ... It's only by really putting a very clear choice to Israel that you will get a result – either you get US aid, or you continue the occupation. The US also stops Europe from boycotting Israel.'

Danish journalist Uffe Taudal found it 'very odd' that the US Congress was prepared to applaud Israeli Prime Minister Benjamin Netanyahu, who openly advocated policies contrary to Washington's. 'Netanyahu went to the US Congress and said

Jerusalem will always stay united,' he told me. 'Everybody stood up and clapped – it has been official American policy for at least 40 years that the US wants Jerusalem as a capital for the Palestinians and a capital for Israel – except for four people they stood up and clapped against stated American bipartisan policy for Republican and Democratic presidents ... At the heart of this [Israeli] strategy is very clever lobbying and very clever political diplomacy. The Israelis make sure that in Europe and the US whatever you say about this conflict you risk paying a huge political price.'

I put to Jody Rudoren that many of Israel's laws governing Palestinians would be illegal under the US Constitution – for example, limiting the number of Palestinians who can assemble to 10, or taking children from the age of 12 for night-time interrogations. She agreed, adding that one could look at examples in Israel itself, rather than the West Bank: 'There are communities here where there are racial criteria for entry to live, all sorts of things that nobody in America would ever accept. But ... Americans by and large accept that Israel is a different type of place. They don't apply their standards. They buy this idea of Israel as a Jewish State created out of the worst moment of history and that it may be an anomalous ethnocracy ... they simply buy this Jewish–Israeli notion of a Jewish and democratic State.'

Jodi Rudoren believes the future of Israel was likely to be decided in a political battle between Europe and the US. 'There are a lot of really simple things that Europe could do and whether they are prepared to do them instead of just saying them over again is an interesting question.'

In the US, as in Australia, unconditional support for Israel is beginning to be challenged. A program has been started in Israel to offer a broader view than traditionally sponsored trips have taken. A group called Extend has been started, taking advantage of the fact that thousands of young American Jews come to Israel on Sheldon Adelson's Birthright trips. Participants are offered a different perspective if they are able to 'extend' their trips. One organisation that offers a briefing to these youths is Military Court Watch, started by Australian lawyer Gerard Horton to monitor the treatment of Palestinian youths before Israel's military court. Referring to Extend, Horton told me: 'These participants get a briefing from Military Court Watch and they sometimes go back to their hotel rooms and are shell-shocked because they realise everything they have been taught is under question.'

However, while Europe is becoming impatient with Israel, it appears that, if anything, US policy under Donald Trump will only further entrench the occupation.

For 50 years, since Israel began the settlement enterprise on which it has based its occupation, the US has supported Israeli policy. With occasional exceptions, Washington has stood by as Israeli politicians have methodically steered their country towards the abyss of apartheid.

CHAPTER 15

The Lobby

June 2013

THE QUESTION STUNNED ME. IT WAS 16 JUNE 2013 AND THE
email was from Paul Israel, head of the Israel–Australia, New
Zealand and Oceania Chamber of Commerce. 'How much
longer are you here?' he wrote. 'Want to make sure we get time
to catch up ...'

It was an odd message – where had Paul got the idea I
was leaving? I needed to dispel these rumours straightaway. If
it caught on that I was about to leave then I'd become a lame-
duck correspondent. I was pleased to be able to let Paul Israel
know that my term had recently been extended and my bosses in
Sydney were happy with my work. 'I'm here for quite a while yet',
I told him.

About the same time, I began to hear from colleagues on the
paper in Sydney that I was coming under increased attack by the
Israeli Embassy. The editor of the *Weekend Australian*, Nick Cater,
had invited Einat Weiss, the spokesperson for the Israeli Embassy

in Canberra, to *The Australian*'s head office in Sydney. As I would later discover, she'd wandered the floor telling various editors that the embassy was not happy with me. To me, the idea of an officer of a foreign government wandering the floor of my newsroom criticising me was outrageous. I made clear my feelings to Editor-in-Chief Chris Mitchell, who had not known anything about Weiss's visit.

Meanwhile, the Israeli Embassy began trying to work out who my successor might be, even though there'd been no announcement that my term was ending – because it wasn't. I heard from *The Australian*'s national security correspondent, Paul Maley, who told me later: 'I'm getting a lot of attention from the Israeli Embassy. They're not happy with you, mate.' Maley promised to keep me informed of developments. 'I'm not going to let them play one journalist against another,' he said.

On 2 May, the embassy cranked up its efforts against me. Einat Weiss made another visit to my paper. She was about to finish her posting in Australia and had arrived – ostensibly – to bid farewell. But it seemed she was more interested in who my successor would be. Among others, Weiss sought out Paul Maley, who told me later that she'd asked about how much longer I'd be the Middle East correspondent. Maley replied that postings at *The Australian* were open-ended and that she should understand I was the principal point of contact on matters to do with Israel.

*

It had been clear to me for some time that the stories I'd written about Palestinian children in the Israeli military court had angered Israel's hardline supporters. I'd been reprimanded by the

Israeli Army – not for inaccuracy but for choosing to do the story. Now the Israeli Embassy had attempted to discredit me.

I'd also been given the brush-off by the Australian Embassy in Tel Aviv. Since arriving in Israel, I'd been invited each year to an ANZAC Day ceremony in Jerusalem by Ambassador James Larsen and his successor (as of early 2010), Andrea Faulkner. In my 'Stone Cold Justice' story for *The Australian* I'd reported that Faulkner had been told by Australian lawyer Gerard Horton of the sorts of things being done to the children in the West Bank military court. Horton had also told Faulkner that members of the UK Parliament and most European countries had visited the court. But Faulkner had never followed up Horton's allegations – despite promising to do so – and Australia remained one of the few Western countries whose diplomatic representatives had never visited the military court. After this story was published in November 2011, I was no longer invited to embassy functions.

But the most sustained criticism of my article had come from AIJAC, a powerful Israeli lobby group in Australia. When I later returned to Australia, I interviewed Chris Mitchell about these events. By then he had retired. He told me: 'Most of the attacks on you came from Colin Rubenstein and Bob Magid [the owner of *Australian Jewish News*]. The stories you did on Palestinian children were the ones that most upset Colin Rubenstein. My view was that in an elected democracy on the other side of the world we should be able to openly and honestly canvass an issue like this without the interference from a lobby group in Melbourne.'

The joint investigation that Sylvie and I did for *Four Corners* on this subject with Sue Spencer, Janine Cohen, Mary Fallon and Neale Maude won the 2014 Walkley Award for Investigative Journalism. After it was shortlisted, *The Australian*'s Editor, Clive

Mathieson, sent me a note: 'I'm exceptionally pleased it's made the shortlist after all the bullets we – and you – took.'

*

AIJAC had been a problem for me from the start. Criticism can and should happen in every field of journalism. Reporters should be subject to challenge; a lot of the criticism is simply lobby groups doing their jobs. But it became more and more clear to me that AIJAC was behind much of the backlash against my reporting.

Meanwhile, the head of AIJAC, Colin Rubenstein, seemed to have the sort of access to *The Australian* that I could only dream of. Newspapers are very competitive publications, with plenty of journalists competing to get their stories run in limited space. Getting a good run in the *Weekend Australian* – considered the prize 'real estate' because weekend papers have higher audiences – meant that I had to begin lobbying my editors early in the week. But one instance confirmed to me Rubenstein's influence.

In March 2010, Rubenstein criticised me for quoting 21 words of Yossi Beilin – three times a minister and one of Israel's negotiators during the Oslo peace process – in an article about US Vice-President Joe Biden's visit to Israel.[1] In the same week he sent an email to Cater alerting him to a long story by one of AIJAC's favourite journalists, Yossi Klein Halevi. That piece argued that President Obama, rather than Israel, was to blame for the lack of progress in peace talks. Cater sent the email and story on to the World News desk, with the message 'Good piece for Saturday?' Even though it was late in the week, Rubenstein's email resulted in the clearing of an entire page for Halevi's story.

The Yossi Beilin case angered me because I realised that I was being pressured not to report a view that when reported in Israel caused few complaints. And the Halevi story showed me how AIJAC works. Given the limited audience of their website, it's important for AIJAC to try to get their stories and preferred commentators published in the broader media. Once the Halevi piece had been published in the *Weekend Australian*, AIJAC was able to run it on its own website, pointing out that it was from the *Weekend Australian*. In my view, this was a lobby group with way too much influence: a point I made strongly to my editors.

The more AIJAC attacked me, the more determined I became not to back off. I came to the view that there was no point in being a correspondent if you could only tell part of the story. I knew I had the backing of Chris Mitchell from an unequivocal email he sent me: 'I had no idea things were this bad. I have NO relationship with Colin and think him a bully so feel free to come to me whenever you need. I am obviously sympathetic to Israel but I am just as keen to get things right. And I am keen on a range of views.'

Around this period I learnt that there were times when Chris Mitchell would refuse to take Rubenstein's phone calls – at which point Rubenstein would go through Cater. Mitchell told me at the time that he had asked Cater to keep Rubenstein 'more at arm's length'.

Later, back in Australia, Mitchell would tell me: 'Sometimes with Colin Rubenstein I'd say, "Send a letter or write a column," but other times if I wouldn't take his call he'd go behind my back to Nick Cater. I got upset with Colin when he rang me and attacked [*Australian* reporter] Elizabeth Wynhausen as "a self-loathing Jew". I thought it was inappropriate for him to be making that kind of comment about one of my staff. For some time after that I stopped taking his calls.'

At the same time I heard that Cater did not want my work to appear in 'Inquirer', the flagship section of the *Weekend Australian*. This was devastating. When I'd been the paper's Washington correspondent under Paul Kelly, the 'Inquirer' section (then called 'Focus') had been what all the correspondents aimed for. I phoned Cater and he confirmed that he'd asked for my work no longer to appear in 'Inquirer'. He told me that 'the Middle East is such a complex part of the world that a correspondent should spend the first 12 months learning about the area and just writing news'. I'd never heard of this happening to a correspondent in my more than 30 years in journalism; normally if a newspaper funds an overseas bureau they want as many features and analysis pieces as possible, rather than just straight news stories, which they can get from the news agencies, or 'wires'.

But I wasn't just having problems with the 'Inquirer' section. I discovered that Cater had commissioned a freelance journalist in Jerusalem to do a story on something that I'd been covering for more than a week.

At nine o'clock on the morning of 31 May 2010, the news broke that Israeli special forces had stormed the *Mavi Marmara*, one of six ships in the 'Gaza Freedom Flotilla', which was seeking to break Israel's three-year blockade of Gaza. Among those on board were Australians and New Zealanders, including journalists. There was serious violence on the *Mavi Marmara* and nine Turkish citizens were killed; a tenth later died in hospital.

I drove south to the port of Ashdod, where the boats with people from the flotilla were being landed by the army. When I arrived, many of the media were up on the hill overlooking the Mediterranean to see the flotilla coming in, and a huge demonstration was taking place. From their crocheted caps – kippahs – I could tell they were mainly young right-wing religious protesters who were on the side of the army. They were carrying signs such as 'It should have been more than nine.' The mob was starting to turn against the media – putting their signs in front of an Israeli reporter from *Al Jazeera*, for instance, every time he tried to do a live cross.

There were three Palestinian women sitting on the hill, and a mob of perhaps 100 protesters gathered around and chanted: 'Go home! Go back to where you came from!' These women were actually Israeli citizens. I thought, this is going to get ugly.

Some of the foreign media there went and spoke to the head of army PR, Avital Leibovich, about the situation but she said, 'Look, that's not my problem. Talk to the police about it. It's not an army issue.' So we then went and saw Micky Rosenfeld, the head of PR for the police, and he said, 'Oh look, it's fine. They will be OK. There are a lot of high emotions here.'

By now the women were starting to be pushed, and we began having an argument with Micky Rosenfeld, telling him: 'You should do something!' Then the police started arguing among themselves about what to do. Finally, some of them moved in and helped the women get away as a group of the young Israelis brought their faces up close to the women, shouting: 'Go home!' It was a very ugly mood and my first taste of the dark side of a section of Israeli society.

As we talked to various people it was difficult to tell whether the army or the activists had started the violence in the flotilla. In the Middle East, one side always disputes the other side's version. Just after the incident Israeli journalists were going on TV and one of them said, 'The flotilla was not in international waters, it was in Israeli waters.' After a day or two it was confirmed that the flotilla *had* been in international waters, but by then seeds of doubt had crept in. I came to see this occur over and over again. Often when there was a story critical of Israel, or a war, some Israeli journalists would quickly appear on television and muddy the waters by claiming an incident was not true or adding enough doubt to make the foreign media hold off reporting it as fact, to soften it with qualification.

I spent the week investigating the claims and counter-claims of the army and the activists who had been in the flotilla. The army was making all sorts of assertions for which there was no evidence. Avital Leibovich held a press conference to be broadcast live on Israeli TV. Two Israeli soldiers who had allegedly taken part in the raid were presented to us – but we were told we could not name them, and they had their backs turned to us to make sure no one could identify them. They read a brief statement, and then the PR staff said there could be no questions. This was hardly a press conference – I stood up and made that point to the organisers.

Day by day, the various claims Israel had made disintegrated. *The Australian* was running my stories prominently through the week. But without telling me, Nick Cater had commissioned Abraham Rabinovich, a freelancer who lived a kilometre from me in Jerusalem, to do an 'Inside Story' for the *Weekend Australian*. It must have seemed strange to readers: all week they'd been reading how the Israeli Army's assertions were coming under fire, but on Saturday all those claims I'd been deconstructing were presented on page one of the paper as fact.

I could see my posting disintegrating. I'd tried to resolve previous disagreements with Nick Cater without enlisting Chris

Mitchell. I knew from my time as Editor of the *Sydney Morning Herald* that the last thing you want is to be constantly called upon to sort out problems. But now that I'd been sidelined from 'Inquirer', I needed to resolve this ongoing problem with getting my stories in. I let Mitchell know that, from my point of view, the exclusion from 'Inquirer' was just the latest in a long series of disagreements with Nick Cater.

As I'd found him to be ever since we'd first worked together in 1984, Chris Mitchell was rock-solid. He intervened and told Cater that excluding me from 'Inquirer' was not acceptable. When another senior editor of *The Australian* was coming to Jerusalem – on a lobby trip, ironically – Cater spoke to him about his 'regret over the difficulties with your [my] stories and the intervention of Colin Rubenstein'.

When I returned to Australia at the end of my posting, I telephoned Cater and arranged to meet. He had left *The Australian* and joined the Menzies Research Centre. Over a pot of tea, I told him that as part of this book I wanted to talk to him about my experiences dealing with him from the Middle East. He told me he did not want to be interviewed for the book.

*

In April 2012 I was confronted with a new attack from AIJAC that typified the way they would try to undermine my reputation even when I wrote an article that was completely factual. My mistake on this occasion was writing about settlements, the one issue the lobby is most sensitive about.

I wrote that under Benjamin Netanyahu there had been 'a major growth of settlements'. This was based on an official government figure: Israel's Central Bureau of Statistics had reported that settlements had grown 660 per cent in the first half of 2011. I was confident that 'major' was an accurate description; to me 660 per cent is 'major'.

But for reporting something factual I was the subject of a new attack on AIJAC's website. AIJAC set up a straw man: they attacked me for something that I hadn't written. They claimed I'd stated that settlement growth was at record levels and 'historically high', then began a long demolition of that. I would never have used the expression 'historically' high. For a journalist reporting on Israel, repeated attacks by AIJAC, even if based on something you have not said, can be damaging.

When I drew the AIJAC attack to the attention of the Editor, Clive Mathieson, he contacted Colin Rubenstein to express his concern. Rubenstein privately conceded to Mathieson that the AIJAC blog post about me was wrong. He assured Mathieson that the matter would be dealt with – which both Mathieson and I assumed meant the item would be taken down. But we discovered the next day that AIJAC had simply reworded the post, turning it into a different attack on me that relied on a contributing blogger.

This brought a strong response from Mathieson. He wrote to Rubenstein:

> You've made it clear to me in the past that you don't agree with some of John's analysis. That's fine and I always take that on board. If your contributor wants to pick apart his analysis piece based on facts then that's OK too. But in this case, the repeated attempts by your contributor to accuse John of fostering a 'perception' about something he has not written border on the malicious. I also note that the original

AIJAC post, which you have conceded privately was wrong, has now been picked up and repeated by blogs. You and I both know that you can't control blogs but this, without a public correction by AIJAC, exacerbates the unfair slur on John's reputation.

Colin Rubenstein replied that he remained convinced the new posting was fair but he would remove the reference to me in the interests of AIJAC's relationship with *The Australian*.

*

Living in Jerusalem, one thing that surprised me was how something that could be reported freely in the Israeli media brought a fierce response from the Israeli lobby in Australia. I saw the government of Benjamin Netanyahu boasting about the swelling of settlements, and I saw this reported by the Israeli media. Meanwhile, AIJAC in Australia insisted that settlements were not growing.

Chris Mitchell would tell me when I was back in Australia: 'I thought the reaction to some of your stories inside Israel was more rational than the reaction of the Israel lobby in Australia. Israel, as far as I could see, took your reports seriously and launched investigations. I found it odd that they could have a more open debate in Israel than in Australia. Of all the Jewish groups I found AIJAC the most hardline.'

The longer I was in Israel, the more I realised that key figures in the Australian Jewish community sat on the far right of the Israeli political spectrum. In Israel I was able to have meaningful discussions with key army or intelligence figures about the

Palestinian issue. But with many of Australia's Jewish leaders this was just not possible. It was almost as if they felt that, given they were not living in Israel, they needed to take a harder line than many people who were living there.

On 25 April 2012 – Israeli Independence Day – Sylvie and I were at a function put on for foreign journalists by an Israeli research group at Jerusalem's Mamilla Hotel. We found ourselves talking to a senior Israeli Army officer. He happened to be extremely familiar with Australia, having visited several times and had had regular contact with the Australian Jewish community. Over a drink, this officer opened up. He painted an extraordinary picture of the Israeli lobby in Australia. 'The Israel lobby in Australia,' he said, 'is the most powerful lobby in the world in terms of impact it has within its own country.'

I replied that surely AIPAC – the lobby group so feared in the US by aspiring members of Congress – must dwarf AIJAC, the equivalent in Australia. He insisted I was wrong.

I have looked at the diaspora in the United States, the UK, France and other places, and in my view, pound for pound, Australia's Jewish community is the most influential in any country.

Firstly, Australia has the highest number of Holocaust survivors per capita outside Israel. This helps shape the political view of the lobby and that view is not really challenged by anyone. The lobby in Australia is small but united – it does not have the sort of competition AIPAC has in the US from J-Street. Groups such as J-Street have emerged and are now getting access to both the Congress and the White House. In Australia, while the

Jewish community is small – 100,000 or something – it is extremely united.

The Jewish community in Australia is also very wealthy – look at the Rich Lists each year and you will see in the top 20 or so a strong representation of Jewish businessmen. And these are businessmen who strongly support Israel.

And then the community itself is much more strongly Zionist than in the US. It's not as intermarried as the US Jewish community and about 70 per cent of Australian Jews have been to Israel.

According to the *Jerusalem Post*, Australia's Jewish community numbers about 120,000, out of a population of 25 million. Most live in the big cities – about 60,000 in Melbourne, 45,000 in Sydney and 8000 in Perth. A leader of the community, Dr Ron Weiser, has estimated that approximately 10 per cent of the community – about 12,000 people – had made Aliyah and moved to Israel, while many others travelled there regularly. 'The Australian Jewish community is one of the most pro-Zionist and Israel-connected in the world,' he said.[2]

The high level of support for Israel in Australia's Jewish community is often reflected by Australia's politicians. I was invited to a lunch for Israeli journalists in Jerusalem. One had just been to Australia on an organised trip, and when we were introduced she said to me: 'I love Australia! You guys talk Zionism better than we do!'

I asked her what she meant. 'Everybody down there loves Israel. We met your Opposition Leader [Tony Abbott], who told us how much he loved Israel. We thought he was fantastic, but then we met Prime Minister [Julia] Gillard. She was even better. They were saying things you would not normally hear an Israeli say!'

*

The relentless efforts of the pro-Israel lobby have been reaping political benefits for hardline supporters of Israel.

On a warm summer's evening in Jerusalem, a who's who of Australian politics arrived for a banquet at the magnificent King David Hotel. It was 27 July 2014, and the group included prominent members of the Liberal Party such as Christopher Pyne, the Leader of the House; Queensland Senator James McGrath; and Brian Loughnane, the party's Federal Director. Key figures in the Labor Party were also arriving, including West Australian Senator Glenn Sterle, MPs Michael Danby and David Feeney, and former MP Mary Easson, a key player in shaping the Labor Party's policy towards Israel. Australia's Ambassador to Israel, Dave Sharma, had also come along. Excellent food was being served and fine wine was flowing. I spoke later to several people who were there.

The banquet was being sponsored by Elbit, one of Israel's largest arms manufacturers. They specialised in state-of-the-art bombs, mortars and cyber-warfare systems. One of their weapons, they have boasted on their website, had 'unprecedented lethality'. On this particular night, business was booming because the Gaza War was in full flight. The Gaza Strip, an hour's drive south of the event, was under attack. The strip is an area of 365 square kilometres, and the Israeli Government Press Office (GPO) told me later that over the 50 days of the war there were 6231 targets in Gaza hit by Israeli bombs, missiles and mortars. This meant on average 17 bombs per square kilometre. Or, with 5000 people per square kilometre, one Israeli bomb for every 294 Gazans. (The GPO told me that during this same period there were 4594 rockets and mortars fired from Gaza into Israel.)

Bloomberg news reported that the war had pushed Elbit to its highest share price since 2010. It added: 'Two Israeli civilians and 43 soldiers have been killed, while more than 1100 Palestinians have died in three weeks of fighting.' Over the next three weeks, Israel would destroy 18,000 homes in Gaza, while Hamas destroyed one in Israel.

There is, of course, no such thing as a free banquet. Two days later, several members of the group travelled north to Haifa, Elbit's corporate headquarters. A lunch was put on – but the group also had to sit through an Elbit presentation. Some of Australia's most influential politicians sat listening while the company spruiked their products of war.

The banquet was one of the events on these regular trips for sympathetic politicians and journalists organised by Melbourne property developer Albert Dadon. Each December, a group was flown to Israel, the UK and Washington for the Australia–Israel–UK Leadership Dialogue. Dadon once asked me if I wanted to fly to London – with Sylvie – to be on a panel during his 'dialogue' about Israel. He seemed surprised when I said no. 'Why would you decline an invitation like this?' he asked.

I replied: 'Because if I'm part of your club I cannot write about it if at some point I need to.'

I did, however, speak to the visiting delegation in 2009 at the request of one of my editors, after I had returned to Jerusalem from covering the 2009 Iranian elections, and attended some of the group's functions as a working journalist. Dadon told me the decision to visit Elbit was his and that 'no one has the choice as to where the Dialogue will open or close except for myself'. He added that it was 'a fun trip for everyone'.

Over the years Dadon has hosted scores of politicians, including Kevin Rudd, Julia Gillard, Peter Costello, George Brandis, Bronwyn Bishop, Mark Dreyfus, Michael Danby, Kimberley Kitching, Andrew Landeryou, Tim Wilson, Tim Watts and Bernie Rippoll. The most enthusiastic invitee is Christopher Pyne, who has taken seven trips to Israel, four of which were organised by Albert Dadon.

In 2010, over dinner in Jerusalem, Dadon began talking to his group about Morocco, his country of birth. 'Who would like to go to Morocco?' he asked the group. Several guests were delighted to accept the offer – including Christopher Pyne. Dadon's secretary booked the flights. Dadon told me that the Government of Morocco had agreed to pick up the bill for all airfares, accommodation and other expenses while the group was in Morocco. Even years later, Christopher Pyne was not sure who had paid for that trip, telling me: 'I understood the [Dadon] Dialogue covered the costs.'

Life was good.

*

Albert Dadon had undoubtedly been influential in shaping Australian attitudes in Israel. But how much of the reality of the Israeli–Palestinian conflict did he really know?

Dadon and I had never met back in Australia, but in late 2010 he phoned to say he was going to arrive in Israel a few days before his annual December 'dialogue' and wanted to catch up. He asked me for suggestions about what he could do before his guests arrived.

I suggested he should travel to Hebron with Sylvie and me and take a tour with Breaking the Silence. This is a group of serving and retired Israeli combat soldiers who have provided testimony of what they have done or witnessed in the West Bank or Gaza, in the hope that the Israeli public will realise that an occupation is, by its nature, destructive.

I told Dadon that in Hebron he'd see the conflict up close. 'Is it safe to go?' he asked.

'Sylvie and I would not be going there with you if it wasn't safe,' I replied. 'We have no intention of making Jack an orphan.'

And so it was that Dadon agreed to come to Hebron on 6 December 2010. Sylvie and I jumped into our car and picked him up at his Jerusalem hotel, then picked up Mikhael Manekin, a former Israeli Army officer and member of Breaking the Silence. I drove and Dadon sat next to me, with Sylvie and Mikhael in the back. The drive to Hebron took about 45 minutes. Along the way we saw two completely different mindsets: that of Dadon, a supporter of Israel who lived in Australia, and Manekin, a supporter of Israel who lived in Israel.

Dadon peppered Manekin with questions; it soon became clear that he was checking Manekin's credentials. There was a distinct undertone of: 'If you are going to be part of a group that criticises Israel you need to have earned the right to do so.' I looked in the mirror at Manekin and detected a certain bemusement. It was, indeed, a bizarre situation: Dadon – a Moroccan-born French-speaking property developer from Melbourne – checking the credentials of a Hebrew-speaking

Israeli-born Israeli who had been part of the Israeli Army and still served in its reserve forces.

As we drove into Hebron, Dadon asked why there were so many Palestinian women walking up the hill on either side of us. 'Because they're not allowed to drive on this road,' I answered.

Dadon was stunned. Despite having hosted dozens of conferences about Israel, it was clear he had never experienced the reality of the occupation. Hebron was having exactly the same impact on him as it had on me all those years ago. After walking around Hebron for a while, Dadon wanted to leave. I told him that he hadn't seen the worst of it – including the sections where the Palestinians' front doors had been sealed by the army. 'I've seen enough,' he said. 'I'm upset that all this is being done in my name.'

On the drive back to Jerusalem, Dadon was silent for a while. Finally, he said: 'John, there are two people that you should bring to Hebron for one of these tours with Breaking the Silence – Michael Danby and Itamar Marcus.' Danby was the Federal Labor member from Melbourne and a strident supporter of Israel, and Itamar Marcus was the publisher of *Palestinian Media Watch*. 'It might change Michael's view and Itamar's presentations,' he said. Dadon would tell me later: '[The trip] opened my eyes. This is the dark side of a society that you don't want to face but when you face it you come out more informed. What I saw that day was not Jewish.'

Without realising it, when Dadon said that what he'd seen in Hebron was 'not Jewish', what he was saying was that the occupation of the West Bank was not Jewish. Israeli lobby groups realise that Hebron is a public relations disaster so like to portray it as an oddity, but what happens in Hebron is exactly the same as what happens throughout the West Bank.

*

Five days later I was in Cairo, covering a visit by Foreign Minister Kevin Rudd. At a news conference, he spoke about his desire for Iran to agree to regular international inspections of its nuclear facilities. An Egyptian journalist asked: if Iran and other nations had to agree to inspections, why shouldn't Israel? Rudd remarked that he could not dispute the logic, and agreed that all countries with nuclear weapons should have to submit to regular inspections.

My ears pricked up. I knew Israel preferred that nobody even referred to their nuclear weapons, let alone talked about inspections. In fact, under Israel's archaic military censorship system, the Israeli media are not even allowed to report on Israel's nuclear weapons unless they are drawing on foreign media sources.

So after the news conference I asked Rudd if he could elaborate on his comments. He told me: 'Our view has been consistent for a long period of time, and that is that all States in the region should adhere to the NPT [Non-Proliferation Treaty], and that includes Israel. And therefore their nuclear facility should be subject to IAEA [International Atomic Energy Agency] inspection.'

Soon afterwards, Rudd was a guest at one of Albert Dadon's banquets at the King David Hotel in Jerusalem. Sylvie and I went along to cover the event. The evening had been going calmly – Christopher Pyne had given a passionate speech about his commitment to Israel – when the mood in the room suddenly changed. An unwelcome guest had just arrived at the banquet, courtesy of the internet. My interview with Kevin Rudd in which he declared that Israel should not be exempt from international inspections had just been published online. People were standing looking at their phones and reading the story. The anger started bouncing off the walls.

Sylvie came over to me: 'That man over there is telling people that you've verballed Kevin Rudd in your interview!'

'That man' was Yuval Rotem, Israel's Ambassador to Australia – who had travelled to Jerusalem for this trip. Last time I'd spoken to Rotem was in the cafeteria at *The Australian*'s head office in Sydney when, ironically, he'd praised me for a series of articles about Kevin Rudd. But tonight it suited him to attack me instead.

By now it was fair to say I was pretty fired up. So often people instinctively blame the messenger if they don't like what someone has said. And so I went looking for Rotem. 'Ambassador, I hear you are telling people that Kevin Rudd did not make those comments about nuclear inspectors.'

Rotem seemed uncomfortable that I had challenged him. 'Well, no Australian foreign minister has ever said that before,' he answered. 'Why would Kevin Rudd say it?'

'Don't you think that's a question for you to ask Kevin Rudd?' I responded. There are two tapes of that interview – I have one and Mr Rudd's staff have one. Would you like a copy? And Mr Rudd is just over there ...'

Just then Rudd's chief of staff, Philip Green, walked past. I beckoned him over. 'Philip, Mr Rotem is saying Foreign Minister Rudd never called for international inspectors for Israel's nuclear facilities.'

'He did,' replied Green. 'We have no problem with your story.'

I then went looking for Danby, who was also telling people in the room he doubted the story, and explained the same thing to him. Danby then switched his anger from me to Rudd. 'I'm going to take this up with Andrea Faulkner,' he said, referring to the Australian Ambassador to Israel. (Rudd was standing 20 metres away – but Danby had backed Julia Gillard when she deposed Rudd, and I knew he and Rudd rarely spoke.)

Now that it was clear that the quotes were not made up, the gates of fury opened against Kevin Rudd. The next morning I saw huddles in the foyer of the King David Hotel as different groups from Dadon's delegation discussed the issue.

Dadon told me that while theoretically Israel should be under the same regime of inspections as anyone else, in reality they should be exempt. He was going to talk to Rudd and insist that he say at his upcoming press conference with Israeli Foreign Minister Avigdor Lieberman that Israel had 'unique security circumstances'.

At the press conference, Lieberman addressed the nuclear issue. 'What is important is not whether any country is a member of the NPT [Non-Proliferation Treaty] but whether it is responsible,' he said. 'Israel does not regard any inspection as necessary, as it is a responsible country, and we have proved this for many years.'

Then came Rudd's turn to speak. He concentrated more on Iran's situation, saying Australia was deeply concerned about Iran's nuclear program. Then he mentioned Israel. 'We recognise ... Israel's unique security circumstances ... but in terms of our fundamental position on the Nuclear Non-Proliferation Treaty, as it applies to this region ... all States should be in, including Israel.'

And so, while he had restated his position, he had added the words that Dadon told me he had wanted him to add.

Dadon could not come to the press conference but, knowing that I was going along, telephoned me at home that night. He asked: 'Did Kevin use the phrase "unique security circumstances?"'

'Yes,' I said.

'Good.'

*

Fast-forward to late 2012, and a new foreign minister, Bob Carr, was facing the diplomatic quandary of how Australia should vote on 29 November when the United Nations General Assembly considered a resolution to upgrade the UN Observer status of the Palestinian delegation from 'Entity' to 'Non-member State'. It would mean Palestine could call upon assistance from the UN, and even prosecute for war crimes.

Former Labor Foreign Minister and head of the International Crisis Group Gareth Evans told Carr that to vote against it would be the worst Australian foreign policy decision in a generation, and put Australia on the wrong side of history. Evans carried a message from former Labor Prime Minister Bob Hawke reiterating the opinion that Australia could not vote against the motion and kill any Palestinian hopes of their own State. Within the Labor Party this was a powerful trio; Hawke, Evans and Carr, all from the right wing, all long-time supporters of Israel.

When I interviewed Carr for this book, he told me: 'From my point of view, I believed that voting in favour of the upgraded status would send a message to the Palestinians that there was hope for them, they had friends and supporters in the world, including nations who have strongly supported Israel's right to exist provided they continued to cleave to the peaceful path. It would send a message to the Israelis that their arrogant expansion of settlements and their mistreatment of Palestinians on the West Bank and Gaza was losing them nations that had previously been strong friends. It could only do good.'

Carr was also surprised by how many on the centre and right of the Labor Party supported his position. The initial thinking was that Australia would abstain from the vote, but he became convinced that there was enough support for Australia to vote yes. 'It's as if years of watching the news out of the West Bank had produced this shift,' Carr reflected. 'That is the only way I can explain it, the impact of what had been happening year in, year out in the West Bank. In the Labor Party, no one could defend the expansion of settlements which are clearly designed to prevent the establishment of the Palestinian State and no one could overlook the heartlessness and the cruelty that a right-wing Israeli cabinet under Benjamin Netanyahu was now directing at a majority Palestinian population.'

Armed with the knowledge that his own New South Wales right-wing faction was supporting him, Carr entered the Cabinet room in Canberra on 26 November. He told me that when the UN vote was discussed, 'I was surprised by the strength behind a pro-Palestinian vote. There were people there who I had not spoken to about the issue. I had no idea that Simon Crean, for example, given his background with the Victorian right, would launch out strongly, or that Craig Emerson would lay down his support. I had no idea that was Peter Garrett's view. I had never had a conversation with him about it.'

But there was one obstacle to Carr's push to change Labor Party policy: the Prime Minister. Gillard had made public the fact that her personal position was to support Israel and oppose the resolution. This was not the first time Gillard and Carr had clashed on issues concerning Israel. Carr explained to me: 'As Foreign Minister I was blocked from making criticisms of Israeli settlement expansion by Bruce Wolpe in the Prime Minister's Office.' Wolpe had been tasked by Gillard with liaising with Australia's Jewish community.

At the Cabinet meeting, Julia Gillard adopted what in Carr's view was an 'utterly remarkable' position. 'The bottom line of what she was saying was that despite the opposition from Cabinet it was still her call. For someone like me who had chaired Cabinet meetings, it was surprising. I thought the wiser course would be to say, "Well, you have strong views on this, and I will consider the opinions around the Cabinet table and I might reflect further overnight."'

As they left Cabinet, Carr made a plea to Gillard: 'Please reconsider your position overnight. It's very clear, despite all the free trips to Israel, that at the Cabinet table and in the Caucus, based on the evidence out of the West Bank, there is a majority who want to vote yes to upgrading the Palestinian status.'

That night, working late, Carr wandered through the ministerial suite in Parliament House. He came across Treasurer Wayne Swan, who was in his office talking to Defence Minister Stephen Smith. Swan and Smith, Carr recalled, were 'just shaking their heads with disbelief' that the situation regarding the vote had got to where it was.

'What do we do now?' Carr asked them. He was conscious of the fact that both Swan and Smith were strong Gillard supporters and determined to prevent any return to Kevin Rudd as PM. Gillard's prime ministership was coming under growing pressure. That morning, *The Australian* had published a Newspoll showing that, as she prepared to begin the final parliamentary sitting week of the year, she was facing electoral defeat by 51 to 49 per cent, based on the preference flow from the previous election. 'This is not a pro-Rudd move,' Carr told them. 'It's just a move on the basis of the evidence, Australia's diplomatic position and Australia's reputation for fair play in the UN, a principled position, it has nothing to do with Rudd's position.'

Carr was surprised that the Rudd forces had been slow to exploit what amounted to a revolt against Gillard. 'At this point, there had been no speculation in the media whatsoever. I sure as hell was not leaking it because of the high probability that at the end of the day my position would not get up,' Carr said. 'I had no interest in leaking it. I did not want to destabilise the government anyway, but as it turned out, from this Cabinet debate there was nothing in the media. The Rudd forces had not caught up with the divisions. It was uncharacteristic of them. Normally they were after any potential mischief to hurt Julia.'

The next morning, Carr dropped around to see Gillard in her office. Despite his words to her the previous night, it was clear that she thought the Carr motion would not pass. Carr repeated that he had no doubt there was sufficient support in Caucus for a motion that Australia should abstain from supporting Israel at the UN. 'When I left her office she was somewhat shocked,' Carr said to me.

Meanwhile, the 102 members of Labor's Caucus gathered with a sense of anticipation. Most were about to vote for a position with which their Prime Minister disagreed. Gillard turned up late and immediately outlined her support for Israel and a two-State solution. But, realising that she had little backing in Caucus, she ended the speech by accepting that Australia would not vote with Israel in opposing the Palestinian upgrading but instead would abstain.

After the meeting, Gillard and Carr met and agreed that Carr would attempt to protect Gillard by appearing as soon as possible on Sky News to praise her for changing her position. They discussed how Bob Hawke had reversed his position under party pressure over the MX missile issue. (Hawke had confirmed an agreement made by the preceding Liberal government for the US to land two MX missiles in the Tasman Sea – but after a party backlash he backed away from it.)

Many in Israel were surprised that one side of the Australian political system had broken from unconditional support for Israel. Israeli journalist Gideon Levy praised the changes Bob Carr had made to the Labor Party's position. 'It always seemed that Australia was a lost cause,' Levy said. 'It's very good news.' According to Levy, if more members of the Jewish community in Australia knew the reality of modern Israel they would push for change.

Meanwhile, the Rudd forces seized on the issue, leaking to the media how Gillard had been 'rolled' after resisting the view of the majority of the Cabinet. The next day the story hit the media, and the rivalry between Kevin Rudd and Julia Gillard took off, leading to Rudd's eventual 'revenge coup' against Gillard. At the following election, which Kevin Rudd and a divided Labor Party lost to Tony Abbott, Carr retired from politics.

*

Carr's first bruising battle with elements of Australia's Jewish community began when he was Premier of New South Wales.

Each year, the Peace Centre at Sydney University chooses a recipient of the Sydney Peace Prize. In 2003, the centre selected prominent Christian Palestinian politician Hanan Ashrawi, a woman who has long argued for a peaceful two-State solution to the Israeli–Palestinian conflict. An invitation arrived on Carr's desk for him to present the award. He decided to accept, reasoning that 'if we encourage Palestinian leaders like Hanan Ashrawi who favour a negotiated peace path to nationhood surely we are helping to produce a peace where Israel is secure'.

But Carr had no idea of what was about to be unleashed upon him by sections of the Jewish community. 'All hell breaks loose,' he recalled in our interview.

The Peace Centre board included two conservatives: Kathryn Greiner, wife of Nick Greiner, Carr's Liberal predecessor as premier; and Lucy Turnbull, the Lord Mayor of Sydney and wife of Malcolm Turnbull, then trying to gain pre-selection for the Sydney seat of Wentworth and who would go on to become prime minister.

> There's talk of an online petition, we are getting protest
> calls at the office, there are attacks in the Jewish media and
> there is pressure on Kathryn Greiner and Lucy Turnbull
> to withdraw support. The Chancellor of Sydney University,
> retired judge Kim Santow, starts to respond to pressure.
> There is pressure on him from donors to the University
> of Sydney to close down this event. It was classic Jewish
> lobbying – classic. Threatening to withdraw money, punish
> people and to extract political retaliation if people did not
> withdraw.

While Carr was coming under pressure, so too was the director of the Sydney Peace Foundation, Professor Stuart Rees. But while both battled opposition, they were receiving extraordinary support. Carr told me there was no other issue during his time as premier over which he received such strong public backing.

Reflecting on the time, Kathryn Greiner told me years later that she withdrew her support for Ashrawi because she thought 'the greater good' was in the preservation of the foundation, and that if they went ahead with the award they would lose corporate funding. She believed the foundation had never recovered from the episode. But she clearly felt resentment at the demands placed upon her.

> There was huge pressure from the Jewish lobby not to go
> through with the award. I withdrew from the award, as
> did Lucy. Malcolm [Turnbull] would have been told in
> no uncertain terms that support for his preselection battle
> against Peter King in Wentworth would have gone back
> to Peter King if Lucy did not withdraw from supporting
> Hanan Ashrawi. I got the impression Lucy was under
> attack from a number of directions.
>
> On reflection, I regret that in this country people so
> forcefully put opposition to our decision. That is not the
> Australian way. The pressure that the Jewish lobby applied
> was far greater than warranted. I think you'd have to call it
> a form of bullying. If attacks come at you from a multitude
> of areas I think you can call it bullying and harassment.

As for Carr, today he considers the campaign against him by elements of the Jewish community as extremely unfair. 'I used to run a factional party school where I drummed into the members of the right faction that support for Israel was in our DNA because we had been shaped by the Israeli Labor Party, because Israel only wanted to survive within secure boundaries, because it was a democracy and a social democracy. And even before I entered Parliament I had launched Labor Friends of Israel in the Sydney Trades Hall in 1977.'

Despite a massive campaign of intimidation, Hanan Ashrawi's voice was heard. Ashrawi, Bob Carr and others refused to be silenced. But such voices of moderation have not been heard enough in Australia, or indeed in other countries.

In 2012, then Prime Minister Julia Gillard convinced Bob Carr to come out of retirement. As Foreign Minister, one of his Cabinet colleagues was Mark Dreyfus, the Attorney General. But that relationship soured after Carr left politics and began the Australia China Relations Institute, funded by Chinese businessman Huang Xiangmo. Carr was outraged when he discovered that in the early weeks of the 2016 election campaign, Dreyfus and Michael Danby had gone to see Mr Huang. Carr told me:

> The purpose of the visit by the two Labor figures was to
> protest that I had the audacity to occasionally criticise Israel
> for spreading settlements on the West Bank. As it happened,
> I simply restated the policy of the Labor government that
> Dreyfus and I had been a part of and I used language little
> different from that used by the Obama administration. The
> implication of the Dreyfus–Danby meeting with Huang
> was that he should use his position as financial supporter
> of the think-tank that employed me to press me to cease
> expressing my opinion about Israel. It was, without any
> doubt, an attempt to pull levers to silence me from making

points I'd made, on behalf of the last Labor Government of which Dreyfus and I were part.

(When told of Mr Carr's claim that the meeting was an attempt to 'silence' Carr, Mr Dreyfus said: 'Bob Carr is not speaking on behalf of the former Labor Government, and should not pretend to do so. The meeting to which Mr Carr refers was private.')

*

In June 2014, the Australian Liberal Government made a dramatic change to the way it saw the Israeli–Palestinian conflict. Traditionally, Australia has accepted the view that the West Bank was 'occupied' by Israel after the 1967 war. This is a term that many Israeli politicians and even military lawyers accept; Israel's Supreme Court stated in 2004 that 'Israel holds the area in belligerent occupation'. Soon after I arrived in Israel, I asked an Israeli military commander, Lieutenant Colonel Eliezer Toledano, the operations officer for the Israeli Army in the West Bank, whether he regarded the West Bank as 'occupied'. He looked puzzled. I explained that for years the pro-Israel lobby in Melbourne had insisted to me that the West Bank was not 'occupied'. 'If this is not occupied then the media has missed one of the biggest stories of your time, our withdrawal from the West Bank,' the commander responded, laughing.

So when, in 2014, Foreign Minister Julie Bishop and Attorney General George Brandis tried to walk away from describing East Jerusalem as 'occupied', it signalled a major shift in policy. It put Australia at odds with most countries, as well as the European Union and United Nations.

Bishop and Brandis issued a statement that read: 'The description of areas which are subject to negotiations in the course of the peace process by reference to historical events is unhelpful. The description of East Jerusalem as "Occupied East Jerusalem" is a term freighted with pejorative implications, which is neither appropriate nor useful.'

The move, however, had an unintended consequence for Australia's farmers: the Arab world threatened to stop their imports of sheep meat, beef and wheat, amounting to billions of dollars. Bishop met 18 diplomats from the region and told them that she was using the word 'occupied' with a small 'o' rather than a big 'O'. While some were bemused by this, when she said that there was no change in the government's position on the legal status of the Palestinian Territories, it headed off a trade crisis.

Three weeks later, SBS went even further, instructing its staff not even to use the word 'disputed'. A 'Dear all' memo to staff dated 19 June 2014 said: 'Palestinians refer to occupied territories and Israelis to disputed territories. Over time, this language has been adopted in discussions at the highest level to indicate a particular political perspective on the ownership of this territory. It is incumbent on SBS to be impartial, so to ensure fairness in our reporting we will use geographical terms.' Somehow, SBS was convinced that the term 'occupied territories' was one proffered by the Palestinians. In fact, it's the term used in international law and, regarding the West Bank, by virtually every country in the world.

An attachment to the email went into further detail: 'When discussing territory whose status remains the subject of negotiation, care must be taken to ensure that the language used is neutral and cannot be interpreted as being favourable to one side over another. The best way to achieve this is to describe the geographic location of the settlements – for example, *Israeli settlements on the West Bank* or *Israeli settlements on the outskirts of Jerusalem* or similar. We should avoid describing settlements as on Palestinian land or on disputed land, or occupied territories.' While those behind the change of policy at SBS might not even have realised it, what they had done was align SBS with the far right of Israeli politics. AIJAC and the rest of the Israeli lobby must have been delighted.

Journalists who write about Israel – even if they do not live there – can enjoy a very pleasant life on one condition: that they never mention the occupation. You can have all-expenses-paid trips to Israel. You can stay at the best hotels and eat at the best restaurants. You can be invited to speak at conferences in Australia, Israel or London. Your spouse will have their airfare paid also. You will be made to feel important. Your editors will be told what a good journalist you are. But to get all of this you must never mention the occupation nor make any serious criticism of Israel. Many journalists comply.

But others do not. The legendary Australian correspondent Peter Cave reported from almost everywhere over a 40-year career at the ABC. Yet after reporting some criticisms of Israel, Cave was attacked, as he told me, by 'a sort of secret society fighting on Israel's behalf against the evil biased media and the ABC in particular'. The group prepared dossiers on him and other ABC reporters and sent them to like-minded journalists and members of Parliament. They took their case against Cave's 'bias' to the Australian Broadcasting Authority. It took two years, but Cave was cleared of bias.

Cave decided to infiltrate the group. Under an assumed name, he joined them 'to keep an eye on them' and began receiving complaints about himself. To build credibility with the group, Cave began defaming himself – 'I'd send them notes such as "You know Cave's got form as a neo-Nazi" or "Cave's a well-known anti-Semite". I busily defamed myself and they clearly loved it by their reactions.'

It worked. Cave's aim was to find out what complaints were being planned against him. He began to receive emails along the lines of: 'We're planning to make complaints against Peter Cave next week.' The group discussed who should complain and about which stories – they even sent Peter Cave the wording that he should use in his formal complaint about himself. He was therefore able to warn his managers of imminent complaints. Eventually, the group wanted him to come to a meeting in Sydney. This presented a problem, of course, for the recognisable Cave. 'I'm very sorry, but I'm disabled and can't leave my house,' he told them. 'I think they cottoned on to me,' Cave told me.

I came to realise that hardline Jewish groups in Australia commonly targeted journalists. One such campaign led to an extraordinary process inside the ABC.

The ABC's Sophie McNeill was targeted from the moment her appointment was announced in February 2015. AIJAC published a dossier which amounted to a comprehensive attack on her. It was authored by Ahron Shapiro and posted onto AIJAC's website. Headlined 'Should the ABC have given advocacy journalist Sophie McNeill the keys to its Jerusalem bureau?', it went on: 'There are serious questions that must be raised about whether Sophie McNeill, who has recently been appointed the ABC's exclusive Jerusalem-based Middle East correspondent, can comply with the obligations contained in ABC's Code of Practice.'

The dossier said that McNeill had appeared on a panel where she was 'speaking alongside' two people who had supported Boycott, Divestment and Sanctions (BDS) against Israel. The case against McNeill included that she once said in an interview: 'One of the saddest things I've seen in my whole life is spending time filming in a children's cancer ward in Gaza.' On this charge, I could also be indicted – one of the saddest things I've ever seen was a baby dying in a children's hospital in Gaza because the hospital could not get through the Israeli checkpoint the medicines required to keep him alive.

The sourcing of much of AIJAC's material was questionable. It said: 'According to the account of a Palestinian student who summarised from a personal video she made of the event ...' AIJAC said McNeill's 'apparent role at the event was to inspire student activities through her first-hand accounts from Gaza, and she appeared eager to play the part'. Apparent role? It continued, 'according to the Tweet of one attendee, she spurred the audience on'. The Tweet of one attendee? McNeill's appearance at the conference, AIJAC said, 'was tantamount to joining a protest movement'. Tantamount to? The standard of allegation made in AIJAC's attacks on journalists often did not come anywhere near the standard of sourcing of material that they demanded from the journalists they were attacking.

The dossier also targeted McNeill for a story she had done looking at Israel's ultra-Orthodox Jewish community. 'McNeill promotes the narrative that Israeli Jewry as a society is radicalising in terms of its Jewish character through the demographic growth of the ultra-Orthodox.' The 'implied message', AIJAC said, was that 'Israel is not really the pluralistic Western society it purports to be but is shifting towards religious radicalism'. Implied message? Of all the absurdities in the dossier, to me this was the most bizarre. Israel's own media is full of stories about the rising number – and power – of the ultra-Orthodox. Given their high birth rates – many have seven or eight children – they are increasing as a proportion of the community.

After publishing the dossier, AIJAC wrote to the board of the ABC, referencing it. The letter set off an extraordinary – perhaps unprecedented – chain of events. The chairman of the board, Jim Spigelman, asked the managing director, Mark Scott, for a response. Scott then instructed the corporation's editorial policies department to prepare a response. Senior managers in the news and current affairs department were also enlisted. Scott believed that the ABC's selection process was thorough, and was unhappy that a lobby group had the power to require the ABC to have to defend an appointment. 'I will not cower to AIJAC,' he told his managers.

The ABC's managers answered each claim, taking more than three weeks. The process included putting to McNeill each AIJAC accusation against her. The AIJAC attack also said that McNeill had credited British journalist John Pilger as being an influence on her – when she was 15. To her ABC managers, McNeill pleaded guilty to this charge but said his influence was in alerting her to the situation in East Timor when she was 15. In fact, McNeill was critical of Pilger – she said that she believed Pilger's politics had 'blinded him' to the situation in Syria.

Mark Scott was particularly angered by the parts of the dossier which attacked McNeill for who she may have spoken alongside on panels. 'Here is a professional journalist like Sophie McNeill subject to a whole lot of attacks which in my view were trying to taint her by association,' Scott told his managers.

Scott wrote for the ABC board a 12-page response to AIJAC's letter. In it he said that while AIJAC did not call for McNeill's appointment to be reviewed or reversed, despite raising a series of critical questions and concerns about her 'past activities' – 'they were letting us know they would be watching'. Scott told the board that he had engaged in dialogue as a media executive for almost two decades. 'In that time, I have seen similar dossiers to the one created on Sophie McNeill on other journalists and around coverage of issues. The AIJAC website contains detailed, negative coverage of many leading Australian journalists who have reported on the Middle East, including Paul McGeough, John Lyons, Ed O'Loughlin and Ruth Pollard, as well as reporters from the BBC and *The Guardian*.'

Scott added: 'The article demonstrates to Sophie McNeill and to the ABC that her every word will be watched closely by AIJAC and she starts on the ground with this key interest group sceptical. We are all aware she will be under even closer scrutiny now. As they seek to influence our coverage, this is a pre-emptive "shot across the bows". It should be noted, of course, that fair, impartial, accurate and balanced coverage from McNeill will not guarantee her immunity from ongoing criticism.' Scott told the board: 'The pre-emptive attack on McNeill is similar to the approach employed by lobby groups internationally. The US reporter, Jodi Rudoren, was targeted when she was appointed Jerusalem bureau chief for the *New York Times* in 2012 and accused of being biased against Israel and unsuitable for the post … The *New York Times* refused to bow to the pressure and Rudoren remained in the position.'

On 30 March 2015, Scott presented the response to Spigelman. The defence, and AIJAC's attack, went to the April meeting of the board. The board supported Scott. The whole process had taken enormous resources inside the ABC. In my view, no other lobby group in Australia would be able to command that level of response. This is real power. And as a journalist I believe that such efforts can have the effect of making a journalist or organisation self-censor. This would not prove to be the case with McNeill. However, in my opinion such a process certainly puts pressure on a reporter, raising the possibility of what is known in journalism as 'the pre-emptive buckle'.

*

During my time in Israel I would come to believe that Australia's uncritical support of Israel is both illogical and unhealthy. In 2012 I talked to Israeli filmmaker Dror Moreh about this. Moreh had just released *The Gatekeepers*, a documentary film in which he interviewed all the living former chiefs of Shin Bet. Moreh had a message for overseas Jewish communities: 'I think that the Jews in the diaspora have a guilty conscience because the Israelis are here, they are fighting for the survival of the country, and we [the diaspora] have to support that no matter what.'

In Israel there's a growing backlash against the hardline position of Australia's Jewish community. Leading Israeli journalist Akiva Eldar, who has family in Sydney and has become familiar with Australia's Jewish leadership, told me:

I'm willing to be on record and tell the AIJAC people and the Australian Government that they are playing with my future, that they don't give a shit about my children, it's about their arses. It is annoying, because it has nothing to do with the real, strategic, existential interests of Israel. Australia should understand that in the US, Israel is a domestic political issue. Australia has to look at its relationship with Israel independently, because the US is not innocently looking at it. I tell my Australian friends and family that you live in Australia and even if you tell your government not to interfere, to take a step back and say nothing, this plays into the hands of the Likud, because this is exactly what Netanyahu wants you to do. He wants business as usual. There is a clear distinction between supporting Israel and supporting the Israeli Government and Israeli policy. If Australia voted in favour of a Palestinian State along 1967 lines it would be very difficult for the Israeli Government to smear them and say they are anti-Semites, because you have a very clean record.

Gideon Levy echoed the warning: 'As long as Israelis do not pay for the occupation and as long as they are not punished for the occupation they will not go for any change. It was true about South Africa and it's true about here. Start to push Israel, economically and politically; that's the only way to deal with Israel. Israel does not know any other language.'

Levy said that, as difficult as it is for him to call for an economic boycott of his home country, this is a better alternative than the current course, which will lead to 'terrible bloodshed'. He added: 'All this policy of carrots will never work with Israel.'

I asked Levy his response to claims from Australia's Jewish community that people like him are 'de-legitimising Israel'.

'One hour of photos from Gaza de-legitimises Israel much more than all my articles together,' he replied.

The fact that – with rare exceptions – Australians have not heard a genuine debate about the Israeli–Palestinian conflict means that the Australian–Jewish community has missed a window when it could have warned Israel that it was going down a dangerous path. A small and hardline group in the Australian Jewish community that does not reflect the views of the broader community has been allowed to limit a debate that could have helped Israel avoid the coming crisis.

For more than 20 years, Australians have read and heard pro-Israel positions from journalists, editors, politicians, trade union leaders, academics and students who have returned from the all-expenses-paid Israel-lobby trips. As someone who has both taken one of these trips when I was the editor of the *Sydney Morning Herald* and then many years later lived in Israel for six years, I am in a position to compare what one is exposed to on these trips and the truth. In my opinion no editors, journalists or others should take these trips: they grotesquely distort the reality and are dangerous in the sense that that they allow people with a very small amount of knowledge to pollute Australian public opinion. Those on the trips return to Australia thinking they have some sort of grasp of the place, but they have spent more time in Tel Aviv's most expensive restaurants and cafes and in settlements than looking at the real crisis behind trying to continue an occupation against another people. The effect of these trips is to shore up opinion behind the hardline pro-settlement elements of Israeli politics. They allow Israel to avoid the public backlash that objective reporting of their settlement activity would bring.

CHAPTER 16

Eight Dead Omars

June 2014

IT WAS SOMETHING MENTIONED IN PASSING ON BAGHDAD RADIO. The Iraqis I was sitting with drinking tea in a café thought there was nothing particularly interesting about it – eight men with the name Omar had been found dead around Baghdad that morning. My Iraqi companions said when things got bad around the city – worse than normal – several Omars were usually found dead.

This is the type of story that stands out to a visitor. It's one of the reasons foreign correspondents are valuable as they can see things with fresh eyes. I told my Iraqi fixer I wanted this to be my next story – why were so many men with the name Omar being killed, often shot in the head or mutilated?

What I discovered in my research helped me to understand the madness of the Sunni–Shia war inside Islam. It also showed me the reality of today's Iraq.

Baghdad, this ancient, biblical city, is at the same time enchanting and horrible. My office sent me there in late 2014 because Islamic State was within 50 kilometres of the city. It was one of those requests that only journalists and aid workers get: the most bloodthirsty terrorist group of our time might be about to take over; could you get there as soon as possible?

Baghdad 'International' Airport has very little international about it. The plane made a steep descent which, I was told, was due to the security threat. Because the authorities could not guarantee that Islamic State or others would not try to shoot down incoming jets, they needed to descend sharply in a corkscrew formation. This meant that the plane descended over a small area which had been secured. To me this said everything. Despite the United States having spent US$1.06 trillion in Iraq since the invasion in 2003 – according to the US Congressional Research Service – neither the airport nor the road from the airport could be secured.

Walking out of the airport, the driver who was meant to pick me up was not there. Given the number of car bombs that had exploded at Baghdad airport, the authorities had come up with a solution – no cars near the airport. That meant you had to walk a significant distance to get a bus, which took you to the outer perimeter of the airport. Soldiers and tanks were positioned every few hundred metres along the road, until you reached a section for taxis. I had no idea who to trust, and knocked back a couple of drivers. Finally, I found someone I could trust – an unemployed journalist. I instantly bonded with this man who had become a taxi driver when his employer retrenched him.

The reality of today's Iraq – which covers much of what used to be Mesopotamia – is illustrated by the use of the 'magic wand' as a security measure. Throughout Baghdad one is stopped at security checkpoints. This is due to the number of car bombings.

To check for explosives, soldiers walk around each car with a black machine – if it detects explosives it will vibrate. Supposedly. The problem is that everyone, including the soldiers using it, knows this is a fraud. The British man who sold these to Iraq was imprisoned for fraud – he had bought parts from China and made the wands in his back shed. But even though everyone knows that, people go along with the sham. What it means is that there is no protection at all against someone going through a checkpoint with a boot full of explosives.

From my hotel balcony I could look down the magnificent Tigris River. The deep-red sun setting over the river was a magnificent backdrop. But due to the growing battle against Islamic State, the scenes played out against it could resemble *Apocalypse Now* – army helicopters snaking their way along the river as they returned to the capital after a day in the field fighting Islamic State, only 30 minutes down the road.

A telling feature of Baghdad on one trip was that as we drove around on every block or two we reached a checkpoint manned by Peruvians. The US pushed for contracted workers to replace US military personnel at the checkpoints so that should any be killed it would not add to the death toll of American servicemen and women. Some of the Peruvians worked in these dangerous jobs for a few months – sometimes paid up to $US500 a day – and then returned to Peru, loaded with cash. If they survived.

But what explained Iraq to me more than anything was 'Omar'. Omar is a name only ever given to Sunni Muslims. No Shiites would ever name their son Omar. Iranian-backed Shia militia have joined Iraqi soldiers – who are also Shia – at checkpoints around the city. If someone was stopped and his papers showed his name was Omar he was liable to be taken aside – not by the army but by the militia. That gave plausible deniability to the army – they could always argue that they had nothing to do with whatever happened next. But often that was the last time that person was seen alive, taken to a remote location, shot and left where they fell.

The worst group for these executions is the Iranian-backed Shia group Asaib Ahl al-Haq – the League of the Righteous. One can always tell whether the Sunni–Shia war is escalating, based on this grim barometer.

The curse of Omar.

CHAPTER 17

Sunset in Gaza

September 2014

SITTING ON A BEACH IN GAZA AS A DEEP, RICH SUN SANK INTO the Mediterranean, I listened to one of Gaza's jihadist leaders as he explained to me why sharia law would be good for Australia. 'Please tell people back home that under sharia there will be no more poor people, that everyone will be equal,' he said. 'All the natural resources of Australia will be divided equally among all Australians. I know that if you adopt sharia Australians will express sorrow and say to themselves, "Why didn't we do this earlier?"'

The speaker was Abu Hafs al-Maqdisi, leader of Jaysh al-Ummah – the Army of the Nation – one of nine Salafist groups in Gaza that believe Hamas is not pushing sharia quickly enough.

Salafism – according to Canadian expert Bruce Livesey, who has spent years studying the subject – is an ideology that claims Islam has strayed from its origins. The word *salaf* means 'ancient one', or 'predecessor', in Arabic, and refers to the companions of the Prophet Mohammed. Until the 1990s, many Salafists stayed out of the political sphere and did not advocate revolution against their rulers; rather, they called for greater adherence in one's daily life to Islam's original teachings and texts. By the mid-1990s, however, Gilles Kepel, a French political scientist and expert on Islam and the contemporary Arab world, noticed that Salafists were increasingly coming to embrace violent jihad in order to achieve their aims.

'The chief rivals of Salafi-jihadis are political Islamists, especially the Muslim Brotherhood, of which Hamas is the Palestinian branch,' the International Crisis Group's Nathan Thrall told me.

'Hamas is a Palestinian nationalist movement, it seeks to establish a Palestinian state with borders that are based on lines drawn by European officials less than 100 years ago. Salafi-jihadis, by contrast, do not have any interest in Palestinian nationalism or in the current borders of the Middle East.' As with Islamic State – their Islamist soulmate cutting a swathe of terror across Syria and Iraq – many of the Salafists in Gaza believe in caliphates rather than the 'artificial boundaries' of countries.

I asked Maqdisi what he thought of the beheadings by Islamic State. 'You must ask Islamic State,' he said. Then he added: 'You are a foreign journalist and have asked me that question, but I am not going to try to behead you.'

These Salafist groups may pose an even greater danger to Hamas than Israel does. Hamas sometimes even denies they exist – but the groups are armed and organised.

I discovered nine Salafist groups engaged in a secret war against Hamas. They are: Jaysh al-Ummah (Army of the Nation); Jaljalat (Rolling Thunder); Jaysh al-Islam (Army of Islam); Ansar al-Sunnah (Loyal Followers of Sunnah); Jund Ansar Allah (Soldiers of the Followers of Allah); the Al-Tawhid Brigades (the One God Brigades); the Al-Haman Mohammed Bin Maslamah Brigades;

the Mujahideen Shura Council (the Defenders of God Council); and Ahrar al-Watan (the Free of the Homeland). All of the groups are Sunni, all want sharia law and some endorse kidnappings.

The Army of Islam helped Hamas kidnap Israeli soldier Gilad Shalit in 2006 and kidnapped BBC journalist Alan Johnston in 2007. It was the Al-Haman Mohammed Bin Maslamah Brigades who kidnapped pro-Palestinian Italian activist Vittorio Arrigoni in 2011, then hanged him after saying he had come to Gaza 'only to spread corruption'.

Gazan journalist Hasan Jaber told me: 'Hamas are not happy to have such groups in Gaza. They don't want anyone in competition, to gain the thoughts or support of people who believe in Islam. They were very worried when they discovered the majority in these groups had left Hamas.' The rivalry has spilt over into gunfights. Hamas often raids the Salafists to seize weapons. 'At first when these groups began to emerge, Hamas began a campaign by their Islamic scholars to convince these groups to return to Hamas, but they failed,' said Jaber. 'So Hamas began to fight and arrest them.'

In 2009 Jund Ansar Allah declared the south of Gaza a caliphate. Hamas surrounded the group's principal mosque and opened fire, and 28 members of Jund Ansar Allah were killed. So deep was the hatred that Hamas then kidnapped the bodies to try to prevent funerals.

Nathan Thrall of the International Crisis Group told me: 'Salafi-jihadis are regularly arrested and suppressed by Hamas. They also have made repeated allegations of having been tortured by [Hamas] Gaza security forces. Salafi-jihadis have attacked a number of sites within Gaza that they believe to have been places of immorality.'

Added to this lethal cocktail is Islamic Jihad, a formidable rival to Hamas. While Hamas has aligned itself with Sunni powers – particularly Qatar – Islamic Jihad has aligned itself with Iran, leader of the Shia world. (Both Qatar and Iran would be more than happy for Gaza to be a problem for Israel.) One Western intelligence operative specialising in arms movements in the Middle East told me that in the 2014 war with Israel, Islamic Jihad had more lethal weapons than Hamas because theirs had been supplied by Iran, while many of Hamas's missiles were made in Gaza. The Salafists are not just at war with Hamas but also with Islamic Jihad.

The International Crisis Group warned in 2011 that isolating Gaza benefited Salafists. 'The international community's policy of snubbing Hamas [and others] and isolating Gaza has been misguided from the outset, for reasons Crisis Group long has enumerated', it reported. 'Besides condemning Gazans to a life of scarcity, it has not weakened the Islamist movement, loosened its grip over Gaza, bolstered Fatah or advanced the peace process.

'To that, one must add the assistance provided to Salafi-jihadis, who benefit from both Gaza's lack of exposure to the outside world and the apparent futility of Hamas's strategy of seeking greater engagement with the international community, restraining, until recently, attacks against Israel and limiting Islamising policies advocated by more zealous leaders.'[1]

The threat to Hamas is increasing as the Salafist groups consider becoming one entity. 'It could be bad for Hamas but it may also have benefits,' journalist Hasan Jaber said. 'Instead of talking to eight or nine groups, they will talk to one.'

Under pressure from these groups, Hamas is pushing sharia law harder. 'Hamas tried but did not succeed to establish sharia in Gaza,' Salafist leader Maqdisi told me. 'We are working with all those who want sharia.'

In 2010 a Salafist group called Free of the Homeland said that at a summer camp the United Nations Relief and Works Agency for Palestine Refugees in the Near East (UNRWA) was 'teaching schoolgirls fitness, dancing and immorality'. Two days later the camp was attacked, prompting UNRWA chief John Ging to declare: 'It is an attack on the happiness of children.' Three years later Hamas banned girls from the annual Gaza marathon, despite the fact that a record 1500 schoolchildren had registered. The UNRWA, which organised the marathon, pulled out in protest. Now Hamas will not allow boys and girls to attend the same camps.

Many in Israel say these groups are more dangerous than Hamas. I asked Maqdisi for his thoughts on Israel. 'For Jews, as humans, they have the right to live,' he told me. 'But Jews as a State, and an occupier, must not exist in Palestine and it must be destroyed from the universe. Israel must be destroyed.'

But these groups need to defeat Hamas before they can launch their own attack against Israel.

*

Maqdisi was nervous about our meeting, changing the venue several times. He had reason to be paranoid: both Israel and Hamas see him as an enemy. Hamas imprisoned him once during a crackdown; he hobbled to our table because of injuries from battles with Israel.

He asked whether there was any chance sharia law would be implemented in Australia. I told him I thought it would be a tough sell – for starters, women, 50 per cent of the electorate, may not like sharia status. 'Women are weak,' he responded. 'Men can protect them. Men can work more than women.'

I told him I did not think this approach would be a winner in Australia. He seemed not to understand. We bade farewell and he hobbled off into the sunset.

*

By now we had only a few more months before we returned to Australia. *The Australian* was happy for me to extend the posting, but Jack had just turned 14 and we thought it would be best for him to be settled into school in Sydney in the lead-up to his HSC. Knowing that this would probably be my last trip to Gaza, I drove back to the Erez Crossing to return to Israel feeling quite depressed. The fact that after 50 years of occupation of the West Bank a Palestinian State is further away than ever only strengthens Hamas's support – they tell their supporters that Fatah's policy of negotiating with Israel and cooperating on security issues has failed. Their argument is that any policy which has resulted in more Israeli settlers, more settlements and more outposts is the wrong approach.

Hamas survives politically because, to this point, the moderates of Fatah have not been able to deliver anything substantial for their constituency. Hamas retains significant political support by peddling the promise that a more militant approach might get better results. This is, of course, irrational. With the strongest army in the Middle East, Israel is not going to be forced into any sort of political accommodation by the militant forces of a trapped enclave.

Former Israeli Ambassador to the US Michael Oren observed that Israel's preferred outcome in Gaza was a 'de-fanged Hamas'.[2] And despite its often violent past, there are indications that Hamas may be heading in that direction. As a study commissioned and published by the United States Institute of Peace concluded: 'Hamas has, in practice, moved well beyond its charter. Indeed, Hamas has been carefully and consciously adjusting its political program for years and has sent repeated signals that it may be ready to begin a process of coexisting with Israel ... Although Hamas would not directly participate in peace negotiations with Israel, Hamas has indicated that it would be willing to be part of a Palestinian coalition government with Fatah under which Fatah would negotiate the actual treaty.'[3]

The only real solution is if Israel makes a deal with the moderates in the Palestinian movement – the Palestinian Authority – and Hamas makes good these declared intentions to focus on political rather than military means.

I walked through the long cage to the crossing and back to Israel. The concrete door at the Erez terminal opened. A voice said: 'Open your bag. Put everything on the table.'

For the next ten minutes, I would once again walk through the state-of-the-art facility between Gaza and Israel, following instructions but seeing no one. I was being directed again by the iron, but invisible, hand of Israel's security apparatus.

Re-entering the world of corridors and cameras, my overwhelming sense was that it does not need to be like this. I remember standing there amid all that metal, concrete and high-tech security equipment thinking that ultimately this was a failure of communication, and real human contact and leadership.

CHAPTER 18

Returning to Iran

Late 2014

OUR SIX-YEAR POSTING DRAWING TO AN END, SYLVIE, JACK and I made plans to visit Iran with Jack's older brother Nicolas, who was visiting from Sydney. This could have been the only chance we'd ever get to go as a family; who knew whether Iran might close again to the outside world?

When I left Iran almost six years earlier, I felt angry. This was one of the most brutal regimes I had ever seen. I was keen to discover what had changed since the Ayatollahs had crushed the June 2009 Green Revolution.

Iran can be an enchanting place for tourists with its absolute wonders. There is a wealth of treasures – vaulted bazaars stretching for kilometres are filled with beautiful Persian handicrafts. The architecture and the mosques are spectacular. The palace complex of Persepolis is mesmerising. The mud-brick alleyways of Yazd and Kashan are breath-taking. The local food is, mostly, wonderful, and Iranians are, in general, very welcoming. They are clearly keen to encourage tourism. We found travel to be both safe and easy – we travelled by bus, train and plane.

In Tehran, a man sitting next to me in a barber's shop – an insurance broker – told me he'd joined the demonstrations during the Green Revolution because he wanted more freedom and did not like Mahmoud Ahmadinejad. 'The Basij and Ahmadinejad are too strict,' he said, adding that '19 out of 20' people did not support the Basij. Ahmadinejad's successor Hassan Rouhani, elected in 2013, better reflected the views of the Iranian people, he told me. Although a religious man, he said Ahmadinejad was 'too religious'. This was ironic, as Ahmadinejad was a civilian politician while Rouhani is a cleric.

There seemed to be a strong view among Iranians I talked to that Rouhani is more reasonable and less dogmatic. Iranians frequently told me they thought he was much better for Iran's image than Ahmadinejad, who was famous for his firebrand speeches denying the Holocaust and pledges to wipe Israel from the map. The man in the barber's shop told me: 'What Ahmadinejad was saying about the Holocaust was ridiculous.' It is important for the West to see a sign of hope in the Iranian people – Rouhani won the election by running on a platform to re-engage with the West. Once elected he made an agreement that he would allow nuclear inspectors to monitor Tehran's nuclear program and to open the country to tourism.

A few streets away, in a Persian carpet shop, a 21-year-old man echoed positive sentiments about Rouhani. 'I don't know how Ahmadinejad ever became president,' he said. 'Rouhani is much better for the country and young Iranians – six years ago our universities had many empty places because there was not enough funding but now they are all full.' The man, who had recently spent 18 months in the army doing compulsory service, also said Rouhani was better for tourism, giving Iran a better international face and freeing up visas for visitors.

Yet, just as I had seen back in 2009, there were two Irans: one modern and secular, and the other devoutly Islamic. The majority of young people we met identified as Iranian first and Islamic second. They described their language, culture and sense of nationhood as Persian, not Muslim. In one part of Tehran we came across energetic young people crowding into a five-level store that sold computers and electronics. In another part, we saw women wearing black robes rushing in and out of mosques.

We saw a legion of young women – usually in their 20s – with bandages on their noses, having just had plastic surgery. The nose-of-choice could be seen in local cafés – a 'ski-slope nose' similar to that of pop icon Michael Jackson. We met a mother and her two daughters who had come from Kuwait for the operation. In a society where women are not permitted to show off other parts of their body, the nose is one feature that can be flaunted. We found out from talking with many women that, because such operations are expensive, some young women even put a bandage on their noses before they go out at night – without even having had an operation – to try to give the impression that they are wealthy enough to have had one. It's a status symbol.

Women in Iran are far from having equal rights; discrimination is entrenched in the law. If a driver injures a male pedestrian they must pay them double the compensation they would pay a female. The rationale for this is that men are the major income-earners. Nonetheless, women are far more visible than in many Middle Eastern countries. We had a female taxi driver on one journey. In Saudi Arabia women are not allowed to drive: leading Saudi cleric Sheikh Salah al-Luhaidan claimed it had been scientifically proved that driving 'affects the ovaries' and leads to clinical disorders in children.[1]

The Iranian regime says there are no nightclubs in Iran. This, however, is as ludicrous as the claim by Mahmoud Ahmadinejad that there are no Iranians who are homosexual. We were told there were many parties around Tehran, but all behind closed doors. We also heard about big 'rave' events for young people in remote desert locations, where they can dance far from the disapproving eyes of the regime. Despite being banned, alcohol is a rising problem, as is alcohol poisoning from home-made brews. According to Reuters, the country opened its first alcohol rehabilitation centre in 2014. The Revolutionary Guards were reported to be major players in the smuggling and illegal sale of alcohol.[2]

And while Rouhani may be a more attractive international face, hardline elements around the Supreme Leader still hold significant power. In government-run bookshops at railway stations I noticed Adolf Hitler's *Mein Kampf* for sale – prominently positioned. When I asked one bookseller what it was about, he said: 'Hitler – My Fight. It's a very good book.'

Along the streets of Tehran, quotes from the Koran in Farsi, Arabic and English were posted on government buildings. They included: 'Do not be inquisitive about other people's lives and do not backbite one another'; 'Do not walk the earth arrogantly.'

Travelling around Iran, our preconceptions were further challenged.

In the southern city of Shiraz, we spent a day with a 25-year-old primary school teacher who acted as our guide. He'd recently served his compulsory 18 months in the army, and his views of the Basij surprised me. 'The Basij militia is unpopular with younger Iranians because of how brutal they were during the 2009 problems. But they can also do good things – they're an emergency team. Whenever the government needs them, and for whatever, the Basiji will help. Iran is surrounded by countries with problems and chaos such as Iraq, Syria and Afghanistan but Iran has calm and stability and I think that is because of the Basij.'

At a museum in Shiraz we met an Iranian sheikh in his 50s who lectured at the University of Shiraz. He was surprised to see foreigners in Iran. He invited us to dinner that evening, along with a friend of his who spoke good English, a 26-year-old international law student at Tehran University who managed his family's business. This student was from a wealthy family, possibly part of the next generation of leaders in Iran.

The student had reservations about the regime of Ayatollahs that imposes religious restrictions. But when it came to the security of Iran he displayed a deep nationalistic sentiment: the brutal eight-year war between Iran and Iraq is seared into the consciousness of all Iranians. 'Since 1979 we have not lost a centimetre of our land in any war,' he told us. 'The Iran–Iraq War lasted eight years and we had 13 countries against us but we fought courageously and won. The only country that helped us in that war was Syria.' Despite the deep divisions in Iran between those loyal to the Islamic leaders and those who want a Western-style democracy, we came across this mindset wherever we went. The streets of many cities were lined with posters of 'martyrs' from that war.

The student also gave us an insight into the way many young Iranians view Israel. There is a sense in Iran that Israel is unlikely to attack, because Israel understands that even if it did prevail over Iran it would be dealt serious damage. This student did not want a war with Israel, but he made it clear that deeply held Persian pride would rise up should one begin. 'In any war with Israel both of our countries would lose. But If Israel attacks us we will fight back and we will flatten Tel Aviv and Haifa. We are not frightened to fight if attacked. The Jews fear death more than we do. Iranians believe that it is better to die young defending our homeland rather than to die as a sick old man in hospital.'

He spoke about Iran's mentality of proxy wars. 'In Iran our military commanders have made a decision that a direct war with Israel would bring upon us too great a cost. That is why we prefer to fight through other people – that is why we give support to Hezbollah and Hamas and the Assad regime.' Asked what support Iran gives Hamas, he said: 'Weapons and advice. Some of the top Iranian military officers go to Gaza.' But how do they get into Gaza? 'Egypt does not want them going through the Egyptian end, Rafah, so they get in there by boat.' When I pointed out that Israel is running a naval blockade of Gaza, he smiled. 'They get in there.' The commander of Iran's Revolutionary Guards, Mohammad Ali Jafari, is reported to have confirmed that Iran has not sent weapons to Gaza but 'gave them the technology of how to make Fajr-5 missiles and now they [Hamas] have their hands on plenty of them'.[3]

In Shiraz we also met a 24-year-old female photographic student, who told us: 'Things are good in Iran for the young. The scarf is not a problem for me. I keep it back at this level but if I go into a mosque I pull it forward.' Social media such as Facebook and Twitter had been banned in Iran since the Green Revolution, but she told me young Iranians know how to circumvent the restrictions. 'We just need to know the filter. That way we have access to everything. It's not something we talk about. We can basically do anything we want to as long as we don't show off. We have a good life. It's a relaxed place.'

In fact, within minutes of arriving at one of the hotels we stayed in, Jack and Nicolas were given by hotel staff the information needed to circumvent the government ban on Facebook.

In the city of Isfahan, deep in the religious and geographic heart of Iran, two Islamic clerics from the Imam mosque had their own views on the regime's restrictions. Over a cup of tea, they gave us an insight into the thinking of the younger generation of clerics.

Sheikh Davoud Jafari was a cleric with perfect English who had studied abroad. His ambition was to become an ayatollah, 'but it is in the hand of God how long this will take'. While conceding the need for reform in Iran, he supported many of the regime's policies. He said that the internet had been used to organise protests against the government in Iran, but he added, 'I think the government should relax its limitations on social media. Social media has been used by the students in Tehran, who are not the majority of Iranians. In 2009 there were probably 58 per cent of Iranians in favour of Ahmadinejad and 42 against because of the strong support for Ahmadinejad from country areas.' He said 'a group of people' wanted change but there was an even bigger group contented with the status quo. The protest movement had been based in the cities, but the majority opinion – which he claimed supported the regime – had 'won'.

Sheikh Jafari watched the BBC and CNN for foreign news. I asked him if, unlike their former President Ahmadinejad, Iran's imams acknowledged the Holocaust. They do, he said, adding that President Hassan Rouhani 'is cleverer than Ahmadinejad'.

He told us there was a synagogue close to our hotel and said we should visit it to see that there was no problem with freedom of religion in Iran. (Later we did just that. There was no security; we simply walked in and introduced ourselves. We spoke to many worshippers, who insisted it was not dangerous being Jewish in Iran.)

The other sheikh sharing a cup of tea with us, Sheikh Mohammad Reza Zamani, was more conservative. Unlike Sheikh Jafari, he defended his regime's internet restrictions. 'Our government acts like a parent for the nation. There are a lot of very bad images on the internet that would not be good for the young, that will invade their minds, and it is better they do not have it. Our government tries to act like a good parent to the nation.'

Elsewhere, though, views of the regime were much more negative. In Yazd, southeast of Isfahan, a shopkeeper at a handicrafts store shook his head, indicating 'no', when I asked if life in Iran was good. When I asked what he thought of the Supreme Leader Ayatollah Khamanei, he looked towards a woman wearing a black chador – a religious woman – and waited until she left the shop. 'No good,' he said. I asked what would happen if that woman heard him say that. He gestured a finger across his throat, as if to suggest beheading, then added: 'People hanged. No good in Iran.' This was another reminder that in the Middle East beneath appearances the reality can be dark.

*

Iran will be crucial in determining the future of the Middle East. I'd become convinced of that after seeing what was going on in Syria, Lebanon, Iraq and so many other parts of the region.

The international community needs to understand how modern Iran sees the world. The national outlook is dominated by the battle against Sunni Islam.

The theme pushed by the State-owned media in Tehran is that Iran is the leader of a Shia – rather than merely Iranian – army. That Shia army also includes the regime of Bashar al-Assad in Syria and Hezbollah in Lebanon. Iran is thus able to command a 'Shia crescent' from Iran through Syria to the Mediterranean in Lebanon. This is, in effect, the front line for the Shia forces in the Battle for Islam.

The Shia army also includes key commanders and forces of the Iraqi Government – although the situation there is more complicated than in Syria and Lebanon. The Shia government in Iraq is the only government openly, and strongly, supported by both Iran and the US.

The Shia crescent and its supporters are now facing the traditional Sunni crescent, which includes Saudi Arabia, Qatar and Bahrain. Iran sees Saudi Arabia and Bahrain as its main enemies – much more of a threat than Israel.

In Bahrain, whose Sunni royal family is protected by Saudi Arabia, the Shias form 70 per cent of the population and made up the majority of the pro-reform demonstrators during the Arab Spring. Iran supported the Shia majority in their efforts to overthrow the minority Sunni royal family. Saudi Arabia's interest in this strategic play was obvious when it sent tanks across the 25-kilometre-long King Fahd Causeway linking the two kingdoms to help put down civil unrest and protect the Bahraini royals in March 2011.

But a new, much more extremist Sunni crescent has opened up to Iran's northwest: northern Iraq and northern Syria. This crescent was established in 2014 after the dramatic victories of Islamic State.

Iranians view Islamic State as a creation of the Wahhabist sect based in Saudi Arabia. There is a strong sense in Iran that Saudi Arabia has got what it has deserved by nurturing al-Qaeda and other Sunni groups: an even worse terrorist group that is now out of control.

Ultimately, the Battle for Islam – the battle between Shia Muslims and Sunni Muslims – can be resolved only by the two powerhouses of each side – Iran and Saudi Arabia. The only solution is if these two superpowers in the Islamic world decide to call off the dogs of war and sue for a genuine peace. Which means instructing their followers – including the most fanatic among them – to end this conflict.

This is unlikely to happen, but it is not impossible. It would require both sides of the Islamic civil war to put aside 1400 years of animosity. Both Iran and Saudi Arabia are now paying the price for this war – from acts of terrorism against against each other to having to spend enormous resources fighting this war.

Both Iran and Saudi Arabia need to decide which is more important: pragmatic self-interest or religious fanaticism. If they decide on pragmatism, they can end this quickly. If they decide fanaticism, the world is set to become a much more dangerous place as the rest of us get caught up in this unholy war.

CHAPTER 19

The View from Palestine

January 2015

ON A FREEZING EVENING ON 4 JANUARY 2015, TWO DAYS
before we left Israel, Sylvie and I sat by a fire in Bethlehem with
a group of journalists, diplomats and NGO (non-government
organisation) workers. The man sitting next to me – a leading
Palestinian businessman – was regarded as a moderate. But what
he had to say was chilling.

Any Palestinian businessman in the West Bank needs to deal
regularly with Israeli officials, who have control over all aspects
of business, including tax. While he opposed Israel's occupation,
this man believed it was important for Palestinians to work to
improve their lot.

But what had angered him were events surrounding a vote
by the 22-member UN Security Council on 30 December, just
six days earlier. Jordan had submitted a resolution demanding a

full Israeli withdrawal from the West Bank by 2017. Nine votes had been needed for the resolution to pass; 15 members had voted yes, five had abstained, and only the US and Australia had voted no.

Chief Palestinian negotiator Saeb Erekat had commented that Palestinian leadership had known that the resolution would fail because of the make-up of the Security Council, but that they had decided to push it anyway. The businessman told me that had the Palestinians waited three days until Australia was off the Security Council, Malaysia or Venezuela would have gone onto the council and voted to support the Palestinians. He saw it as stunning incompetence. (Australia was a rotating member of the Security Council. The US, as a permanent member, had a power of veto, which they would have used. What angered the businessman was that Australia added a certain 'respectability' to the US position and that he would have preferred if the US had been shown to be alone in its Security Council support for Israel's ongoing occupation of the West Bank.)

Then the businessman really opened up: 'Armed struggle is coming. I can guarantee you 100 per cent that Palestinians are going to take up weapons.'

I told him it was my understanding that the Israelis, through their massive system of informants, knew what was happening in every square inch of the West Bank.

'Israeli propaganda,' he retorted. 'The Israelis' strongest town in the West Bank is Bethlehem – they know everything. But in other places the Israelis are not so strong. I could take you to places where the Israelis know nothing. The weapons are already there – and when the time comes they will get more from the mafia. The mafia in Israel will sell weapons to anybody.'

Most Palestinians are reluctant to talk about armed campaigns. They talk about 'peaceful resistance', but once you get to know them they become more honest: a new armed conflict, or 'uprising', against Israel remains an option.

According to this businessman, about 2000 militants would join an uprising against Israel. 'They will not fight in the open, as they know they will lose. It will instead be by stealth – it will be bombings, it will be snipers, it will be attacks in different parts of Israel. They will terrify Israelis. It would not be hard to get 2000 people out of 2.9 million in the West Bank to join the fight. The weapons are already there.'

The businessman cited the case of Palestinian prisoner Jamal Tirawi, who was released from prison in 2013. Before he was returned to the Balata refugee camp, the Israeli Army searched the refugee camp for weapons and found none. Then the Palestinian Authority security forces searched the camp and found none. Yet a couple of hours later to celebrate the release of Tirawi, scores of Palestinians came out carrying weapons. A European diplomat who was present was stunned by the number of weapons that had appeared despite the searches.

*

In our six years in Israel, one of the most interesting conversations I had was in December 2009 with Ahmad Aweidah, among the most powerful financial figures in the West Bank. Born in Jerusalem, he was educated at the University of St Andrews in Scotland, and worked for the Société Générale banking group in France and then Paltel (Palestinian Telecommunication), the largest company in the Palestinian Territories. He now ran the

Palestine Securities Exchange – responsible for US$7 billion in deposits.

I wanted to meet Aweidah because of his reputation as one of the brightest of his generation. He was not regarded as an 'Israel hater' and was often mentioned as a future leader. So I drove to meet him at his office in Nablus in the West Bank.

Aweidah called himself a moderate – which is why it was ominous that he wanted a one-State solution.

'In terms of one State, I think we should go with the Martin Luther King call of one man one vote ... It's better than continued conflict, is it not? I think the two-State solution is no longer viable. I think the only solution now is one State where the Palestinians are the majority and the Jews are a protected minority, just like the whites are now in South Africa.' The new State, Aweidah said, could be called 'Israeltine': 'a combination of Israel and Palestine'.

Aweidah outlined how it would work. 'Under one State, Jews and Arabs would share power at a local level for things like education and health, while things like water would be decided at a national level. The Jews would have their own canton and the Arabs would have their own canton. It would be a federal structure. The Palestinian canton would not be responsible for the defence of the country. I am happy for the Jewish canton to remain in charge of defence through the IDF. Not a single Palestinian would serve in the IDF. Jerusalem would be everybody's. Jews would be able to live in Hebron not as settlers but as full citizens. The Irish and the English resolved their conflict. The English and the Scots. There have been many other conflicts that have seemed as intractable as this one.'

I suggested there would be a lot of resistance from Israelis because it would mean the end of the Jewish State. 'But it would be the birth of the Jewish canton,' he retorted. 'Don't worry, we will be good to them – they will be treated as a protected minority. We are not interested in oppressing them. Historically we don't have a problem with Jews. Anti-Semitism is not an Arab or Muslim thing, it's primarily been a Christian thing.'

While the US still talks about a two-State solution, most Palestinians I met had abandoned the idea. They said the last chance for this was under Netanyahu. Indeed, it is usually only visiting foreigners who cling to the idea.

The parents of the Palestinian children at Jack's school had given up on a two-State solution. When Barack Obama was elected in 2008, they rekindled some interest, but after Benjamin Netanyahu blocked Obama's efforts they gave up hope.

'What have we got from 15 years of negotiating since Oslo?' asked Aweidah.

> Today we're sitting behind a wall with 600,000 Jewish
> settlers. So what will we get from another 15 years of
> negotiations – one million settlers? The Jews say 'Never
> again' about the Shoah [Holocaust]. We now say 'Never
> again' about losing more years negotiating and getting
> nothing. The settlers are actually rendering the two-State
> solution impossible and pre-empting the one-State solution.
> With the current growth of settlements, soon it will be
> impossible to divide the land anyway.

The attitudes of many Palestinians hardened after the election of Netanyahu in 2009. 'Netanyahu still believes we are going to get up and leave,' said Aweidah. 'They have tried every trick in the book to push Palestinians out. They want the land, they don't want the people. We say 15 years and we are the majority.'

Israeli journalist Akiva Eldar revealed one of the methods that Israel used to dramatically lower the number of Palestinians in the West Bank:

> Israel had used a covert procedure to cancel the residency status of 140,000 West Bank Palestinians between 1967 and 1994. The legal advisor for the Judea and Samaria Justice Ministry's office admitted this in a document obtained by *Haaretz*.
>
> According to the document, Palestinians who wished to travel abroad via Jordan were ordered to leave their ID cards at the Allenby Bridge border crossing. They exchanged their ID cards for a card allowing them to cross.
>
> If a Palestinian did not return within six months of the card's expiration … [they] were registered as NLRs – no longer residents. The document made no mention of any warning or information that the Palestinians received about the process.
>
> The Central Bureau of Statistics reported that the West Bank's Palestinian population amounted to 1.05 million in 1994 – which meant the population would have been greater by about 14 percent if it weren't for the procedure.
>
> Today, a similar procedure is still in place for residents of East Jerusalem who hold Israeli ID cards; they lose their right to return if they have been abroad for seven years.

Ahmad Aweidah gave a different perspective: 'There are people here now who are young and energetic and who believe in the future. Palestinians have one of the highest birth rates in the world. In Gaza alone in the first six months of this year [2009] there were 53,000 births.' Time and demographics, he said, were on the side of the Palestinians: a mirror image of the view of Israel's settlers.

He went on to say that the Palestinian economy was in 'tatters'. 'It's an economy completely disfigured, a servile economy for Israel. We import 80 per cent of our needs from Israel. Palestinian companies are not able to trade as they wish, its people are not able to move as they wish. Gaza is a complete catastrophe. The Palestinian economy is at 10 per cent of our potential. Palestinians have about $70 billion of their assets abroad (particularly in the US and Arab world).'[1]

How did Aweidah interpret Netanyahu's claim that Israel was trying to help the Palestinian economy?

It's bull. It's just for media consumption. Netanyahu doesn't want to pay the price for peace. He's not interested in removing the settlements, he's not interested in a two-State solution, but he has to say something. What he actually believes is that Palestinians should pack up and go to Jordan …

In 1948 we were not supposed to be staying here. But we are still here. We have strong population growth, we are building things, we're constructing things, we're having kids, we're getting married, we have a thriving culture, we have a thriving film industry now and we're not going anywhere. We are a people who have a will to survive and who know how to survive. And Palestinians in the diaspora are successful – they are doctors, investment bankers, lawyers. The game is not lost. Far from it – we have survived against almost insurmountable odds. This is 62 years on. That plan did not go the way it was intended. The plan was that we would be completely emptied out of this land. [David] Ben-Gurion completely fucked up. He should have finished the job then.

The Israelis have even alienated the Israeli Arabs. The Israelis could have so easily made Israeli Arabs part of their society and defenders of their society, but instead the way they have treated them has made them more extremist over the years.

As I sat listening to Aweidah, one of the brightest young Palestinians, outlining his vision for the future of his people, I wondered whether Israel had failed to reach out to the next generation of moderate Palestinians. Aweidah, 40, should be a bridge to a future in which Israelis and Palestinians live alongside each other.

As I drove from Nablus back home to Jerusalem, I kept thinking to myself: if this is how the moderate Palestinians are talking in public, how are the extremist Palestinians talking in private?

*

Many people believe that if the Palestinian Authority disbanded itself it would precipitate the end of the occupation. That is, they believe that the PA helps Israel to maintain the occupation.

'The role of the Palestinian Authority cannot be underestimated in how it's easy and relatively cheap to run the occupation,' Israeli Sarit Michaeli from human rights group B'Tselem told me.

If the PA didn't exist Israel would have to fix traffic lights
in Ramallah, set the curriculum and print schoolbooks
in Nablus, paint zebra crossings in Bethlehem, prosecute
criminals on issues other than security – a Palestinian who's
a rapist or thief would have to be found and brought to trial
by Israeli courts – and anything to do with running water,
sewerage would have to be done by Israel ... This money
would have to be provided by Israel.

Israel uses the existence of the PA as a retort to people
who criticise the occupation. It's a very common thing from
Israeli spokespeople and media to say that Palestinians run
their own lives ... The existence of the PA ... has allowed
them [Israel] to posit the claim that there is really no direct
occupation. This is important, because a lot of people buy
this argument in Israel. If you have a situation where the
control is indirect it's easier to mask this control.

Michaeli argued that the PA had very little authority. 'The
Palestinian economy is completely subjugated to the Israeli
economy.' The World Bank found that restrictions imposed by
Israel cost the Palestinian economy $US3.4 billion per year: 35
per cent of Palestine's GDP.[2]

*

For the first two years we were in Jerusalem, the Israelis said it
was impossible to have peace with the Palestinians – how could
Israel make peace with the Palestinian Authority when it was
divided from Hamas? Interior Minister Eli Yishai said that 'First
they [the PA] should make internal peace with Hamas and then

they can try talking to us.' But when PA leader Mahmoud Abbas did try to 'make internal peace' with Hamas, Netanyahu said that this was the reason why Israel could not make peace. After the PA and Hamas announced a 'unity government' in April 2014, Israel suspended peace negotiations with the Palestinians, and Netanyahu would later tell his security cabinet: 'Today, Abu Mazen [Mahmoud Abbas] said yes to terrorism and no to peace.'[3]

This was despite the fact that Abbas insisted not a single person who had been a member of Hamas could become part of the new Palestinian Government. Apart from Abbas's own distrust of Hamas, he had another reason to ensure that no Hamas figure was part of any new government: money. The US lists Hamas as a terrorist organisation, so the US Congress would cease funding the Palestinian Authority should it have any involvement with Hamas.

When Hamas made it clear it was prepared to agree to a Palestinian State along 1967 lines and recognise Israel, Netanyahu came up with another condition: that the Palestinians must recognise Israel as a Jewish State – a condition no previous Israeli prime minister had introduced.

It almost seemed as if Israel was coming up with an excuse for every development. The more I talked to Israeli officials, the more it became clear: I was watching in slow-motion as a government sabotaged perhaps its last chance for peace.

I asked *New York Times* Jerusalem bureau chief Jodi Rudoren whether Netanyahu's new condition of recognising Israel as a Jewish State was a negotiating ploy or a legitimate claim. Her answer was surprising. 'My feeling is that it might be both things,' she replied.

It's certainly possible that Netanyahu made it a priority to scuttle the talks, because we don't see real evidence that he really wanted them to succeed. But I buy his argument that 'Until they officially acknowledge this is the nation State of the Jewish people I cannot be convinced based on incitement or whatever that this agreement won't be a precursor for them to try to destroy this State' ... If I were the Palestinians I would have said, 'We already recognised you, basically, and we won't take away the Arab rights and we won't let this affect the right of return but sure, if you want to be the nation State of the Jewish people go for it. From now on you're the nation State of the Jewish people, and by the way, since you want that so badly we'd like the land swaps to be this way or we want this on the refugees.'

Crispian Balmer of Reuters was also critical of the Palestinians, and believes they should be placed under greater scrutiny. 'I also do get frustrated because I think sometimes the Palestinians are given a free ride. We're all very critical of the occupation and they [the Palestinians] are the underdog, but at the same time, last year we did a story on honour killings in the Palestinian Territories ... They do some pretty foul stuff themselves.'

And Balmer has pointed out, it is not just the Israelis who are hostile to the foreign media. 'It should also be said the Palestinians are pains in the arse too when it comes to some of this stuff. I've had significant problems with the Palestinians, be it Hamas gunmen smashing into our newsroom in Gaza and threatening to throw one of our people from the 12th storey or in the West Bank.'

*

It was 23 September 2011. President Mahmoud Abbas had just submitted an application for Palestine to become the 194th member of the United Nations. The PLO had been given UN Observer status way back in 1974, long before it declared the independent State of Palestine in 1988. The Oslo Accords – which created the Palestinian Authority – had offered a brief ray of hope, but since then the peace process had stalled as Israel continued to aggressively expand its settlements in the West Bank.

Frustrated by the lack of progress, and emboldened by the events of the Arab Spring, Abbas and his team had been courting the international community for many months before arriving for the 66th Session of the UN General Assembly in New York. Their hope was that full membership of the UN would take them to the brink of statehood. The next step after official recognition by the UN would be for Palestine to become a sovereign country, consisting of the West Bank and Gaza, with East Jerusalem as its capital.

I was there to cover the proceedings at the UN, along with a huge contingent of international media.

Benjamin Netanyahu rose first to address the assembly, delivering a speech fit for prime-time American television: perfect English with an American accent. (Netanyahu lived in the US for many years.) The speech ticked all the boxes, painting Israel as the David against the Goliath of Iran. His message amounted to: 'We won't have a State imposed on us. The only solution is one that the Israelis and Palestinians work out for themselves through direct negotiations.'

Compared with this, Abbas's address later in the day was one of the worst crafted speeches I had heard. He raced through his words, barely stopping to allow the generally friendly audience of diplomats from 190 countries to offer him the applause they clearly wanted to give. He spoke entirely in Arabic and made no attempt to pitch his message directly to key players by using occasional phrases in English, French or Hebrew. He could easily have rehearsed some targeted phrases for the international media along the lines of 'Why should we be one of the last people on earth to live under occupation?' A simple message which could have been run on news bulletins around the world – not just in the Arab world.

Worse still, he made no effort to appeal to the very people who would be crucial in deciding whether Palestinians ever got a State: the Israeli public. Apparently playing to his own constituency, he mentioned Muslims and Christians but made no reference to any Jewish connection with Jerusalem. It was an appalling misjudgement by Abbas, displaying a real lack of courage. There can't have been too many times when a speaker with the attention of the world on him has lost an opportunity so comprehensively.

The next day I was walking along Fifth Avenue and ran into two Israeli journalists with whom I'd flown from Israel, Shimon Shiffer and Nahum Barnea. They are two of the elder statesmen of Israeli media, both from *Yedioth Ahronoth* – the largest selling newspaper in Israel and generally a centrist paper. They were sitting in the sun outside a café in a plaza, reading the papers, so I joined them. We started talking about the UN speeches.

With no warning, Shiffer snapped: 'I now talk to you as an Israeli, rather than a journalist. As an Israeli, I was outraged at Abbas's speech! I'm a supporter of Abbas and the Palestinians, but for him to wipe the Jews out of the history of Jerusalem … this outrages me!'

If he'd outraged an influential supporter, I thought, what impact had he made on the less sympathetic Israeli public? I realised how the Israelis were wiping the floor with the Palestinians in terms of how to play public relations. There really was no contest.

After 50 years of occupation, the Israeli–Palestinian conflict has become a media war. The Israelis are winning this war, without question – not because they have the better argument, but because they have a better resourced and more intimidating media and lobbying machine. Living in Israel, I experienced Israel's *hasbara* machine on a daily basis. When a missile was fired into southern Israel from Gaza and landed in towns such as Sderot or Ashkelon, the Israeli PR people would send out texts along the lines of 'Rocket lands in Ashkelon – Russian-speaking media can contact [name and phone number included], Japanese media can contact [name and number], German media can contact …' It would then go on to say that if you wanted to speak to a woman who had a child at the school you could call her on the number provided or if you wanted to speak to a paramedic on the spot you could call his number. It amounted to a rapid-response media special forces team.

The machine worked even harder during the time of the Gaza wars. During the 2012 Gaza War, three Israelis were killed when a missile from Gaza hit their home. I needed to get to the front line and our car was not working. An email arrived saying that the think tank Israel Project had a bus leaving Jerusalem, which I joined. With about 30 journalists on board, staff from the Israel Project handed out 'Fact Sheets'. Their staff also walked up and down the bus with baskets of sandwiches: 'Pastrami on rye or vegetarian?' they asked. Many journalists live off organisations like the Israel Project. In Israel, you can be driven to war while being fed facts, figures and pastrami on rye.

The Palestinian side, in contrast, were appalling – highly disorganised and suffering from the fatigue of a 50-year occupation. Which made me wonder: given that Israel's image around the world was probably the worst it had ever been, due largely to the wars with Gaza and the occupation, and the Palestinians' image was probably as good as it had ever been, what would be the situation if the Palestinians ever learnt to do public relations the way the Israelis do it?

*

By November 2012, facing the prospect of a US veto after its application was referred to the UN Security Council, Palestine had decided to reduce its ambitions and pursue an upgrade to 'Non-member State'. The resolution was approved by a majority of UN members – with Australia, on the initiative of Bob Carr, taking the historic decision to abstain. Palestine had partially achieved its objective – no thanks to Abbas's appalling speech in front of the UN.

One day in 2010, a year into my posting, I ran into the chief Palestinian negotiator, Saeb Erekat, at the American Colony Hotel in Jerusalem. While I had spoken to him on the phone, I had never met him so I introduced myself. 'I'm having real problems getting any information out of your side,' I said. Then I added, 'Compared with the Israelis.'

Erekat looked at me and said, 'Yeah, the Israelis are good, aren't they?'

My only thought was, well, you're getting a billion dollars a year in funding from the European Union, Australia and other countries and you still can't put together a functioning public relations department?'

Fifty years on, the Israelis have set up a largely remote-controlled machine and have got every inch of Gaza and the West Bank mapped out. Yet the Palestinian are just playing with the same old blunt instruments. But while the Israelis are able to maintain military control over the Palestinians, they will not win the real contest. As Israel continues to rule over an increasingly large population – a minority Jewish population (based on demographics) is now on the brink of controlling the lives and movements of a majority Palestinian population in Israel, the West Bank and Gaza – Israel's occupation is, inevitably, doomed.

The only question is whether what comes next will be an orderly, political process or a violent, chaotic one in which many people will die. I am by nature an eternal optimist. But after six years of living amid this conflict I fear that the latter is now almost inevitable.

CHAPTER 20

Netanyahu's Israel

January 2015

OUR TIME IN THE MIDDLE EAST WAS DRAWING TO A CLOSE. As a family, we'd arrived with such enthusiasm.

We'd spent some of our best years in Israel. But during these six years, Sylvie, Jack and I had realised something was very wrong. We'd come to this realisation in different ways and at different times – after all, Jack had spent this time in primary and secondary school, so his experience here had been very different from mine and Sylvie's. But from our varied lives, we'd each come to the same conclusion: the State of Israel is in deep trouble.

We each felt a disappointment with what we'd found here – a sadness that there was so much suffering and that it showed no sign of stopping. But as a journalist I had a very different perspective: astonishment that the reality of modern Israel goes largely unreported.

What is going on in Israel today is a dramatic story. What is occurring is the extinguishment not just of any chance of a Palestinian State but also of the vision by the international community, as agreed by the United Nations in 1947, to find a sustainable peace through a two-State solution. However, unless you read between the lines or have sources of information outside the mainstream media, you would barely know this.

The other conclusion I'd come to was that the end of a Palestinian State also meant the arrival of a horrible new reality. As Israel approaches the 70th anniversary of its founding, there is a formidable threat confronting it. If not addressed, Israel will not survive in its current form.

*

As the correspondent for *The Australian*, I'd had extraordinary access to Israel's military and political elite. When Yuval Diskin, head of Shin Bet, decided to have a rare media briefing, I was one of 10 foreign journalists invited. At one dinner I was asked to commence proceedings: a daunting task, given there was a former Prime Minister of Israel, Ehud Olmert, sitting opposite me. We'd gathered in the Jerusalem home of a leading lawyer. There were 20 Israelis – lawyers and politicians – and four foreign journalists present.

'Now that you've been here four years, tell us how you see Israel's future,' the host asked.

'To me Israel is like a train,' I began. 'It's one of the best trains I've been on. It's not just the fastest train, but also the quietest. It showcases Israeli technology. Every carriage has wi-fi and each seat has its own TV. The buffet car has magnificent food and wine. But there's one problem: in two hours this train is going to have a head-on collision, and a lot of people are going to be killed. The collision is going to be with the occupation of the Palestinians. In my opinion no society can keep another people under occupation for 50 years. Unless there's real change I think this will end in tragedy.'

I stopped.

There was silence. Finally, a woman said: 'John, I think every person in this room agrees with everything you just said.'

Ehud Olmert then told us how close he'd come to achieving peace with Palestinian leader Mahmoud Abbas. Olmert stunned Abbas when he walked in with a map of a Palestinian State that he believed he could convince the Israeli public to support. While this is frequently cited in the media, what he went on to tell us debunked the version often quoted by Israeli lobby groups of that famous meeting, that Abbas rejected the peace offer. He said Abbas asked if he could keep the map. 'Only if you sign it!' Olmert replied. Abbas said he could not sign a deal as momentous as this without consulting others. Before he could do this, however, Olmert was hit with massive corruption charges and went to jail. The two men never met again. Olmert told all of us at the dinner that night very strongly: 'Abbas neither accepted nor refused. To say that he rejected that offer is wrong.'

*

As argued earlier, overwhelming evidence now exists that Israel determined from 1967 that it would aggressively execute its settlement push to make a Palestinian State impossible. Israel has been moving towards an extremist position for many years.

Israeli documents show Golda Meir (1969–1974) could have done a peace deal with Egypt much earlier, while Ariel Sharon

(2001–06) saw off two peace attempts: the 2002 Arab Peace Initiative and the Geneva Initiative of 2003. Sharon was both a formidable military strategist and a wily politician. As a military commander, he successfully took Israel into Gaza to establish settlements; as Prime Minister he successfully took Israel out of Gaza in 2005.

Withdrawing from Gaza was a political masterstroke. Sharon was able to tell the US that he was committed to withdrawing from 'the territories'. As one European diplomat explained to me: 'But what he didn't add was that at exactly the same time he was massively boosting the number of settlers in the West Bank. This was what was important to Israel – it had no real religious and political connection to Gaza but it did to the West Bank.' Sharon withdrew 10,000 settlers from Gaza, but was responsible, according to Israel's *Maariv* newspaper, for 100,000 new settlers in the West Bank.

The growth in settlements was strongest under Shimon Peres (1995–96) and Ehud Barak (1999–2001) – both Labor Party prime ministers. Until, that is, Benjamin Netanyahu, who proved to be the biggest booster of settlements of any prime minister in terms of financial incentives for people to move there.

Netanyahu has now become Israel's longest serving prime minister. He could bring peace to Israel if he wanted to. From a position of unprecedented strength, Netanyahu could force a solution by defining clear borders for Israel and Palestine. Instead, he has enmeshed the two, meaning that the two partners in perhaps the world's most abusive marriage have been forced to live in the same house indefinitely. Many people who follow Israeli politics closely know this but an entire industry relies on continuing the fantasy that a two-State solution is still viable.

So who is Benjamin Netanyahu? Over my years in the Middle East I was able to observe him up close. He is the shrewdest politician I have ever seen. He is the great survivor. In the highly factionalised world of Israeli politics, he has always managed to cobble together a new alliance or to do another deal to stay in power. And when the history of the Middle East is written, I have no doubt that he will be recorded as the man who has consigned Israelis and Palestinians to decades of conflict.

To try to understand Netanyahu, I spoke to Israelis who have known and worked with him. This included having lunch with a senior official from the Israeli Foreign Ministry whom I liked and trusted. He not only had regular access to Netanyahu but had also known his family for decades.

I asked him: did he think Netanyahu was serious about peace?

He grinned and said there were two seminal figures in Netanyahu's life: his brother, Yonatan, and his father, Professor Benzion Netanyahu, and to understand Netanyahu you needed to understand these two influences.

Yonatan Netanyahu led the bold rescue of more than 100 Israeli passengers held hostage by Palestinian and German terrorists at Entebbe Airport in Uganda in 1976. The operation was seen as flawless, except for one Israeli death: Yonatan Netanyahu. My contact told me that it was the death of Yonatan while defending Israelis that motivated Benjamin to enter politics.

The other key to understanding Benjamin was his famous historian father, Benzion (who would die in 2012). The official told me that if Benjamin tried to 'cross the Rubicon' to bring peace, he would be halfway across when his father would shout: 'Bibi, come back!'

The official pointed to an interview Benzion gave *Maariv* newspaper soon after his son's re-election in April 2009 that Benjamin tried, unsuccessfully, to stop *Maariv* from running. In it, Benzion said the two-State solution was a charade. 'There are no two peoples here. There is a Jewish people and an Arab population ... there is no Palestinian people, so you don't create a state for an imaginary nation.' When the interviewer suggested that Professor Netanyahu did not like Arabs, he replied: 'The Bible finds no worse image than that of the man from the desert. Why? Because he has no respect for any law. Because in the desert he can do as he pleases.'

There was no solution, Professor Netanyahu insisted, except for 'strong military rule'. He said there was 'valuable experience' to be gained from how the Turks treated the Arabs during Ottoman rule: 'The Arabs were so badly beaten, they didn't dare revolt.' Asked how the Arabs in Israel should be treated, he said: 'I think we should speak to the Israeli Arabs in the language they understand and admire – the language of force.' Benzion said a war with 'the Arabs' should include 'withholding food from Arab cities, preventing education, terminating electrical power and more'.

Finally, the reporter asked how much the professor thought he had influenced his son Benjamin. 'I have a general idea,' Professor Netanyahu replied. 'Bibi might aim for the same goals as mine, but he keeps to himself the ways to achieve them, because if he gave expression to them, he would expose his goals.'

When I pointed out to the official that the views of a father could not be assumed for a son, he replied: 'Indeed – but his father is the man he most admires. Do you think that Benjamin did not absorb many of these views?'

*

On 4 November 1995, right-wing activist Yigal Amir watched then Prime Minister Yitzhak Rabin speak to thousands about peace in Tel Aviv. Amir was a 25-year-old Yeshiva student who believed the settlements in the West Bank should continue and who opposed any peace agreement with the Palestinians. When he watched the famous handshake at the White House between Yitzhak Rabin and Yasser Arafat in 1993 – the same handshake which so inspired me as a young correspondent in Washington all those years ago – he was devastated. As the *New York Times* reported, that handshake 'spelled the end of the world that Yigal Amir believed God had given the Jews'. The paper reported: 'At the Institute for Higher Torah Studies, where Mr Amir was a diligent, argumentative student, the moment of reconciliation between the Israeli and Palestinian leaders that was greeted so warmly around the world seemed a catastrophe; the celebration at home [in Israel] obscene … Yigal was in a state worse than depression.'[1]

That night in Tel Aviv, Yigal Amir watched Yitzhak Rabin talk about peace. Once Rabin had finished speaking, Amir made his way through the crowd, hiding a gun. He then went up to Rabin, pointed the gun at his back and fired three shots, killing both Rabin and the Oslo peace process.

Israeli journalist Akiva Eldar told me Netanyahu was 'absolutely complicit in incitement against Rabin'. While Rabin was negotiating peace with the Palestinians, Netanyahu, then Opposition Leader, campaigned against Oslo. 'At one rally Netanyahu was filmed on a balcony addressing extremists, many of whom were carrying mock coffins for Rabin and Oslo,' said Eldar. 'Standing on that balcony with a coffin – he did everything to destroy [the Oslo peace process].' Netanyahu addressed another rally at which an effigy of Rabin dressed in a Nazi uniform was held aloft. Shortly afterwards, Rabin was shot dead.

After Rabin's assassination, *Haaretz* noted that he had been a war hero – the military's chief of staff during the 1967 Six-Day War, including the triumphant taking of the Western Wall. 'But Prime Minister and Defence Minister Yitzhak Rabin was slain in the wake of systematic incitement led and orchestrated by Netanyahu,' the paper's journalist Sefi Rachlevsky wrote. 'At the height of the incitement and under his direction, Netanyahu managed to turn a Zionist hero into a figure at which thousands and tens of thousands of people shouted "traitor," with hoarse throats and leaps of hatred and ecstasy. And continued to the conclusion: "With blood and fire, we will oust Rabin."'[2]

Rabin's widow, Leah, blamed the Likud leaders – including Netanyahu – for the climate in the lead-up to the assassination. After listening to Netanyahu calling for reconciliation after Rabin's death, Leah Rabin said: 'It's too late. What happened wasn't a bolt of lightning from the heavens. It grew from the soil, a very particular soil.'[3]

Just seven months later, Israelis elected Benjamin Netanyahu as their new Prime Minister.

During his first term (1996–99), the US became highly suspicious of him. After Bill Clinton met with Netanyahu in 1996, Clinton adviser Dennis Ross wrote: 'In the meeting with President Clinton, Netanyahu was nearly insufferable, lecturing and telling us how to deal with the Arabs. Clinton said "He thinks he is the superpower and we are here to do whatever he required."'

Netanyahu knew there was one thing that would kill the peace process: settlements. 'He approved Har Homa, the first new settlement after Oslo,' Akiva Eldar told me. This happened in 1997. 'People don't realise the importance of Har Homa: its purpose was to put a barrier between Jerusalem and Bethlehem. President Clinton gave his word to Palestinian leader Yasser Arafat that after Oslo was signed he would not allow Netanyahu to build a new settlement, and he even sent Dennis Ross on a secret mission to Netanyahu to tell him not to build Har Homa. But the Israelis said, "We're not going to stop." This said to Arafat that you cannot rely on the Americans.' Netanyahu's fast-tracking of Har Homa dealt a serious blow to the peace process.

When speaking to the international community, Netanyahu had a mantra: two States for two peoples. But for settlers, in private, he had a different message.

In 2001, two years after he lost the prime ministership, he drove to Ofra, an Israeli settlement in the Palestinian Territories, 20 minutes from his home. The settlers there believed that during his prime ministership he had not done enough for settlements – even though, like every PM before him, he had encouraged 'the settlement enterprise' through financial incentives. But for the settlers who want Greater Israel – a complete takeover of the West Bank – enough is never enough. To effect his political comeback, Netanyahu needed to win over the settlers – the most powerful lobby group in Israel.

The reason this meeting is important is that it explains why the Israeli–Palestinian conflict is worsening today. Here were the real thoughts of the man who would return to power and become Israel's longest-serving PM.

Not realising he was being filmed, he boasted about how as Prime Minister he had sabotaged the 20-year peace process set in place by the Oslo Accords. 'I know what America is,' Netanyahu told the settlers. 'America is a thing you can move very easily, move it in the right direction. They won't get their way [in terms of a two-State solution]. They asked me before the [1996 Israeli] election if I'd honour [the Oslo Accords]. I said I would but … I'm going to interpret the accords in such a way that would allow me to put an end to this galloping forward to the '67 borders.'

A key element of Oslo was that Israel would give the Palestinians limited autonomy in certain areas. But to allay Israel's security concerns, President Clinton had agreed that 'defined military zones' would remain under Israeli control. The Oslo process relied on Israel acting in good faith in relation to these zones.

'Why is that important?' Netanyahu asked the settlers in his private meeting. 'Because from that moment on I stopped the Oslo Accords. How did we do it? Nobody said what "defined military zones" were. "Defined military zones" are security zones; as far as I'm concerned the entire Jordan Valley is a "defined military zone". Go argue.' Then came the punchline. 'I de facto put an end to the Oslo Accords!'

Oslo was meant to be a five-year interim agreement culminating in the creation of the State of Palestine in the West Bank and Gaza. The Oslo process would then continue for several years, as both sides were required to adhere to ongoing conditions. But as Netanyahu said, he had used 'defined military zones' so that land intended for the Palestinian Authority would be under the control of the Israeli Army. Israel has in fact declared more than half of Area C in the West Bank to be 'defined military zones'.

Washington had never been able to prove that Netanyahu was trying to derail Oslo. Yet the video found its way onto Israeli television.[4] It has now been played several times, so Israelis are clear about what Netanyahu thinks of the peace process. Yet they continue to vote for him.

Akiva Eldar told me: 'I think history will look at Netanyahu's first term as the beginning of the end of the two-State solution. It started when he was taped saying he would destroy Oslo. The turning point was the incitement that led to the assassination of Yitzhak Rabin.'

*

Shortly after Netanyahu became Prime Minister for the second time – in 2009 – indications emerged that he was yet again running interference with US efforts for peace. In the first eight months of his government, Netanyahu issued tenders for 25,000 units in the West Bank and East Jerusalem. Israel's *Maariv* newspaper reported in May 2010: 'Netanyahu is pleased by the fact that the Americans failed, so he said, to twist his arm and that ultimately, in the dual between him and the Obama administration, he was the one who emerged with the upper hand.'[5]

While defenders of Greater Israel, particularly in countries like the US, Australia and Canada, supported Israel's obfuscation on the basis that 'the situation is extremely complex', for Netanyahu the game was simple. By not sitting down with the Palestinians he was guaranteeing his own re-election – he had already suffered the political trauma of being thrown from office in 1999 – but he needed to give the appearance to the US that he was serious about peace.

As Akiva Eldar said: 'Netanyahu, when he was second- and third-time prime minister [2009–15], did everything to waste time. He wants history to remember him as the prime minister who saved Israel from the tragedy of a Palestinian State – that he was able to manipulate the entire world to save Israel from Oslo.'

*

In September 2011, I was one of a group of reporters who flew from Tel Aviv to New York with Netanyahu, for his appearance at the UN in connection with Palestine's push for membership. I'd rung Netanyahu's Australian-born press secretary, Mark Regev, and expressed my interest in being part of the media contingent. There were about 35 Israeli journalists on board, and two foreign journalists, including me.

The security was extraordinary. We'd boarded in a special part of Ben-Gurion airport, with massive concrete barriers and dozens of security men surrounding the plane. On board, security men sat every few seats. There were doctors on board and a huge medical kit in the cabin.

Mid-flight Netanyahu came down to the back of the plane with his wife Sara to say hello to us. The Israeli media weren't won over, though. One of them, *Yedioth Ahronoth*'s Nahum Barnea, said to me, 'There are 35 Israeli journalists on this plane and 34 of them don't trust Netanyahu.' When I asked him who was the journalist who did not hate Netanayahu, he said: 'That guy over there,' pointing at the reporter from *Israel Today*, US billionaire Sheldon Adelson's free pro-settlement newspaper.

Many of these journalists would openly describe the Prime Minister in print as a liar or a hypocrite. Their general view was that 'unless the occupation was dealth with, their children and grandchildren were destined to live in conflict.' Nahum Barnea's son was killed in a bombing in Jerusalem that he went to cover as a journalist, not knowing his son had been involved. Barnea and most of his journalistic colleagues believed there had to be a solution.

Sometimes Netanyahu would talk about media bias, but generally he would deal with the problem by going through friendly media such as *Israel Today*.

Netanyahu knew how to read people and managed to play the United States very well on this visit. After his pitch-perfect speech to the UN, he spoke to Congress and received something like 30 standing ovations.

Israel won a reprieve when Palestine downgraded its membership bid. But fourteen months later Palestine approached the UN seeking non-member status. When Israel tested the strength of its support the result was not good: only eight countries out of 192 voted with Israel. So remote and obscure were some of these countries for the Israeli public – such as Palau, Micronesia and the Marshall Islands – that Benjamin Netanyahu issued 'talking points' to his Cabinet to explain where they were.

Someone leaked the Cabinet document to me. It said: 'These are small island states, situated fairly close to one another in the Pacific Ocean, have very close ties to the US and vote with Israel in the General Assembly.'

A black humour developed among Israel's diplomats. 'There's a joke that if all else fails we have two guaranteed votes: the US and Micronesia,' one told me.

*

Immediately following the vote upgrading the status of Palestinians, the Netanyahu Government announced approval for zoning and planning of building work in the E1 zone of the West Bank. With this announcement, Netanyahu crossed another of Washington's red lines. Only 12 square kilometres in area, the E1 lies between Jerusalem and the settlement of Maale Adumim. Settling this area would make a contiguous Palestinian State virtually impossible. Israel quietly began construction in the area. As Israeli website +972 Magazine reported, the development plan included the transfer of the West Bank police headquarters, the construction of at least 3500 residential units and a large commercial centre, and more. The plan made no reference to the local Palestinian population.[6]

'The E1 would kill the idea of two States,' Alon Liel, former head of Israel's Foreign Ministry, told me. 'The strategic location of the E1 is going to cut Palestine into three geographic units: Gaza, the north West Bank and the south West Bank. This is also playing into the hands of the enemies of Israel who are saying Israel is developing a Bantustan system.' Liel added: 'The Israeli Government in its response said: "Who is the international community? We don't recognise the international community."'

The continued escalation of settlement growth made the attempts by the US under John Kerry at peace negotiations virtually impossible. The number of West Bank new settler housing commencements increased by 132 per cent in the first quarter of 2013, according to the Israeli Central Bureau of Statistics.

Over my six years in Jerusalem, I watched as the government of Israel – at a critical time in history – sabotaged peace. It was a critical time because it was not too late to form a Palestinian State and because Netanyahu, as someone from the far right, had the credibility with the right wing to deliver a deal.

Yet because Israel has been so successful at running interference with this reality, a perception has been created that it is earnestly chasing peace – if only the Palestinians would come to the party. Without doubt, there have been occasions when the Palestinians have blocked an agreement.

But the power to make an agreement has, mostly, been with the more powerful partner – Israel. They are the occupier. They have the ability to withdraw from the West Bank to allow the creation of a Palestinian State. And any withdrawal would be backed by the fierce – and legitimate – deterrence that comes from being the most powerful military in the Middle East should a new Palestinian State pose any security threat to Israel.

Debate about a Palestinian State has been going on, one way or another, since 1947 when the United Nations created the State of Israel alongside a new Arab State. Netanyahu said, occasionally, that he would be prepared to consider a Palestinian State. Surely, then, the proof of this would be to present a map showing boundaries Israel would accept. Despite all his rhetoric, Netanyahu has never been prepared to present a map to the Palestinians – something that surely someone would do if they were serious about negotiations. Acceptance of the boundaries in the map would, of course, be dependent upon the Palestinians agreeing to various conditions.

As mentioned, the financial support given to settlements by the Netanyahu government has been unprecedented. Investigations by Israeli media have revealed that much of the financial support has been given 'under the table' through the World Zionist Organisation, founded by Theodore Herzl at the first Zionist Congress. *Forward* magazine reported that 'for decades, the Israeli government, with the tacit consent of diaspora Jewish leaders, has taken one branch of this group, the Settlement Division, and turned it into a covert cash box for bankrolling settlement activity off the government's own books'.[7]

Various Israeli politicians have protested about the unaccountability of government spending on settlements. According to official Israeli figures, from 2008 to 2012, spending on settlements increased 1000 per cent. In 2014 alone, it increased by 800 per cent.

It has taken considerable investigation by Israeli politicians to track funding for the settlements, as it comes from several different departments – the interior, agricultural, transport, education, welfare and health ministries. One Knesset member who has been frustrated by the opaque nature of the funding is Elazar Stern, from Tzipi Livni's Hatnuah Party. 'I'm a member of the finance committee and I'm telling you, I'm being conned,' he told Reuters. 'Funds are hidden. Clauses are lumped together so that you vote on an item that is justified and then they slip it in.'

Another member of the Knesset, Stav Shaffir, who sat on the Finance Committee, later said that when she got onto the committee she realised that Israel had two budgets, 'one budget that has been passed legally on the Knesset floor, another secret budget that is being transferred in the finance committee, secretly, sometimes with no Knesset member even sitting inside and with no supervision on where this money is going'.[8]

*

On the election of Netanyahu's fourth government in 2015, after I'd left the Middle East, the push for Greater Israel would become stronger still.

The ministry Netanyahu chose in 2015 reflected the growing extremism in Israel. As the country moved to a more hardline position, politicians actively paraded their pro-settlement credentials. The new Minister for Justice was Ayelet Shaked, who previously ran a radical right-wing group called My Israel. In 2016, Netanyahu appointed Dani Dayan, a settler leader, to be Israel's Consul General to New York. Dayan is openly opposed to a two-State solution. He once said: 'I am willing to commit injustices on behalf of the existence of the Jewish people.'

It's one thing to encounter racism among ordinary Israelis, but much of it seems to be driven by political figures. According to the *Jerusalem Post*, Naftali Bennett, a senior minister in Netanyahu's government, is reported to have said during a debate about terrorism: 'I killed a lot of Arabs in my life – and there's no problem with that.' Ben Dahan was appointed to run the Civil Administration (the body which is in charge of the West Bank) despite having said of Palestinians: 'They are beasts, they are not human.' Dahan – a rabbi – once told *Maariv* newspaper: 'A Jew always has a much higher soul than a gentile, even if he is a homosexual.'[9] In countries like the US and Australia, such comments would disqualify someone from high office.

Many politicians openly flaunted their racism. In Upper Nazareth, a traditional Christian area, Israeli councillors made their views of Arabs clear – with impunity. Councillor Zeev Hartman, when asked his wish for Israeli Independence Day, said he wanted 'all the Arabs to disappear'.[10] The Mayor of Upper Nazareth, Shimon Gapso, said that since the establishment of Israel, 'racially-pure kibbutzim without a single Arab member and an army that protects a certain racial strain have been established, as have political parties that proudly bear racist names such as "Habayit HaYehudi" ["Jewish Home"]. Even our national anthem ignores the existence of the Arab minority – in other words, the people Ben-Gurion did not manage to expel in the 1948 war. If not for all that "racism", it's doubtful we could live here, and doubtful that we could live at all.'[11]

The new public mood was reflected in political slogans. Said journalist Akiva Eldar: 'The slogans of the 1990s were that only the Likud [Party] could make peace. Now peace is not on the cards any more. The average Israeli would like to wake up in the morning and find out that there are no Palestinians around, including Israeli Palestinians. For the average Israeli, a Palestinian is a terrorist until proven otherwise.'

In 1991, fresh from high school, journalist Gil Yaron left Germany and moved to Israel to work as a journalist. He wanted to live where he was 'self understood' as a Jewish person. But Yaron told me, 'I think ... [Israel] is moving in a very problematic direction.' Language that was once used on 'the outer rims of the political spectrum' had become mainstream. He pointed to the way Arabic had been downgraded and how Benjamin Netanyahu had told Israeli Arabs 'if you don't like it here, you can go to Gaza'. Yaron said: 'That used to be the talk of the extreme right, it should not be a sentence from the Prime Minister.'

Award-winning Norwegian journalist Sidsel Wold had been a great supporter of Israel. She lived on a kibbutz for three years and came to love the country. She learnt Hebrew and began converting to Judaism. In 2007 she became correspondent for Norway's NRK because 'I wanted to show a more positive side of Israel and Israelis'. However, what she saw changed her mind. 'After living in Jerusalem for five years one gets a very different picture, unfortunately a negative one,' she told me. 'But that is also because Israel has changed. There is no ideology, no idealism like in the 1980s, the solidarity has gone. What I see is the beginning of another apartheid state, with a different system than South Africa but with segregation.' She came to the view that 'Israel's greatest enemy is its own politics, its occupation and its arrogance.'

I arrived in Israel having been exposed to all the myths pushed by Israel's lobby groups. One myth was that inside Israel there had been a fierce debate about the future of the country. Living in Israel, I quickly realised it was untrue. Veteran Agence France Presse bureau chief Philippe Agret agreed: 'Even the left are united behind Zionism … All of them are Zionists. Today a lot of Israelis are driven by fear. If not indifferent, they condone what's happening in the occupied territories, and the discrimination within Israel.'

The dominant Israeli viewpoint today is that Israel is now 'managing a problem' in much the same way that a police force manages a troublesome neighbourhood. Most Israelis have moved on from seeking any change. They're comfortable with the status quo. They take some international criticism, but it's not great enough to deter them from Greater Israel. This is a term usually heard from visiting foreign ministers.' Most Israelis can get on with their lives and not even have to think about the conflict; the Israeli Army manages that for them. People living in Tel Aviv never need to think about the settlements – they happen 'out there'.

Over lunch in Jerusalem in late 2014, towards the end of my posting, I asked an Israeli official – one of my contacts – whether Israel had in fact won the Israeli–Palestinian conflict. He smiled, as if he were surprised it had taken me so long to figure it all out. 'It depends what you mean by won,' he said. 'If by won you mean that we are in total control of the West Bank, then yes, we have won. The debate at senior levels of our government now is what comes next – do we cede back some of the territory for a Palestinian State, or do we decide we are going to hold on to it permanently and make it part of Israel?'

But the 'victory' that Israelis believe they have won is, in my view, corrosive. It is changing the character of Israel. The continuation of the settlement enterprise confirms that many Israelis now believe it is a right for 600,000 Jewish settlers to live on land that is not within their recognised borders. The values upon which Israel was founded are being violated on a daily basis.

The mood in Israel is hardening. One reason for this was the Second Intifada (2000–05). While the previous 40 years of the conflict had occurred mainly in the West Bank, the Second Intifada brought violence into Israel. Many Palestinians engaged in attacks on civilian targets. Suicide bombers hit bus stops and cafés. In my view this was unforgivable.

Sylvie and I came to realise how crucial the Second Intifada was to understanding the Israeli mindset. Talking to Israelis helped us realise how many families had been touched. Our landlord, Avi, told us how it ended his relationships with Palestinians; this situation was common. I realised there was a major disconnect between the high importance that Israelis place on the Second Intifada and the low importance given to it by many journalists.

The Second Intifada largely wiped out the centre and left in Israel, and the whole country veered to the right. It gave political momentum to the national religious movement, which argues that the decision of the United Nations in 1947 to create a Palestinian State was irrelevant.

The First Intifada, from 1987 to 1991, was confronting; the Second Intifada was dreadful. And if the next round of violence comes it will almost certainly be far worse than the last.

Within Israel, more and more security experts are realising that there is something their country can do to address the violence: end the occupation. More than 200 key national security figures in Israel and the US have posted comments on the site of the New York-based Israel Policy Forum (IPF),[12] urging Israel to change direction. Yuval Diskin, a former head of Shin Bet, wrote: 'The unsolved Israeli–Palestinian conflict represents an existential threat. We need to reach an agreement before we reach "a point of no return" in the Israeli–Palestinian conflict, a point from which we will not be able to return to the option of the "two states for two people."' Shabtai Shavit, a former head of Mossad, wrote: 'Some values are more sacred than land. Peace, which is the life and soul of true democracy, is more important than land.'

Many of the former heads of Mossad and Shin Bet – who understand both Israel's strength as well as the consequences of not finding a resolution – have urged their country to agree to a Palestinian State. It is the politicians, not the security experts, who are resisting.

The Israeli media has grown louder in its warnings. Even *Israel Today* has expressed concerns. Columnist Dan Margalit referred to 'the last remnants of Israel's good name in the democratic world'.

Warnings have also been heard from some Israeli politicians. Former President Shimon Peres warned: 'We're galloping at full speed toward a situation where Israel will cease to exist as a Jewish state.' Former Prime Minister Ehud Olmert said: 'We don't have unlimited time. More and more Palestinians are uninterested in a negotiated, two-state solution because they want to change the essence of the conflict from an Algerian paradigm to a South African one. From a struggle against "occupation", in their parlance, to a struggle for one-man-one-vote. That is, of course, a much cleaner struggle, a much more popular struggle – and ultimately a much more powerful one. For us, it would mean the end of the Jewish state.'[13]

Arnon Soffer, an academic from Haifa University, has advised several Israeli governments about the 'demographic threat' of the Palestinians. 'When 2.5 million people live in a closed-off Gaza, it's going to be a human catastrophe,' he told the *Jerusalem Post*. 'Those people will become even bigger animals than they are today, with the aid of an insane fundamentalist Islam. The pressure at the border will be awful. It's going to be a terrible war. So, if we want to remain alive, we will have to kill and kill and kill. All day, every day. If we don't kill, we will cease to exist. The only thing that concerns me is how to ensure that the boys and men who are going to have to do the killing will be able to return home to their families and be normal human beings.'

Israel is losing many of its most loyal friends. Over our six years in Israel, we watched international support for the country deteriorate. In his second and third terms, Benjamin Netanyahu crystallised in the minds of many the idea that Israel was no longer interested in a two-State solution. In November 2011, French president Nicolas Sarkozy, who had been one of Netanyahu's confidants, was caught telling President Obama that Netanyahu was a 'liar'. In October 2014, Richard Ottaway, the Conservative chairman of the UK's Foreign Affairs Committee, explained his reasons for abandoning support for Israel: 'Looking back over the last 20 years, I realise now Israel has slowly been drifting away from world public opinion.'[14]

Strangely, outsiders recognise the coming crisis better than many Israelis. The country has been immersed in so many conflicts for so long that its public now finds it difficult to make objective assessments. Jewish diaspora communities have been told for so long that everything is fine that they do not realise the coming dangers.

Prominent British lawyer David Middleburgh warned that diaspora Jews have a duty to visit the Palestinian Territories to understand the problem. 'If we do nothing, can we complain if we awake one day and Israel has sleepwalked into the status of a pariah country?' he asked.[15]

The *New York Times*'s Jodi Rudoren said: 'I don't think [Netanyahu] has a real plan to deal with the pariah issue. I think his basic feeling is to avoid. This problem is not solvable, he thinks, because the way to solving it through a road map is unacceptable to him. The way he would like to solve it with the [Israeli] military staying in place is obviously unacceptable to the Palestinians, so let's keep going and make sure they [the Israelis] don't get blown up today.'

I asked Rudoren for her thoughts on the conflict generally:

I actually don't think it is more complicated than I thought.
I think it's less soluble than I thought. I think the outsiders'
understanding of this situation is basically like two peoples
with reasonable claims to the same place trying to figure out
some sort of way to split it up. There are a few nutty issues
like what do you do with Jerusalem and the refugees but
they should be figure-out-able and what's taken so long? But

I think the more you get into it the more you understand the
hatred, the racism, the distrust, the invisibility of one to the
other, the deeply held belief that each set of people wants
to destroy the other's right to exist as a people, as a nation-
State, all those things make what should be a fairly simple,
straightforward project – all the work has already been done
on the maps etc – makes it really complicated. This question
– is there really a will to resolve it?

German journalist Gil Yaron told me:

The occupation is not only hazardous but dangerous to
Israel, though I can think that it could be fatal, because
it endangers Israel's connection to the Western world. It's
becoming worse by the day and because of what it does to
Israeli society, that lawless vacuum in which ideological
organisations act with impunity, which teach generation
after generation of Israelis [in the army in the West Bank]
how to solve problems with violence … and they take
this knowledge and bring it back home to Israel and it is
affecting our society back here. The anti-democratic trends
that we have in Israel I think are in part as a consequence
of the occupation and at the same time I belong to the
school who fervently believes that this problem is unsolvable
in the foreseeable future because I do not think that the
maximum concessions that both sides are willing to make
will satisfy either side.

Within Israel there is an inherent contradiction. Israeli land
expert Dror Etkes told me: 'How do you on the one hand keep the

narrative you tell yourself – that you are a democracy, that you are a villa in the jungle, that you are a place which differs from the entire area around it – and on the other hand you are pleasing the most tribal and territorial and chauvinist and nationalist and violent needs or interests of your own society. Israel is not willing to give up either one of these desires.'

Over six years, the thing that most surprised me about Israel was that it is two totally different things: a triumph and a tragedy.

It is a triumph because of what it has achieved in the first seven decades of its life. Israel rose from the Holocaust to become a State three years later. It became a dynamic economy and was able to defend itself against any threat. It revived Hebrew, turned a desert into a bread basket and became a dream for Jews.

It is a tragedy because that dream is being destroyed by a greed for more land.

*

By 2017, Benjamin Netanyahu had been Prime Minister for a total of 11 years. After four terms of Netanyahu the settlement enterprise was so firmly entrenched that a Palestinian State was virtually no longer viable.

It seemed the Oslo peace process could not survive Benjamin Netanyahu. I believe that more than any other leader, he has been responsible for consigning Israel to long-term war.

It's now highly unlikely that there will be a peaceful resolution to the Israeli–Palestinian conflict. As the occupation passed its 50th year in 2017, an indefinite future of violence set in. The Israeli public has been so inculcated, for so long, to believe that they cannot make peace with Palestinians – the savages – that peace would now be almost impossible. As Benjamin Netanyahu told Israelis of Palestinians: 'They murder – we build.'

Netanyahu has killed off the two-State solution. A Palestinian State is dead before it has been born. As far as the majority of Israelis are concerned, they have won the conflict with the Palestinians. And in a military sense they have. Because this is the world's slowest war, the international community has, largely, grown tired of it. Because, on average, there are one or two Palestinians killed every week (excluding wars with Gaza), they rarely make the headlines; they are 'the norm'. Virtually no media outlet in the world will run a story about the deaths of one or two Palestinians.

In 1989, towards the end of apartheid, I met a South African diplomat in Sydney who told me that the aim of his government was to maintain an 'acceptable' level of violence between the white and black populations. Incidents such as the notorious 1976 Soweto massacre were not acceptable. But in daily life, with a hostile black community, there would always be some violence; the aim was to ensure that it did not cause South Africa problems internationally.

Israel has reached a similar situation. As long as, on average, only one or two Palestinians a week are killed, the world can live with it. But maintaining an 'acceptable' level of international criticism does not solve the underlying problem.

The occupation of 2.9 million Palestinians cannot go on forever – especially when that number becomes 4 or 5 million. Unlike the South African regime, which ultimately was brought down by economic sanctions, Israel has shown that it can sustain a long international campaign. But what it cannot sustain is the cancer growing from within: a cancer that one day will be fatal if not cut out. The internet and mobile phones are destroying Israel's ability to manage its message by *hasbara*.

The editorial board of the *New York Times* has written about 'increased talk among Israelis of the "one-state solution", in which Israel subsumes the West Bank formally while incorporating the Palestinian population or somehow shifting the Palestinians to Jordan and Egypt. The likeliest outcome, given the growth rate of the Arab population, is that Israel would be confronted with a miserable choice: to give up being a Jewish state – or to give up being a democratic state by denying full voting rights to Palestinians.'

And so, after 50 years of occupation, the reality has come to this. That Israel is faced with 'a miserable choice'. But many would argue that the Palestinians no longer have a choice, miserable or not.

*

Benjamin Netanyahu has, finally, got what he wished for. Israel's hundreds of settlements and outposts are firmly entrenched. A Palestinian State is now almost physically impossible. This is victory for Netanyahu and his political base, the Likud Party, with its nationalist–religious core.

But in coming years, there will be tragic consequences of Netanyahu's sacrifice of peace on the altar of Greater Israel. It will be unthinkable tragedy.

Israel is a country steeped in military tradition. In many militaries around the world the term 'Code Red' means a state of high alert and imminent danger. After six years of living in Israel, I have come to a very clear, but regrettable, view: Israel, Code Red.

Farewell, Jerusalem

6 January 2015

IT WAS OUR LAST DAY IN JERUSALEM. SYLVIE, JACK AND I
woke up at the American Colony Hotel. It was almost six years
to the day since we arrived here to begin our great adventure.
Six years since we landed at Ben-Gurion Airport in Tel Aviv,
excited but uncertain about what lay ahead. A few days earlier
we'd moved out of our house, and since then we'd been based
here, saying goodbye to friends and contacts and doing tasks such
as closing bank accounts and trying to convince a bureaucrat in
the water company that we wanted our programmed payments
to cease.

Early in our time here, Sylvie and I had talked about how,
when we finally left, we'd have a farewell party to which we'd
invite our Israeli and Palestinian friends. How naïve we'd been.
We now realised how absurd that idea was. The days when
Israelis and Palestinians would share social occasions were long
gone.

On this, our last morning, we gathered for breakfast. There was a certain sadness for the three of us. The Middle East had become such a major part of our lives. Jack had virtually grown up here. He came here as an innocent, wide-eyed, eight-year-old boy and was leaving a 14-year-old on the verge of young adulthood. Most of his real friends were here. Likewise, Sylvie and I had enjoyed a golden period in our marriage, travelling for work and pleasure, and building up a wonderful circle of friends.

However, the conflict was with us until the very end. The American Colony Hotel, which is in East Jerusalem, ordered a Palestinian taxi driver for us – what the Israelis call a Jerusalemite. He told us his family had stayed here during the violence of 1948 when Israel was established, and he only had Israeli residency, not citizenship. This meant he had limited rights – for example, Israel did not allow him to vote in national elections.

As we arrived at the security gates leading to Ben-Gurion Airport, he wound down his window. When dealing with armed Israeli security officers at these checkpoints, Palestinian drivers often try to speak Hebrew with thick Israeli accents, in the hope that they won't be taken aside.

On this, our last trip to the airport, this strategy failed as dismally as such attempts usually did. The Israeli officers could tell immediately that he was a Palestinian, which meant we would have a much longer security check and he would be given a serious interrogation.

Finally we were allowed into the terminal. We sat at the gate waiting to board.

'What an extraordinary time we've had,' Sylvie said to Jack and me. We discussed where we thought Israel was heading. The conversation had a sad personal note for Sylvie: two days earlier, a Palestinian woman she knew from the village of Nabi Saleh in the West Bank was shot by Israeli soldiers, although had survived.

I asked Jack how he looked back on his time here. 'It's been fun,' he said. 'But I think the political situation is terrible. Some of my friends from school have to stop themselves from speaking Arabic in the street for fear that they will be attacked. It's sad.'

My own thoughts wandered across the extraordinary stories I'd covered while based here. I'd been an eyewitness to the optimism of the Arab world as it tried to find democracy then watched it all come crashing down so violently. My view was that the Arab Spring failed not because 'Arabs and democracy don't go together', as some say, but because countries cannot go from dictatorships to democracies in one step. Democracy will come, one day, to various Arab countries, but first they need to set up independent institutions such as police forces and civil services. I'd covered the funeral of Nelson Mandela, who I regarded as the greatest man of the 20th century. I'd covered three wars between Israel and Gaza, and seen the senselessness of that conflict.

Finally our plane took off. As I looked down at Tel Aviv's high-rise buildings glistening beside the Mediterranean Sea, I felt a sadness that these years had passed – so quickly. Professionally, I felt proud that I'd done my job honestly. The Israeli lobby made all sorts of efforts to get me to soften my reporting. I was pleased I hadn't buckled.

This had been the toughest assignment I'd ever had – by far. But those who'd read my reports over those six years could have been confident that they were reading facts, not propaganda. Back in Australia, I will often run into people, both Jewish and non-Jewish, who remark that they were surprised I was able to get published what I did, and that they appreciated it. That, in the end, is what journalists should do: report what's in front of them. Then it's over to the politicians and the public to decide what they do with that information. But without facts, they cannot know what they are dealing with.

Several crucial events had occurred during our six years in Jerusalem. Firstly, Israel reached its demographic tipping-point between Israelis and Palestinians: a crucial factor in any potential solution. Depending on whose figures you accept, the number of Palestinians in Israel, the West Bank and Gaza equalled or passed the number of Jews in Israel and the West Bank (since 2005 there have been no Jews in Gaza).

Professor Sergio DellaPergola is regarded as Israel's foremost demographer. According to him, as of 2016 the Jewish population of Israel, the West Bank, the Golan Heights and East Jerusalem was 6,336,400. This compares with the Palestinian population of 5,967,100 – made up of 1,757,700 living in Israel, 2,448,800 in the West Bank and 1,750,600 in Gaza. However, the Israeli Civil Administration estimates that there are 2,919,350 registered Palestinians in the West Bank. This would mean that the Palestinian population has passed the Jewish population. Whichever figure one accepts, the tipping-point has either arrived or is arriving, with faster birth rates of Palestinians than Israelis.

The reason this is so important is because it means, now or in the near future, a minority Jewish population has control over the lives and movements of a majority Palestinian population. While Israel does not occupy Gaza the way it does the West Bank, it controls movement in and out of Gaza with its naval blockade and it controls entry and exit points, along with Egypt in the south.

The other major event that happened in our time in Israel was a dramatic escalation in settlement growth. When we arrived in 2009 there were 296,000 settlers in the West Bank, excluding East Jerusalem. When we left, there were 385,000, according to the Israeli human rights group Peace Now. This meant the number of settlers had grown by 30 per cent.

As we sat for the first time all those years ago on our balcony over Jerusalem, there was so much we didn't know. We did not truly understand either Israelis or Palestinians, and we did not understand that the powerful side of the equation – Israel – has, for now, pushed away the desire for peace.

Six years on, we had seen so much. We had lived and breathed this place, the good and the bad, the wonderful and the dreadful. We had met good people on both sides of the conflict who yearned for peace, and for their children to have better lives than they'd had.

But we were also leaving disappointed and sad. We knew that what is coming could have been avoided. And we got to know too many of the people – both Israeli and Palestinian – who will face this coming storm.

This tragedy now seems inevitable. Almost 3 million people in the West Bank cannot be denied all civil rights for more than 50 years without dire consequences and almost two million people in Gaza cannot be locked forever in the world's largest open-air prison. One day many of those five million people will rise up.

*

We arrived back in Australia on 10 January 2015. Shortly after our return, we were invited to a Bar Mitzvah in the northern Sydney suburb of Neutral Bay. The son of some friends of ours had come of age.

Something occurred at the event that surprised me. Towards the end of the ceremony, the rabbi asked us all to pray for the Israeli Defence Forces. He drew on Deuteronomy 20:4: 'For the Lord, your God, is the one who goes with you, to fight for you against your enemies, to save you.'

I was surprised both by the explicit message and the fact that it was being delivered in Australia. I'd heard many such exhortations in Israel, but hearing this in Sydney jarred. My reading of the prayer was that virtually anything the IDF do in battle is justified because, after all, God is not just with them, but fighting against the enemy to save them.

I'd covered three Gaza wars and found it hard to believe that any god could justify the dropping of white phosphorus onto heavily populated areas. The fact that we were being asked in a relatively modern Jewish community in Sydney to pray for a foreign army confirmed how deeply the propaganda of 'the most moral army in the world' had seeped into Australia.

*

Another event occurred after our return that confirmed why the Israeli Government believes it has the support of countries like Australia in continuing its occupation. In February 2017, Benjamin Netanyahu made an official visit: the first by a sitting Israeli prime minister. The reception he received was extraordinary; I had no doubt that he would never receive such adulation in Israel.

Prime Minister Malcolm Turnbull's office invited me to a lunch for Netanyahu in Sydney. It was attended by about 400 business men and women, including leaders of the Jewish community. This was a serious show of business power; I walked past six billionaires before I even found my table.

That night, Netanyahu received a rapturous reception at the Central Synagogue in Sydney's Bondi Junction. Soon afterwards, I had lunch with Rabbi Levi Wolff, chief minister at the synagogue. Over chicken soup and a bottle of kosher wine in Bondi, Rabbi Wolff told me he'd never seen anything like the interest the Netanyahu visit evoked. Two Holocaust survivors who were desperate for a seat in the synagogue on the day came to see Rabbi Wolff and rolled up their sleeves, displaying their tattooed numbers from the Holocaust. For them the opportunity to see Netanyahu rounded out their circle of survival.

Rabbi Wolff and I talked about some of the themes of this book. He predicted that I would be hit by some criticism, but he toasted me with a glass of wine: 'You have an important job to do. As Dick Cheney said, "Dogs never bark at parked cars." If you're moving and actually doing something in life then people will attack you.'

*

A year and a half after we returned to Australia, we went back to Jerusalem. It was our first overseas holiday after coming home and the three of us all nominated Jerusalem as the place we'd most like to visit. For all its problems, we were drawn back. Leaving Israel had made us realise the depths of the friendships we had made there, both Israeli and Palestinian. 'Welcome back to your second home!' Israeli journalist Akiva Eldar quipped when we went to dinner at his apartment in Netanya.

When you live in conflict, friendships and family become even more important. We were keen to experience the strange magic of Jerusalem again. The city may be, as Amos Oz once wrote, 'an old nymphomaniac who squeezes lover after lover to death, before shrugging him off her with a yawn', but we were enchanted by her. We visited our neighbours from Avi's apartment, Ilan the historian and Stephanie the museum curator. Ilan had developed lymphoma, but was being successfully treated. 'My doctor is an Arab woman,' he told us proudly, explaining that hospitals remained perhaps the only place of coexistence. Ilan and Stephanie were old-time Israelis who were distressed at how the occupation was sabotaging their country.

While I was there, I checked the situation in the military court. After my various articles, the Israeli Government had vowed to improve the system. The Israeli Foreign Ministry's Yigal Palmor had two years earlier told me that his government had taken note of my reporting about children. 'You've made a difference,' he said.

But in fact I found the situation had worsened. Detention rates for Palestinian children were up 93 per cent in 2016, according to Military Court Watch. I realised that this situation could never really improve as long as the occupation continued. There might occasionally be a dip, but the ongoing detention of Palestinians is a key weapon in maintaining settlements and enforcing the occupation.

*

For many years, Israeli lawmakers had given lip service to the idea of a Palestinian State. But they'd always fallen back on a range of excuses as to why this was not possible – most commonly that the Palestinians were not 'partners for peace'.

But in 2017, the Israeli Government dropped all artifice when the Knesset passed the Regularisation Bill. This law allows Israel to retroactively legalise Israeli settlements in the West Bank. It allows Israel to expropriate private Palestinian land and give it to Jewish settlements for their exclusive use. In effect, it makes 'theft' an official Israeli policy.

Even leading lights of the Likud Party expressed their concern. Former Likud Deputy Prime Minister Dan Meridor described the law as 'evil and dangerous', explaining that 'the Arabs of Judea and Samaria did not vote for the Knesset, and it has no authority to legislate for them'. Another Likud heavyweight, Benny Begin – the son of former Prime Minister Menachem Begin and considered one of the most right-wing members of Netanyahu's government – called it 'the robbery Bill', saying it allowed for the 'looting' of Palestinian land.[1]

The leader of the Labor Party, Isaac Herzog, predicted that the law would see Israel's leaders face international justice one day. Speaking before the Bill was passed, Herzog said: 'It is not too late to stop the horror of a freight train. The train that leaves from here will only stop at the Hague': a reference to the International Criminal Court. 'Its car will carry international indictments against Israeli and Jewish soldiers and officers.'[2]

But the ruling extreme right wing applauded the passing of the Bill. Bezalel Smotrich, a member of Orthodox party the Jewish Home, called it 'an historic day for the settlement movement', adding: 'From here we move on to expanding Israeli sovereignty [in the West Bank] and continuing to build and develop settlements across the land.'[3]

The Knesset also pushed ahead with a range of new laws that weakened the position of Palestinians still further. Documented by the Association of Civil Rights in Israel, they included a law allowing the State to revoke someone's citizenship in absentia. It prevented a citizen who is outside Israel from returning home if the State has a 'concern' that their return could endanger Israel's national security. It also permitted courts to sentence someone convicted of throwing stones to 20 years' imprisonment, and even to impose fines on the parents of stone-throwers. Another law allowed the banning of entry to Israel or the West Bank of someone regarded as an advocate of the pro-Palestinian Boycott, Divestment and Sanctions movement.

The Israeli–Palestinian 'marriage' has become so abusive that every sign of conciliation goes nowhere. In January 2017, Hamas announced that it would rewrite its charter, in response to claims that its old charter was anti-Semitic. It agreed to change the language of the charter to make it clear that it did not oppose Jews but the occupation. The draft of the new charter said that Hamas 'considers the establishment of a fully sovereign and independent Palestinian state, with Jerusalem as its capital along the lines of 4 June 1967'.[4] This meant that Hamas was accepting the existence of Israel up until its occupation of the West Bank began – that is, accepting the boundaries set out by the United Nations in 1947.

This was big news: it essentially meant that Hamas accepted a two-State solution, putting it in line with countries such as the US and Australia. But that change led to nothing: a few weeks later, Hamas leader Mazen Faqha was shot dead outside his home in Gaza City, a killing Hamas claimed was a targeted operation by Israel.

*

It is still important to cling to hope, no matter how forlorn this hope may be.

One idea that former Prime Minister Yitzhak Rabin put forward involved developing a large parcel of land between Israel, Egypt and the Gaza Strip into one massive hospital complex. Patients and doctors from all three places would come together for medical care. Those advocating the idea saw it as a way of building on one of the few areas of common interest, and seeing enough relationships develop from this to create a well of goodwill. From that well of goodwill, it was hoped that greater understanding of each other could be found.

Developers and architects were engaged for the project – but they were sworn to strict confidentiality. A Turkish benefactor offered US$800 million as a contribution. Rabin's advisers also looked at building a similar complex at a site where Israel, Jordan, Lebanon and Syria meet. Doctors from Gaza could sit in the cafeteria next to doctors from Israel, while children from Lebanon would be lying in beds next to Israeli children.

But one day it all came to a halt. The Israeli Ministry of Defence informed those involved in the project that it would not be proceeding. Their reason? That they could not guarantee security of the hospitals. Even though an Israeli prime minister had come up with the plan, Israel's defence establishment sank it. It confirmed my view that the Israeli military establishment was sometimes more powerful than the country's elected officials.

My own suggested solution draws more broadly on the fundamentals of the Arab Peace Initiative of 2002. I believe that that plan stands the test of time. The great advantage –

from Israel's point of view – is that in one document it delivers a peace agreement with the 22 members of the Arab League.[5] The economic power that this would deliver to Israel is unimaginable: the commencement of business and diplomatic dealings with countries as regionally powerful as Saudi Arabia and Qatar would unleash a new economic bloc on the world. Business dealings already go on between Israel and the Gulf States – indeed, even discreetly with Iran – but they are done at an unofficial and under-the-radar level. Enacting the 2002 Arab Peace Initiative would exponentially increase trade and joint ventures.

One factor rarely considered when people discuss the Arab Peace Initiative is that it would deliver to Israel a new peace agreement not just with 22 countries but with 57. This is because the Arab Peace Initiative was also endorsed by the Organisation of Islamic Cooperation, a group of 57 countries that include Iran.

'Israel is in the region but not part of the region,' a senior Jordanian official – a supporter of the Arab Peace Initiative – told me during a visit I made to Amman in 2012. 'To become part of the region they need to solve the Palestinian issue, and that means helping to create a Palestinian State.'

The world was given a taste of what peace could bring to the Middle East after Israel and Jordan signed a peace agreement in 1994. The change within Jordan was profound. Before that deal was signed, the conflict with Israel – and the potential for war at any time – had consumed Jordanians and their political dialogue. But once peace was made, Jordan began to focus on internal issues: creating employment, alleviating poverty and building schools and hospitals.

The enthusiasm of a move towards Israeli–Palestinian peace ended, of course, in 2000, amid the disappointment of the failure of the Middle East Peace Summit at Camp David, and the beginning of the Second Intifada after Opposition Leader Ariel Sharon famously visited the Temple Mount (one of the contentious topics of the peace talks). Four years later, around 4000 Palestinians and Israelis were dead.

Israeli writer Amos Oz believes that the end to the conflict will not be a happy one, but continues to hope that it will not be marked by violence. 'The Israeli–Palestinian conflict is a clash of right and right,' he wrote. 'Tragedies are resolved in one of two ways: the Shakespearian way or the Anton Chekhov way. In a tragedy by Shakespeare, the stage at the end is littered with dead bodies. In a tragedy by Chekhov, everyone is unhappy, bitter, disillusioned and melancholy but they are alive. My colleagues in the peace movement and I are working for a Chekhovian not a Shakespearian conclusion.'[6]

*

Historian Simon Sebag Montefiore wrote in *Jerusalem: The Biography* that the city belongs to no one and exists for everyone in their imagination. 'And this is the city's tragedy as well as her magic; every dreamer of Jerusalem, every visitor in all ages from Jesus' Apostles to Saladin's soldiers, from Victorian pilgrims to today's tourists and journalists, arrives with a vision of the authentic Jerusalem and then is bitterly disappointed by what they find.'[7]

Like so many through the ages, I, too, left Jerusalem bitterly disappointed. For me, though, it wasn't a disappointment with my vision of Jerusalem but with the decisions of modern politicians – led by Benjamin Netanyahu. He and his government today have unprecedented power. They could give the Middle East its best chance – its only chance – for decades to resolve one of the region's most destabilising conflicts – the Israeli–Palestinian conflict (the other being the Shia–Sunni conflict whose resolution will rely on Iranian and Saudi Arabian leadership). As long as Palestinians living with no rights and no hope keep increasing in number, a time bomb ticks away. Israel does not need to pretend any confected warmth towards the Palestinians. Now is the time to act, not when another round of sustained violence envelopes Israel in the distrust of the international community.

Twenty years ago, when Sylvie and I first visited Israel, debate among Israelis was fierce. Now, as the country becomes more isolated, many Israelis want to cut contact with those who challenge what their government is doing in the West Bank.

When Sylvie, Jack and I arrived in Jerusalem, we had hope. As we sat on that balcony at the beginning of our great adventure, we looked across Jerusalem with awe and excitement. But now we've seen the reality.

If the whole world could see the occupation up close, it would demand that it end tomorrow. Israel's treatment of the Palestinians would not pass muster in the West if the full details were known. The only reason Israel is getting away with this is because it has one of the most formidable public-relations machines ever seen, and enormous support from its diaspora communities. But while this worked for the first few decades of the occupation, now virtually every incident between an Israeli soldier and a Palestinian is filmed by a mobile phone. Military occupations look ugly because they are ugly. Israel's reputation will bleed as long as its control over another people continues.

I predict – with sadness – that one day history will catch up with Israel. The longer that takes, the more tragic it will be.

Former *Washington Post* publisher Philip Graham once said that journalism is the first rough draft of history. From our balcony over Jerusalem, I've written this first draft of an extraordinary period. I deeply hope that the final version of history is not what it is shaping up to be.

We must avoid a coming tragedy.

ENDNOTES

Author's Note

This books draws on conversations during my six years in Jerusalem. Extensive interviews were done with Chris Mitchell, Bob Carr, Kathryn Greiner, Tim Fischer, Jodi Rudoren, Philippe Agret, Crispian Balmer, Dominic Waghorn, Dror Etkes, Gideon Levy, Chris McGreal, Gil Yaron, Akiva Eldar, Daniella Weiss, Jonathan Cook, Gerard Horton, Ahmad Aweidah and Uffe Taudal.

Prologue: The Handshake

1 Thomas Friedman, 13 September 1993, http://www.nytimes.com/learning/general/onthisday/big/0913.html

2: My Long Journey to Jerusalem

1 Council on Foreign Relations, 10 April 2008 and 1 August 2014.
2 https://www.theguardian.com/world/2003/aug/22/israel1

3: Arriving to a War

1 http://www.haaretz.com/israel-news/bill-clinton-s-russian-immigrants-are-obstacle-to-peace-comment-draws-fire-in-israel-1.315244
2 https://www.theguardian.com/commentisfree/2010/feb/04/israel-palestinian-territories-war-crimes
3 https://972mag.com/israels-top-news-channel-govt-asked-us-to-show-more-gaza-devastation/99033/.20 November 2014.
4 As he was about to board his plane in Tel Aviv to travel to New York to address the United Nations, Benjamin Netanyahu said he would tell the UN 'the truth about the heroic soldiers of the IDF, the most moral army in the world' (*Jerusalem Post*, 28 September 2014).
5 http://aijac.org.au/news/article/atrocity-or-atrocious-reporting

6: The French School of Jerusalem

1　Israeli Military Order 101, 17 August 1967.

2　http://www.haaretz.com/middle-east-news/.premium-1.573976

3　Citizenship and Entry into Israel Law (Temporary Order) 5763, 31 March 2003 (extended June 2016).

4　http://www.militarycourtwatch.org/

5　https://www.unicef.org/oPt/UNICEF_oPt_Children_in_Israeli_Military_Detention_Observations_and_Recommendations_-_6_March_2013.pdf

6　www.theguardian.com/world/2012/jan/22/palestinian-children-detained-jail-israel

7　Personal communication.

8　Military Court Watch, 29 January 2015.

9　http://www.theaustralian.com.au/life/weekend-australian-magazine/stone-cold-justice/news-story/832380779022d889cdb491120895b45c

8: The Arab Spring

1　https://www.channel4.com/news/sidi-bouzid-roots-of-the-tunisia-revolution

2　http://www.nytimes.com/2012/09/17/opinion/a-preventable-massacre.html

9: 'I think Egypt is Going to Blow'

1　http://www.smh.com.au/world/fear-on-the-nile--no-place-for-the-fainthearted-20110206-1aii2.html

11: Frankenstein's Monster

1　https://www.adalah.org/ January 2017

2　http://www.haaretz.com/a-civilized-country-doesn-t-traffic-in-bodies-1.371876

3　http://www.haaretz.com/jewish/books/probing-the-bureaucracy-of-occupation-1.453805)

4　http://www.haaretz.com/israel-has-101-different-types-of-permits-governing-palestinian-movement-1.403039

5　Hadas, Ziv, 'The Bureaucracy of Occupation: the District Civil Liaison Offices', Machsom Watch and Physicians for Human Rights-Israel, p. 8.

6　Women's Centre for Legal Aid and Counselling (WCLAC), 'Life Behind the Wall: Women's Voices from the Seam Zone', accessible at www.wclac.org

7　HaMoked, Case 65164, from 'The Permit Regime: Human Rights Violations in West Bank Areas Known as the 'Seam Zone'', www.hamoked.org/files/2013/1157660_eng.pdf

8　Richard Ben Cramer, *How Israel Lost: The Four Questions* (Simon & Schuster, 2004).

9   http://www.nytimes.com/2009/08/02/opinion/02friedman.html

10 'The Permit Regime: Human Rights Violations in West Bank Areas Known as the 'Seam Zone'', Executive Summary p. 2, www.hamoked.org/files/2013/1157660_eng.pdf

11 https://machsomwatch.org/sites/default/files/InvisiblePrisonersEng.pdf

12 Victor Ostrovsky and Claire Hoy, *By Way of Deception: The Making and Unmaking of a Mossad Officer*, St Martin's Press, New York, 1990.

13 http://news.bbc.co.uk/2/hi/middle_east/685792.stm

14 https://www.yesh-din.org/en/a-court-of-non-convictions-for-israeli-felons/

15 http://www.jonathan-cook.net/2005-02-04/israels-latest-land-grab-is-part-of-an-old-strategy/

16 Personal communication, 1 March 2014, and *Haaretz*, 12 December 2013.

17 972mag.com/this-is-how-settlers-take-over-palestinian-land/115754/.

18 https://www.hrw.org/report/2016/01/19/occupation-inc/how-settlement-businesses-contribute-israels-violations-palestinian

19 http://www.haaretz.com/middle-east-news/.premium-1.562975

20 http://www.haaretz.com/israel-news/.premium-1.733746

21 documents.worldbank.org/curated/en/137111468329419171/West-Bank-and-Gaza-Area-C-and-the-future-of-the-Palestinian-economy

22 Guy Bechor, 'Jewish demographics have won', *Yedioth Ahronoth*, 20 June 2013, p. 24.

23 http://www.washingtonpost.com/wp-dyn/content/article/2006/11/21/AR2006112100482.htm

24 http://files.yesh-din.org/userfiles/Yesh%20Din_Under%20The%20Radar%20-%20English_WEB(3).pdf

25 http://www.haaretz.com/secret-israeli-database-reveals-full-extent-of-illegal-settlement-1.266936

12: Coffee with the Israeli Army

1   http://blogs.timesofisrael.com/an-objective-journalist-the-unicorn-of-the-middle-east/

2   http://www.haaretz.com/blogs/west-of-eden/.premium-1.568875

3   ibid.

4   Sylvain Cypel, *Walled: Israeli Society at an Impasse*, Other Press, New York 2007.

5   http://www.haaretz.com/survival-of-the-fittest-cont-1.61341

6   http://www.timesofisrael.com/poll-half-of-jewish-high-schoolers-think-arabs-shouldnt-vote-in-israel/ URL; and http://www.jta.org/2016/03/08/news-opinion/israel-middle-east/six-surprising-findings-from-pews-study-of-israelis

7   *Jerusalem Post*, 2 July 2016.

8   http://www.jpost.com/Israel-News/Tel-Aviv-cleaning-ad-found-pricing-workers-by-race-spurs-outrage-444122
9   cdn3.phr.org.il/wp-content/uploads/2016/04/Divide-And-Conquer.pdf.
10 *Haaretz*, 21 October 2012.
11 *Haaretz*, 28 March 2015.
12 *Haaretz*, 15 May 2015.
13 http://www.haaretz.com/black-like-me-1.281530
14 Max Blumenthal, *Goliath: Life and Loathing in Greater Israel*, Nation Books 2014.
15 *The Times of Israel*, 1 June 2016.
16 *Haaretz*, 25 May 2016.
17 http://www.haaretz.com/opinion/.premium-1.693502
18 Chemi Shalev, 'Berlin, 1933 and Jerusalem, 2014: When racist thugs are on the prowl', *Haaretz*, 2 July 2014.

14: The American Factor

1   http://jewishjournal.com/opinion/rob_eshman/114519/
2   Thomas Friedman interview, Channel 10 Israel, 14 September 2016.
3   http://www.thedailybeast.com/articles/2014/04/27/exclusive-kerry-warns-israel-could-become-an-apartheid-state
4   http://america.aljazeera.com/articles/2014/5/1/kerry-israel-apartheid.html
5   http://www.cbsnews.com/news/john-kerry-confronted-over-sarcasm-on-israeli-invasion-of-gaza/
6   newrepublic.com/article/117247/contentious-interview-rahm-emanuel
7   http://www.haaretz.com/israel-news/.premium-1.698153
8   http://mondoweiss.net/2016/09/israel-turning-friedman/
9   http://nypost.com/2016/12/06/kushner-foundation-donated-to-jewish-settlements-in-west-bank; *Washington Post*, 5 December 2016; http://edition.cnn.com/2017/02/23/politics/kfile-david-friedman-november-speech
10 http://foreignpolicy.com/2017/02/15/903972-bibi-israel-palestinians-netanyahu/
11 https://www.nytimes.com/2017/02/15/opinion/inching-toward-a-one-state-solution.html?_r=0
12 James Abourezk, United States Senator 1973–79, http://www.honorlibertyvets.org/experts.html#.WT93e1WGPcs
13 Paul Findley, *They Dare to Speak Out: People and Institutions Confront Israel's Lobby*, Lawrence Hill & Co, Chicago, 1985, p 166.
14 Adlai Stevenson III, interviewed by William J Small, United Press International, for publication 28 September 1980.
15 David G Nes, Oral History, Lyndon Baines Johnson Presidential Library.

16 George W Ball and Douglas B Ball, *The Passionate Attachment: America's Involvement with Israel, 1947 to the Present*, WW Norton & Co, New York, 1992, pp 57–58.

17 Thomas Friedman, *New York Times*, 1 August 2009.

18 William Koenig, *Eye to Eye: Facing the Consequences of Dividing Israel*, revised edition 2006, pp. 247–248.

19 http://www.jta.org/2015/09/03/news-opinion/politics/some-jews-have-divined-the-real-cause-of-jimmy-carters-cancer

20 http://www.haaretz.com/settlementdollars/1.689683

21 www.theguardian.com/world/2009/jul/19/us-bingo-funding-israeli-settlements

15: The Lobby

1 John Lyons, 'Defiant Israel turns its back on peace push', *The Australian*, 13 March 2010.

2 *Jerusalem Post*, 29 October 2016.

17: Sunset in Gaza

1 International Crisis Group, 'Radical Islam in Gaza,' 29 March 2011.

2 Michael Owen, 'Israel must not be permitted to crush Hamas,' *Washington Post*, 24 July 2014.

3 www.usip.org/sites/default/files/Special%20Report%20224_Hamas.pdf

18: Returning to Iran

1 http://www.economist.com/news/middle-east-and-africa/21588438-will-saudi-women-ever-be-allowed-behind-wheel-car-ovarian-issue

2 http://www.reuters.com/article/iran-alcohol-idUSL5N0LF1GK20140326

3 www.theguardian.com/world/2012/nov/21/iran-supplied-hamas-missile-technology

19: The View from Palestine

1 http://www.haaretz.com/israel-admits-it-covertly-canceled-residency-status-of-140-000-palestinians-1.360935

2 cdn3.phr.org.il/wp-content/uploads/2016/04/Divide-And-Conquer.pdf; documents.worldbank.org/curated/en/137111468329419171/West-Bank-and-Gaza-Area-C-and-the-future-of-the-Palestinian-economy

3 *The Guardian*, 2 June 2014.

20: Netanyahu's Israel

1 *New York Times*, 19 November 1995.

2 http://www.haaretz.com/opinion/.premium-1.639193

3 *Los Angeles Times*, 14 November 1995.
4 Channel 10, Israel, 18 July 2010.
5 *Maariv*, 27 May 2010.
6 https://972mag.com/resource-what-is-the-e1-area-and-why-is-it-so-important/61298/
7 *Forward*, 4 March 2015.
8 http://www.reuters.com/article/us-palestinian-israel-settlements-idUSKBN0EZ0JA20140624; and *Ynet*, 10 November 2014.
9 https://972mag.com/next-head-of-civil-administration-said-palestinians-are-sub-human/106533/
10 *Haaretz*, 22 April 2009.
11 *Haaretz*, 7 August 2013.
12 www.ipforum.org/
13 *Haaretz*, 13 November 2003.
14 John Cassidy, 'A British friend of Israel speaks out,' *New Yorker*, 14 October 2014.
15 www.thejc.com/comment/comment/take-a-lawyer-s-advice-visit-the-occupied-territories-1.52007

Epilogue: Farewell, Jerusalem

1 http://www.haaretz.com/opinion/.premium-1.769360
2 https://www.theguardian.com/world/2017/feb/06/israel-likely-pass-bill-retroactively-legalising-jewish-settlements
3 Ibid.
4 https://www.theguardian.com/world/2017/may/01/hamas-new-charter-palestine-israel-1967-borders
5 Algeria, Bahrain, Comoros, Djibouti, Egypt, Iraq, Jordan, Kuwait, Lebanon, Libya, Mauritania, Morocco, Oman, Palestine, Qatar, Saudi Arabia, Somalia, Sudan, Syria, Tunisia, the United Arab Emirates and Yemen
6 http://www.nytimes.com/2013/01/29/opinion/global/roger-cohen-sitting-down-with-amos-oz.html
7 Simon Sebag Montefiore, *Jerusalem: The Biography*, Weidenfeld & Nicolson, London, 2011, p. 2.